The Scientific Basis of Astrology

BY PERCY SEYMOUR

Astrology: The Evidence of Science

THE
SCIENTIFIC
BASIS
OF
ASTROLOGY

Dr. Percy Seymour

St. Martin's Press

New York

Book design by Susan Hood

Library of Congress Cataloging-in-Publication Data
Seymour, Percy.
The scientific basis of astrology : tuning to the music of the
planets / Percy Seymour.
p.   cm.
ISBN 0-312-07795-5
1. Science and astrology. I. Title.
BF1729.S34S49   1992
133.5—dc20   92-2684
                                                   CIP

FIRST EDITION: JULY 1992
1 3 5 7 9 10 8 6 4 2

For Michel Gauquelin

Contents

Preface   xi
Introduction   1

PART ONE
  1. The Schedules of Success   19
  2. Calendars—Schedules of Light   37
  3. Timekeeping Schedules of Light   57
  4. The Haven-Finding Art   73
  5. Biological Clocks Linked to Light   89

PART TWO
  6. Gravitation and the Cycles of Light   107
  7. Programming by Weather and Climate   123
  8. Animal Navigators   137
  9. The Magnetic Compasses of Life   151
 10. Magnetic Programming of Biological Clocks   167

PART THREE
 11. Programming by Magnetism and Light   187
 12. Programming by Food and Odor   203
 13. Maps and Shapes in Space and Time   217

14. Scientific Evidence and Theories   233
15. The Astronomy-Astrology Debate   251

Afterword: Michel Gauquelin   269
Bibliography   273
About the Author   279

Preface

Astrology is defined by Fred Gettings in his *Dictionary of Astrology* as "The study of the relationship between the Macrocosm and the Microcosm, which (in material terms) is often defined as the study of the influence of the celestial bodies on the Earth and its inhabitants." When defined in this way then astrology does have a basis in science. This basis shows quite clearly that some of the claims of astrology are valid, but it also puts severe limits on the all-embracing claims made by astrologers that they can predict the futures of individuals, the stock market, global catastrophes, and world politics.

The counter claims, made by many scientists, that astrology is opposed to the basic principles of Western science comes from a total misunderstanding of serious astrology, and an appalling lapse in their understanding of the methodology, philosophy, and history of science itself. What these scientists normally call astrology is in effect the cheap sun-sign astrology of the horoscope columns run by some newspapers. These bear as much resemblance to the research now being done on astrology, as do the scientific reports in these papers bear to what is actually going on in the laboratories and observatories of the world. Yet these same scientists are usually extremely annoyed when people base their appreciation of science on this type of science writing.

Astrology in the ancient world was the first serious scientific attempt to explore the limits of determinism and the predictive powers of an all-embracing cosmology, and in this sense it was precursor of all subsequent scientific efforts at predicting celestial phenomena, terrestrial events, and the outcome of laboratory experiments. This is all very much in keeping with Einstein's observation that "Scientific thought is the development of pre-scientific thought."

Some aspects of celestial and terrestrial phenomena, that in ages past were a prime concern of astrology, have since been taken over by other scientific disciplines and many of the concepts of the subject have become part of our cultural heritage.

For example, astrologers believed that if they could predict the positions of the planets against the background stars, then they could predict the destinies of individuals as well as many other terrestrial events. It is thus not surprising that two of the greatest contributors to our developing understanding of planetary motion, Ptolemy and Kepler, also practiced as astrologers. Since these early days the prediction of planetary movements and eclipses has been divorced from its astrological origins and is now part of the science of astronomy.

The ancient astrologers had also noticed that there was some correspondence between the zodiac constellation that rose and set with the Sun, the weather conditions that prevailed at a given time, changes in vegetation, the behavior of animals and birds, and the farming tasks that had to be carried out at certain times of the year. These observed correlations have since become part of the sciences of meteorology and agriculture. They have also been immortalized in an artistic motif known as the signs of the zodiac and the labors of the month, which was used to decorate churches and illustrate medieval prayer books.

Tidal predication was also very much associated with astrology. Thus when referring to the fact that some magician had made use of the Sun and Moon to carry out a tidal prediction Chaucer dismissed this work, and astrology in general, as an "abominable superstition." Galileo dismissed the idea that the Moon could influence the tides as "occult nonsense." Tidal prediction is now firmly established in the science of oceanography.

Research in astrophysics and geophysics has revealed a variety of ways in which our terrestrial habitat has been molded by extraterrestrial evolution. These subjects have also shown that our local environment is linked to the rest of the universe in ways even more astonishing and exciting than those conceived by ancient astrologers. In a real sense modern astronomers and astrophysicists are cosmic environmentalists, in that they are concerned with investigating the various forces, fields, particles, and radiations that bind our earthly home to the cosmos.

Even *The Times*, one of the most enduring, traditional, and conservative of British institutions, was willing to admit that some aspect of astrology might have a scientific basis. In the Science Report that appeared in *The Times* on December 5, 1970, the science correspondent commented on a report that had appeared in *Nature* on the same day. This paper had drawn attention to some correlations between solar activity and planetary alignments. The item in *The Times* went on to point out that this type of alignment was exactly the kind of relationship studied by astrologers. Further along they draw attention to the fact that variations in the sunspot cycle can affect the terrestrial environment via the solar wind, and suggested that there may be a sound basis for some astrological predictions. The report ended with these words: "The radiation from the sun is one of the prime hazards to manned space flight, so we may find the curious anomaly that the dates of future space flights might be chosen using the textbook astrological techniques of Kepler to predict low sunspot activity."

The task of sorting out the wheat from the chaff of ancient astrology is one that still has to continue, and this book is concerned with making a contribution to the quest. It examines the scientific evidence that shows quite clearly the links between the universe and the bio-sphere. It seeks to clarify those concepts of astrology that can be understood in terms of a theory which does not step outside the current paradigm of science, and it attempts to define the limitations placed on the claims of astrology by this particular theory.

It also examines the so-called scientific arguments against astrology, and shows that these are not really scientific at all, but merely rationalizations of irrational and pseudo-scientific prejudices. The militant terms in which these scientists couch their objection to astrology, and the high moral tones usually evident in these statements, are just a smoke screen with which they attempt to hide the nakedness of their arguments. The attitudes of these scientists are usually strikingly similar to those of some astrologers whom they condemn with such sanctimonious zest—i.e. they are willing they accept "uncritically" those results which reinforce their beliefs and reject those which may undermine their cherished preconceptions. Such attitudes cannot be graced with the word scientific, even if they are held by eminent scientists.

The history of science shows us that scientific theories are constantly being changed and replaced by others, no matter how permanent they may seem at a given time. If we see the body of scientific knowledge as a building, then theories are similar to the scaffolding used to repair and extend the building. If the required additions to the general structure of the building are very extensive, then it is sometimes necessary to reinforce and extend the very foundations of the building. The scientific evidence that supports some of the basic concepts of astrology does not require such an approach to the foundations of present day science. Thus on the basis of what we know at the moment we cannot dismiss some of the basic concepts of astrology, and indeed a few of the contentions of astrologers are underpinned by recent advances in scientific research.

On November 15, 1991 the front page of *The Higher (The Times Higher Education Supplement)*, carried a report of some research undertaken by Professor Peter Roberts, Visiting Professor of Systems Science at the City University of London. His work consisted of giving personality tests to people born on the same day as a few celebrities. He was able to demonstrate that the similarities between personalities increased as the time differences between the actual times of births of these individuals decreased. In other words "time twins" showed more convincing personality similarities than people born at different times on the same day. When interviewed by a reporter from *The Higher*, Prof. Roberts said, "The vast majority of astrologers are not interested in scientific research. They treat it like a religion which is not meant to be questioned.

But scientists should be curious not furious—they are the ones that are unscientific if they will not even look at the evidence."

I would agree with Peter Roberts's statement.

Dr. Percy Seymour
Plymouth, November 1991.

The Scientific Basis of Astrology

Introduction

Science is at a crossroads. As we come to the end of the twentieth century, it is becoming apparent that there are important unsolved problems in many areas of science. Our century has been at the same time one of the most successful periods in the whole history of science. We have solved the problem of atomic structure, we have unleashed the energy locked up in the atomic nucleus, we have used physical principles to crack the genetic code, we have placed men on the Moon, and we have sent space probes to the outer planets. The euphoria associated with all these positive achievements has led many scientists to underestimate the fundamental problems that still face us. A similar time of scientific overconfidence, at least on the part of physicists and some astronomers, existed at the end of the last century. Some physicists in the 1890s said that all the important discoveries in physics had been made by then and it was just a case of filling in the details.

Scientific progress in the early decades of this century showed quite clearly that those who believed that fundamental physics was then almost complete were totally wrong. The start of our own century saw the birth of a completely new approach to science as classical physics gave way to modern physics.

1

Relativity and quantum mechanics are at the very foundations of modern physics. The theory of relativity showed us that many measurements in physics depend on the observer's point of view—hence its name. The quantum theory revealed that in making measurements on subatomic phenomena we actually change the situations we are investigating, and this places limits on the accuracy with which we can know the outcome of certain experiments. This is known as the uncertainty principle. As Dr. Jacob Bronowski said in his book *The Ascent of Man:*[1] "One aim of the physical sciences has been to give an exact picture of the material world. One achievement of twentieth century physics has been to show that that aim is unattainable."

In the latter half of our own century, it has become clear that there is a basic conflict between the quantum theory and the theory of relativity. It was the physicist John Bell who with a mathematical proof called Bell's theorem highlighted this conflict. Gary Zukav in *The Dancing Wu Li Masters* by G. Zukav, Rider/Hutchinson, London, 1979 said this of Bell's theorem: "Bell's theorem tells us that there is no such thing as separate parts. All the parts of the universe are connected in a way previously claimed only by mystics and other scientifically objectionable people."

Bell himself commented on this conflict in the following words:

For me then this is the real problem with quantum theory: the apparently essential conflict between any sharp formulation and fundamental relativity. This is to say, we have an apparent incompatibility, at the deepest level, between the two fundamental pillars of contemporary theory. . . . It may well be that a real synthesis of quantum and relativity theory requires not just technical developments but a radical conceptual renewal.[2]

[1]This book is based on the television series of the same name, published by the BBC, 1973.
[2]This is an extract of an informal talk given by Bell at CERN, Geneva. It is printed in *Speakable and Unspeakable in Quantum Mechanics* by J. S. Bell, Cambridge University Press, Cambridge, 1987.

There are also problems that arise from scientifically collected data in other areas of human activity.

The Scientific Method

The scientific method is a particular way of investigating the natural world. There are a number of stages that can be identified in the development of a new area of science. First there is the data-collecting stage. During this stage scientists make a number of observations or measurements that are normally aimed at relating two or more quantities with each other. For example, the early astronomers related the points on the horizon at which the Sun rose and set with the length of the day and the warmth of the air. The second stage involves looking for patterns in the collected data. If such patterns do exist then it becomes possible to predict some possible future trends in the data. This type of prediction is purely empirical and does not involve any conceptual model. We will see in a later chapter that the mathematical astronomy of the Babylonians represents such an approach to astronomical data.

The next stage consists of constructing conceptual models which can lead to refined predictions. It is necessary to understand that these conceptual models are pure creations of the human mind and do not arise directly from the observations or measurements. However, the predictions of the models do have to be tested against further measurements and observations. One extremely important aspect of the scientific approach which is known to all scientists, but may not be so well known to nonscientists, is that there is no such thing as scientific proof. It is impossible to prove a scientific model or theory. One can only show that for a limited set of circumstances the model makes predictions that turn out to be consistent with the data. It is, however, possible to disprove a scientific theory, and this is a very important facet of the scientific method; if its predictions are not verified by further experiments and observations, then the model is rejected and a new conceptual model has to be constructed. This point was well made by the physicist Niels Bohr, who said, "We must continually count on

3

the appearance of new facts, the inclusion of which within the compass of our earlier experience may require a revision of our fundamental concepts."[3] Albert Einstein was also clearly aware of the limitations of our theories. He said, "The only justification of our concepts and system of concepts is that they serve to represent the complex of our experiences; beyond this they have no legitimacy."[4]

Challenges from Interdisciplinary Areas of Science

Within the general context of the scientific method previously described, there are a variety of ways to proceed with an investigation. One approach that has been particularly useful and successful in laboratory-based sciences is known as reductionism. In this approach an attempt is made to explain whole systems in terms of the behavior of their constituent parts. Thus in physics we try to explain atoms in terms of subatomic particles and these in terms of still smaller particles; in chemistry we try to explain chemical compounds in terms of the atoms of which they are composed; and in biology we try to explain the structure and behavior of living organisms in terms of biochemistry and biophysics. This approach is less successful in environmental biology, the planetary sciences, astrophysics, and cosmology. In these disciplines it is necessary to study living and nonliving systems in the context of their environment.

There is also growing evidence that there are important problems at the interfaces between these disciplines that could possibly be solved using a more holistic approach. Nevertheless, some scientists have ignored this data and others have dismissed the available evidence, not because there is anything unscientific in the way the information was collected but because it conflicts with some of their preconceived ideas. It has been known for some time

[3]N., Bohr, *Atomic Theory and the Description of Nature*, Cambridge University Press, Cambridge, 1934.
[4]A., Einstein, *The Meaning of Relativity* (First published in 1922), reprinted by Science Paperbacks, London, 1967.

that the Sun undergoes a cycle of sunspot activity with a period of roughly eleven years, and that this cycle affects a stream of charged particles—called the solar wind—which in turn causes the magnetic field of Earth to vibrate in unison with it. It has also been known since the last century that the Moon causes tides not only in the oceans and atmosphere of Earth but also in the magnetic aura that envelops our Earth. There also exists a body of evidence which strongly suggests that there is a relationship between sunspot activity and certain configurations of the planets as seen from the Sun. All this information is well documented and several scientists have used the data to make successful predictions of events connected with sunspot activity; yet several scientists, in particular astrophysicists, have dismissed the evidence because it conflicts with the simple and naive models which they set up for test purposes. This shows a complete misunderstanding of the very nature of science. Establishing that a particular model does not explain the data does not mean that no model can be thought of that could possibly provide an explanation of the observations. To make such a claim is to shackle the creative imagination of scientists and to limit the free spirit of scientific inquiry.

There is also a great deal of evidence that the magnetic field of Earth and its many vibrations have effects on a very wide variety of living organisms, including humans. There is further evidence that the personalities of individuals are somehow related to the state of the Solar System at the time of birth. A few years ago I started developing a theory which can explain these data without stepping outside the known and accepted principles of science.

Where I Stand

I am a scientist. As such I cannot propose or understand a model of reality which does not take account of scientific data. I am not an astrologer—in fact, this theory developed out of an examination of the arguments that astrology cannot work! As a theoretical astrophysicist, with an interest in the relationship between fundamental physics and the large-scale structure of the universe, I am searching, as are many others, for a model to explain the current anomalies and paradoxes in these areas. This search has, for me, necessitated exploring many areas that are beyond the domain of astrophysics (i.e., biology, chemistry, and to my amazement, astrology).

My interest in the history and philosophy of science and my examination of the so-called scientific arguments against astrology had shown me quite clearly that these arguments were not scientific at all. They were merely rationalizations of pseudo-intellectual prejudices that are only accepted by some people as scientific because they reinforce their own beliefs. What I found surprising was the fact that some of the defenders of astrological concepts had unearthed scientific data, largely ignored by the scientific community, which led to insights into unsolved astrophysical problems, such as those connected with the sunspot cycle.

This book explores these areas, highlighting the evidence which exists to show that Earth is part of a complex series of interactions, and that the relationship of Earth and everything on it, plants and animals including human beings, with the rest of the Solar System is highly complex and very important for life on Earth.

Outline of the Theory

The building blocks of the nervous system are the neurons, containing a "message transmitter" called an axon. This axon is usually stimulated by electrical activity generated within the neuron, but it can also be activated by electrical stimulus from outside. Since a changing magnetic field generates an associated electrical field (this is the principle of the electric generator) it can also act as a stimulus to the central nervous system. It is as if the nervous system can act as an antenna through which we can detect some of the vibrations of the Earth's field. This field has fluctuations which are linked to the Sun and Moon, and to the spinning of Earth on its own axis. There are further subtle variations on these basic changes which are linked to the sunspot cycle. My theory proposes that this cycle is in itself linked to the positions and movements of the planets, including Earth, around the Sun. This means that the whole Solar System is playing a "symphony" on the magnetic field of Earth.

According to the theory I have proposed, we are all genetically "tuned" to receive a different set of "melodies" from this symphony. While in the womb, the organs of our familiar five senses are still developing, so they are less effective in receiving information than they are once we are born. However, the womb is no hiding place from the all-pervading and constantly fluctuating magnetic field of Earth; so the symphonic tunes which we pick up can become part of our earliest memories. It is in the womb that some of the "magnetic music of the spheres" becomes etched on our brains. The first role of our particular response to this music is to provide the cue for our entry onto the stage of the world. At later stages in life, when the Solar System "plays our tune" again on the magnetic field of Earth, it evokes these memories and our response may influence the way we act in a given situation. This is a very brief and largely pictorial description of the basis of my theory, which will be further developed and expanded in the rest of the book.

"Tuning In" to the Cosmos

The advent of radio several decades ago introduced many new concepts and phrases into our language. We often talk about "being on the same wavelength," "tuning into someone's thoughts," or "picking up their vibrations." The basis of all radio communications is the very important principle of resonance.

Resonance makes it possible for a radio telescope to tune in to the specific vibrations of hydrogen atoms in, for example, the Andromeda galaxy (which is 14 million million million miles away); for us to listen to particular radio stations as we drive along in our cars; and for the Moon to shift a hundred billion tons of water out of the Bay of Fundy in Canada twice a day. All the detailed calculations which supposedly show that the Sun, Moon, and planets cannot affect life on Earth have ignored the possibility of resonant interactions. The theory I have developed makes extensive use of the concept of resonance—resonance between the tidal tug, due to gravity, of the planets on the very hot gases trapped in the magnetic fields of the Sun and Earth, and resonance between the resulting fluctuations of the Earth's magnetic field and the electrical activity of the neural network of the fetus. The important point about resonance is that a small fluctuating force can have large consequences if it has the same natural frequency as the natural frequency of the system to which it is applied.

The whole theory has proved to be controversial for several reasons, but mainly because it gives support to some aspects of astrology, a subject which is treated with fear and derision by most scientists today. Astrology is an ancient discipline, which may be studied in great depth, and I believe it should be studied in this way if we are to understand some of the most important roots of Western culture. "Sun-sign" astrology, so simplistically presented in magazines and newspapers, is all that most people know of the subject, yet many serious astrologers feel this presentation to be almost an abuse of the subject. Many aspects of the subject cannot be supported, as yet, by the scientific theory I am proposing, yet I am forced to the conclusion that some parts of it do reflect physical reality, though expressed in symbolic and nonscientific language.

I first discussed the scientific and mathematical details of the theory at the Fifth International Astrological Research Conference held in London in 1986, and some of its salient features were presented in a more refined form at the First International Conference on Geo-cosmic Relations held in Amsterdam in 1989. The semi-popular version of the theory is given in my book *Astrology: The Evidence of Science*, published in revised paperback form by Penguin Arkana in England in 1990.

Astrology, Time, and Evolution

In this book the theory is again described but there are several radical differences between this book and my earlier one on astrology. The most important difference is that the magnetic joining between our Earth, life on Earth, and the rest of the Solar System is now seen as just one consequence of several different ways in which we are linked to the Sun, Moon, and some of the other planets. However, according to the viewpoint developed here, magnetic fluctuations still provide the basic framework into which many other cosmically induced environmental changes are fitted.

We can explain this by an analogy. Think about the basic principles of a home or office computer. We can store a great deal of information on the magnetic discs supplied with the computer. Each disc contains a large number of tiny magnetic particles that can be aligned by the magnetic fields generated by the computer itself, but to begin with these particles are randomly oriented, and we say that the disc is unformatted. Thus, before a disc can be used it has to be formatted, or in other words, the normally circular disc has to be divided up into segments onto which we can then "write" our information. This is rather like using files with labels to divide up the drawers of a filing cabinet, which would otherwise be full of unclassified pieces of paper and a terrific mess—it would be unformatted. The computer converts the information we wish to store into a magnetic form, using a suitable coding system, and the magnetically encoded information can then be stored at the labeled locations on the magnetic disc.

In this book I am proposing that the magnetic fluctuations of the geomagnetic field connected with the Sun, Moon, and planets have, over the long time-scales of biological evolution, provided a magnetic format or schedule in time into which other environmental changes were stored using a magnetic coding system. This is not dissimilar to the way a video camera can store visual images in magnetic form on a videotape. This shift in emphasis in the role of magnetism in the theory has been necessitated as new data has come to hand and as the scientific framework of my theory has been further refined.

The new concepts are introduced by exploring the parallels between the way our conscious use of astronomical cycles for calendar making, timekeeping, direction finding, and navigation systems have developed, and the way evolutionary processes in biology have given rise to biological clocks, calendars, and navigation systems which are also linked to geocosmic cycles. In both cases the original direct causal linking between the cosmos and the internal referencing systems gave rise to long- and short-term clocks that were constant and stable in themselves, and were thus less reliant on the direct causal connection. The cosmic cycles then, in a sense, became "memorized" within the technological and biological referencing systems, and so it was only necessary to check the synchronization of these two systems on rather infrequent occasions.

It is further proposed that biological clocks of humans are not as simple as those of lower forms of life, in that they involve not only solar, lunar, tidal, and seasonal cycles, but also have cycles which are related to the basic periods of the planets as seen from Earth. These personal internal biological clocks are occasionally checked subconsciously against the environmental cycles which are linked to fundamental cosmic periods. This checking can be done in a variety of ways, but two of the most important ways of phase-locking biological clocks to cosmic cycles are by means of light and magnetism.

Research into human rhythms has revealed that we have several internal biochemical cycles which differ from the mean length of the solar day, and also from one individual to the next. Thus, we all have slightly different internal biological clocks. However, in our dealings with other people we have to use some externally agreed-upon standard form of timekeeping. This standard system is very much the product of astronomical research and horologic development. Thus as individuals we have to adapt our internal schedules to that of the social group in which we live.

Genetics ensures that we share some of our physical and behavioral characteristics with other members of our family. I am proposing that some of our behavioral characteristics are intimately linked with the way our nervous system is "wired up" and that this is also related to the internal biological clocks which we possess and that form the framework into which we slot our personal schedules. With the development of larger social systems people paid less attention to the differences between their internal schedules, and concentrated more on those aspects of their schedules which they had in common with other people. I am proposing that some aspects of serious astrology, which is rather different from the simplistic sun-sign astrology often seen in newspapers and magazines, is an attempt to understand our own internal schedules formed over long periods of time and which we inherit genetically. It is a fairly complex theory that rests on a basis of diverse scientific evidence. For this reason it is necessary to cover quite a lot of physical and biological science in order to understand how the theory was formed. In the rest of this introduction I give a brief synopsis of the book.

Synopsis of the Book

In the first chapter we will consider the importance of schedules to success in life. We will consider how the growth of society has made it necessary to accommodate our own schedules to that of ever larger groups, and how the accelerating pace of travel and communications makes it necessary to accommodate at least some of our schedules to those of the global community of which most of us are now a part. Calendars, clocks, and diaries are essential to all forms of scheduling. Chapter 2 is mainly concerned with the origins and development of calendars in general, and the development of our own calendar in particular. However, the essential point is that early calendars depended on making certain observation of the Moon, Sun, and stars, and that theoretical astronomy arose as a subsequently successful attempt to predict the astronomical phenomena necessary to work out calendars that did not require direct observations. Thus, the calendars we use today embody mathematical techniques that have been developed over many centuries, and for the most part direct astronomical observations are no longer necessary.

The early use of the Sun and stars for dividing the day into convenient smaller units will be discussed in chapter 3. Initially, direct observations were made on the Sun and stars, using shadow and star clocks, but once some standard referencing framework had been established, mechanical methods were developed which could take over the task; but these methods still had to be checked against the daily cycle of day and night. The candle and water clocks eventually gave rise to mechanisms involving gear wheels and pendulums that were more accurate, but this development took several centuries.

The most accurate pendulum clocks eventually gave way to high-precision atomic clocks which used the vibrations of atoms as their basic regulators. Such clocks led to the discovery that the spinning of our Earth had variations of its own. This led to a change in our reasons for checking clocks against Earth's spin. Since we still regulate our lives by apparent motions of the Sun across the sky, we have to alter day length as given by atomic clocks by very small amounts to accommodate the extremely slight slowing down of our Earth. This means that sometimes we have to insert "leap seconds" into our year to keep international atomic time in step with the average solar day.

The use of Sun, stars, and Moon for navigational purposes is the main subject discussed in chapter 4. First we look at the use of celestial objects for finding direction, and then we see how ancient seamen found latitude (distance from the equator) using the stars and Sun. Finding longitude (distance east or west of a given meridian) required methods of comparing local time with the time at some reference meridian. This led to the setting up of the Paris and Greenwich observatories and to the invention of the marine chronometer. Essentially, all the methods worked out for determining longitude combined actual measurements on celestial objects with data in the nautical almanac for a specific time at the reference meridian. It was these developments that eventually led to the establishing of a global time zone system.

In chapter 5 we move on to biological programming by the cycles of light in our environment. In some simple life forms there seems to be no internal biological clocks regulating the responses of these organisms to light (i.e., the organisms respond directly to the cycles of day and night, and in the absence of such cycles do not react in any way). In other examples the organisms seem to have constant and stable biological clocks which can keep on regulating their bodies even when removed from direct access to the environmental cycles. However, if the organism is removed for more than several days then the various functions of the organism can become de-synchronized. The internal cycles then have to be reset by exposing the organism to the environmental cues once more.

Gravitation is a major controlling factor in the regulating of environmental cycles. In chapter 6 we investigate the various roles played by this important cosmic force. The cycles of day and night, the seasons, and changing day length are all controlled by the spinning of Earth on its axis and its motion around the Sun. These in turn are determined by the "traffic rules" for large-scale objects which are Newton's Laws of Motion and the Law of Gravitation, laws that also explain tidal phenomena. We will not only consider the physical causes of phenomena associated with Newton's laws; we will also consider the biological consequences of such cycles associated in some way with gravitation.

Chapter 7 looks at the effects of the seasons on the atmosphere of Earth and the biological consequences of seasonal variations in meteorological conditions. It also notes the long-term effects on climate of changes in Earth's orbit due to the gravitational inter-action between Earth and the other planets. The effect of variations in the radiative output of the Sun, due to the sunspot cycle, is also important.

There is considerable evidence that many animals navigate using the Sun as a compass, while others, like bees, can also use the polarization of the sky, which is linked to the position of the Sun, as a navigational aid. Some species of birds migrate at night, and there is evidence to suggest that they use the stars as navigational aids. These are the subjects to be discussed in chapter 8. We will also look at other navigation aids used by animals.

In chapter 9 we look at the growing evidence that many differ-ent animals, including humans, can use the magnetic field of Earth for direction finding. In chapter 10 we look at biological consequences of changes in Earth's magnetic field. In recent years it has become clear that many biological organisms can detect and respond to systematic changes of the geomagnetic field, especially those connected with the apparent movements of the Sun and Moon, as seen from the surface of the Earth. Some scien-tists have suggested that the geomagnetic field may be second only to the Sun and sky in giving organisms information of time, location, and direction. Dr. Robert Becker has gone so far as to suggest that over eons of time many different species have become locked in step with specific fluctuations of the geomagnetic field.

Chapter 11 discusses biological programming using a combination of light and magnetism. In earlier chapters we saw that many animals can use both light from the Sun (and the stars) or the geomagnetic field to find direction. They thus have a built-in redundancy with regard to direction finding and they must be able, at some physical level, to correlate the two different types of directional data. It is then argued that the large brain capacity of early man was able to use the stars and those planets visible to the naked eye to find direction when hunting or traveling at night. On clear days and nights they would use the Sun or stars, but on cloudy days or nights they would use the magnetic field of Earth for this purpose. It was the discovery of this redundancy that led to the realization that planetary magnetic tides are present in the geomagnetic field.

The food available for eating, and the smells given off by biological organisms, also show a seasonal dependence which could well have played some role in programming seasonal responses in a variety of species, including humans. This possibility is explored in chapter 12.

Chapter 13 looks at the integration of these various forms of environmental programming within individuals. As an analogy, one could see life as an opera, with music, libretto, stage directions, scenery, and costumes. If one has seen a particular opera several times, then if one only hears the music, one can picture the rest, and one knows how the story will unfold. In life we have many more options than the singers in an opera, and there are a variety of triggers in life that could set a particular train of events in action. We do have our own free will to make choices, but the menu does not have infinite possibilities, so we have to choose from the options available.

In chapter 14 we look at some of the evidence, in favor of and against, some aspects of astrology. We look, in particular, at the work of Michel Gauquelin, Alan Smithers, Hans Eysenck, David

Nias, Suitbert Ertel, Peter Roberts, John Addey, and Theodore Landscheidt.

The concluding chapter 15 looks at recent developments in the debate on astrology. In particular, we look at the attitudes of scientists and astrologers to the evidence presented above. We also considered the debate on the theory presented in my book *Astrology: The Evidence of Science.*

PART ONE

PART ONE

The Schedules of Success

It will be well known to most of us that for success in life we have to develop schedules. Although we do not have to stick rigidly to these, we need a framework to organize our time in the most efficient way. We need personal timetables for some form of self-discipline, when we are on our own, but most of us also need schedules because we live and work with other people. These schedules are very necessary in order to live with members of our family; to work efficiently with people at work; to get on with people in our local community; and to make our own contribution to our country. Increasingly we have global commitments, either through travel or modern forms of communications, and this means we have to fit in, to some extent, with the schedules of people in other countries. For any sort of workable schedule we need three things: a calendar, a watch, and a diary. If we travel a great deal we also need railway, bus, and other travel timetables and route maps. In this chapter we are going to take a brief look at schedules in our day-to-day lives.

Calendars, Timekeepers, and Diaries

Some of us buy calendars. Many large firms and other organizations use calendars as part of their advertising schemes, so it is relatively easy to obtain a free calendar at the start of the year. Many people also buy calendars as presents to give to relatives and friends. This essential commodity of everyday life, which we can obtain so easily, is in reality the fruit of one of the first conscious applications of the science of astronomy to life, and, as we will see in the next chapter, it was one of the strongest motivations for early interest in the day and night skies.

A few calendars do have astronomical themes, for example, calendars of astronomy societies, or firms that sell equipment associated with astronomy; but for the most part the large variety of the forms taken by calendars are much more a tribute to the ingenuity and the imagination of graphic designers, artists, and photographers, and the input of astronomy to the calendar's development is largely ignored. Several calendars do have the phases of Moon given for each month, but in general this is the only acknowledgment that the motions of heavenly bodies had anything to do with our calendar.

Most of us are awakened by some form of alarm clock, and some of us might receive an early-morning alarm call from the local telephone exchange, and this event starts us on our daily schedule.[1] Throughout the day we will pace and organize our activities according to the time that we get from wristwatches, or clocks in our home or place of work. Although the physical reality of day and night acts as a constant reminder of the relationship between Earth and the external universe, the timepieces that we use seem, on the face of it, to have very little to do with astronomy. We will see later the extremely important role that astronomy played in developing our consciousness of the passage of time, and the stimulus it gave to the development of timepieces of all kinds. We will also see that the now-accepted convention of twenty-four hours to the day had its origins in the astronomical methods of timekeeping of the ancient Egyptians.

Our calendars and timekeepers represent a social framework into which we fit our personal activities. Most of us lead fairly complex lives, and so although we can remember many of the

---

[1]In England it is possible to arrange for the telephone company operator to give you a telephone call in the morning.

routines of our schedules, we also need prompts for those events and appointments that are not routine, and this is where diaries and personal timetables become important. The personal nature of a diary is apparent in its very definition. *The Shorter Oxford English Dictionary* gives two definitions for the word *diary*. The first says: "A daily record of events or transactions, a journal; specifically a daily record of matters affecting the writer personally." The second definition shows its relationship to calendars: "A book prepared for keeping a daily record; also applied to calendars containing daily memoranda [1605]." Diaries are at least a few hundred years old. They have personal connections and they can be aids to memory. They are also essential to most personal schedules.

Personal Schedules

The factors that affect the setting up of our personal schedules are varied. Some of them are the result of our biological functions. A few of these, such as the beating of our hearts, are for the most part involuntary, although even this can be altered by the use of certain exercises or by biofeedback systems. Breathing is another example of a largely involuntary system, although we do have more control of the rate of breathing than we have of heartbeat. Other voluntary biological functions are also necessary. We have to eat and drink at frequent intervals, and we also have to discharge waste matter at regular times, for the well-being of our bodies. In this case we have, within reasonable limits, some choice as to when we participate in these activities.

Some of our personal activities are dependent on the type of people we are, and this will play a big part in the way we set up our own schedules. For example, the hobbies we choose and the amount of time we wish to spend on them are to a large extent related to our personality characteristics. However, there may be external factors that also determine when we can carry out activities associated with these hobbies. Sailing, gardening, bird watching, or astronomy are dependent not only on the time of year, but also on the more variable weather conditions available at a particular time. Many activities within our schedule will be determined by the fact that most of us do not live as hermits, but in contact with other people.

Family Schedules

Many joint activities are undertaken within families. Very few families have a totally flexible attitude to mealtimes, so for the most part we have to fit in with the schedule of meals, which most of the time is decided by the parents within the family. We may also take our holidays at the same time of year, and to cut traveling expenses, we may travel to our various places of work, or school, using just one car. In some homes with limited facilities, we may have to have a schedule for different members of the family to have a bath. Families may share the housework, and so there will be another schedule for these activities. Joint outings to theaters, cinemas, sport centers, and museums will put further constraints on our own schedules, but here we also start to overlap with those decided by the people who manage these facilities.

Schedules of the Local Community

For life to function smoothly in any community there has to be a large number of interacting schedules. Starting times of schools, colleges, offices, and businesses; opening and closing times of shops and banks; and shift working in some factories and other large organizations like docks and airports—all have to be carefully planned by the management of organizations. Those who work out bus and suburban train tables have to study the use of these facilities by the public at different times of day before they can draw up schedules that are efficient for the people who use them, but that are also cost-effective for the company. Traffic engineers who design the operating schedules for traffic lights at intersections have to coordinate the sequencing of these lights to ensure a steady flow of traffic and to avoid traffic jams.

Coordinating National Schedules

The world now has a standardized time system, but this is a relatively recent development. Even within countries time was not standardized until the 1850s. For example, 9:00 A.M. in New York was not the same as 9:00 A.M. further west. In some countries local time was based on a convenient sundial. This in many cases was the sundial on the parish church.

The coming of the stage coach was to change all this. Humphrey Smith, formerly of the Royal Greenwich Observatory, made this point very well. At the special conference organized to celebrate the 300th anniversary of the founding of the famous institution, he had this to say:

But for each local community, hours of labour and sleep, and times of meals, were adequately regulated by the Sun, or by the Church clock, checked occasionally by a simple Sundial. The first significant step towards the ending of this insolation was the introduction of the stage coach, which made available facilities for travel which had hitherto been the privilege of the minority.[2]

Smith also told the story of timekeeping by the guard on the London-to-Bristol coach in the 1830s. This guard was responsible for the safe custody of the mail carried on the coach, so he carried a cutlass, a brace of pistols, and a blunderbuss to repel any highwayman. He was also responsible for keeping to a schedule, so he also carried a timepiece locked in a leather pouch. At that time the time difference adopted between London and Bristol was twenty minutes—we now known it is closer to ten—so the timepiece was adjusted to lose twenty minutes on the down run and gain twenty minutes on the up journey. The activities of the post office made it necessary to introduce a uniform time system, as was made clear by Henry Booth in 1847:

The managers of this large establishment having its ramifications in all parts of the kingdom, are quite aware of the advantages of

[2]H.M. Smith "Greenwich Time and the Prime Meridian," *Vistas in Astronomy*, 20, 219, 1976.

one uniform system of time, by which alone their vast and multitudinous operations should be guided, and all other arrangements be made subordinate; accordingly all their movements are regulated by 'London Time.'[3]

Railway Time

The development of railway systems in England assisted considerably in the spread of a uniform system of time covering the whole country. The world's first public railway was the Stockton and Darlington Railway, which was opened on September 27, 1825. A few other railways quickly followed. At first they were used for hauling freight, but this was followed by the rapid development of passenger traffic. The great exhibition of 1851 led to a considerable increase in passenger travel. To quote from the *Railway Times* of that year, of the 6.2 million separate visits to the event, "For the most part the visitors travelled by train."[4] The link between the spread of Greenwich time and the railways was well expressed a great deal later by Aldous Huxley: "In inventing the locomotive, Watt and Stevenson were part inventors of time."[5] Along with development of the railways came the growth of the telegraph system. On the Great Western Railway, between West Drayton and Paddington, the electric telegraph was used in public for the first time. The continuing spread of the telegraph system, along with the railway system, eventually led to the adoption of Greenwich time throughout England. On February 11, 1852, *The Times* reported that electrical communication would be established between the Royal Observatory at Greenwich and the London Bridge Railway Terminus. The article in *The Times* listed three main reasons for doing so: "(1) to transmit Greenwich time to the . . . clock shortly to be constructed for the New Houses of Parliament and the Royal Exchange; (2) to transmit Greenwich time throughout those parts of the kingdom which is reached by

[3]Henry Booth, *Uniformity of Time*, London/Liverpool, (Privately published pamphlet), 1847.
[4]*The Railway Times*, October 18, London, 1851.
[5]Aldous Huxley, "Time and Machine," *The Olive Tree*, London, 1947.

the Galvanic telegraph; and (3) to compare the transits of stars at Greenwich with the same at Paris."[6] In his annual report of 1853 the astronomer royal, George Biddell Airy, wrote, "I cannot but feel satisfaction in thinking that the Royal Observatory is thus quietly contributing to the punctuality of business throughout a large portion of this country."[7]

Local Time or Railway Time?

The situation that Airy described in 1853 was not reached until a great deal of debate and argument had gone on throughout the country. For example this letter appeared in *The Times* on October 2, 1851:

Electric telegraph and local time.
    Sir,—Contemporaneously with the advance of railroads, and the invention of the electric telegraph, the difference of time arising from the variation in longitude of places has been considered objectionable; and, for convenience' sake, an uniformity of time—that of Greenwich—has been adopted throughout the Kingdom, with exception of a few places in the west of England.
    By reason of the submarine telegraph, England will now be brought into immediate communication with France and the greater portion of Europe. The question therefore arises, what meridian should be determined on for universal adoption?[8]

A few days later, this letter, by E. S. H., was replied to by "Chronos" from Greenwich, who some people thought might be the astronomer royal Airy himself. Chronos ended by saying:

The convenience of central regulation need not, of course, be lost by keeping true local time. A timekeeper 10 minutes west of London, on receiving his electric intimation that it is noon at Greenwich, set his clock at 10 minutes to 12, which is just as

---

[6]Report in *The Times*, February 11, London, 1852.
[7]The Annual Report of the Astronomer Royal on the Royal Observatory, Greenwich, London, 1853.
[8]Letter to *The Times* by E. S. H., October 2, 1851.

easy as setting it to 12. The only persons who derive any real benefit from the so-called 'uniformity' are the clerks who settle the railway time-tables, who are thereby saved some 20 minutes' trouble in calculating the allowance of time to be made as trains proceed east or west. This appears hardly a sufficient ground for bewildering all the timepieces and headpieces in Europe; and we must be content with humbly entreating what we dare not demand, that they will cease from their desperate attempts to 'annihilate both Space and Time' (which have not even the laudable effect of 'making two lovers happy'), and allow the old legitimate King Time to resume his place in our clocks and bosoms.[9]

As Derek Howse says in his book *Greenwich Time*, this "which only goes to prove that *The Times* has long been able to embrace many opinions, even when the dispute is over a subject embodied in its own name."[10]

Legal Time in England

By 1855 more than 90 percent of all public clocks in Great Britain were set to Greenwich mean time, but as yet there was nothing on the statute book that defined time for legal purposes. This point was well made by a letter to *The Times* from "Clerk to the Justices" published on May 14, 1880:

During the recent elections many members of Parliament and the officials conducting elections must have been much troubled to decide what was the correct time to open and close the poll.

Greenwich time is now kept almost throughout England, but it appears that Greenwich time is not legal time. For example, our polling booths were opened, and closed at 4:13 P.M.

This point as to what is legal time often arises in our criminal courts, but has hitherto escaped a proper decision and discussion. Will not some new M.P. take up this point and endeavour to get an Act making Greenwich time legal time![11]

[9]*The Times*, October 7, 1851.
[10]D. Howse, *Greenwich Time*, Oxford University Press, Oxford, 1980.
[11]Letter to *The Times*, May 14, 1880.

This oversight in the legal system was soon corrected. The first reading of the Statutes (Definition of Time) Bill took place on June 1 of that year, it was referred to a committee that reported back to the House on July 5, it passed through the remaining stages of both houses, and received the royal assent on August 5, 1880. The bill stated very clearly:

Whenever any expression of time occurs in any Acts of Parliament, deed, or other legal instrument, the time referred shall, unless it is otherwise specifically stated, be held in the Case of Great Britain to be Greenwich mean time, and in the case of Ireland, Dublin mean time.[12]

The Atlantic Cable

In 1851 the English Channel was crossed by the first successful submarine cable for transmitting telegraphic messages. In 1852 Wales and Scotland were linked with Ireland, and in 1853 the telegraphic link with the continent was extended to include Denmark and Belgium. In 1860 England became linked with the Indian subcontinent. However, one of the most exciting possibilities at this time was that of a link between Europe and North America. Although the first telegraphic message was sent across the Atlantic on August 5, 1858, communication had failed by September 3, and could not be reestablished. Another, much more successful attempt was made in 1866, by the ship the *Great Eastern*. An important factor leading to this success was that this ship received the Greenwich time signal twice daily by telegraph, from London, during the laying of the cable. In October 1866 Dr. B. A. Gould of the U.S. Coastal Survey, working with Airy at the Royal Observatory, used this new cable to redetermine the longitude differences between the observatories of Greenwich and Harvard University at Cambridge, Massachusetts.

[12]D. Howse, *Greenwich Time*, Oxford University Press, 1980.

Standardizing Time on U.S. Railroads

The task of standardizing time on the railroads in North America was a much more difficult one, because of the sheer size of the country. This problem was solved by Professor C. F. Dowd, who was principal of Temple Grove Ladies' Seminary in Saratoga Springs, New York. Dowd proposed that for U.S. railway purposes, there should be four standard meridians fifteen degrees of longitude apart, the eastern one being the Washington meridian. These meridians would be the centers of four time zones. In each zone the time adopted would be uniform, and it would change by one hour when passing from one zone to the next. This means that Dowd's scheme was identical, at least in principle, to the one in use over the whole world today. The boundaries of each time zone did not follow the meridians of longitude exactly, but were adjusted to take into account local state or county boundaries as well as the regions served by individual railroads. Dowd at first proposed that the reference meridian of this time zone system should be that defined by the transit telescope at the U.S. Naval Observatory in Washington. However, in the Act of September 28, 1850, which set up the *U.S. Nautical Almanac*, Congress stated that "hereafter the meridian of the observatory at Washington shall be adopted and used as the American meridian for all astronomical purposes, and that of the meridian of Greenwich shall be adopted for all nautical purposes."[13]

Later Dowd decided to change to meridians based on Greenwich, and he made the following proposal:

Explanation of standards.
The time of the 75th Meridian (west of Greenwich) is adopted as the standard time for all roads east of Ohio and the Allegheny Mountains; and the time of the 90th Meridian for western roads situated anywhere in the Mississippi valley. These times may be designated Eastern and Western Times, their difference being just one hour. Following westward still, the next hour standard

[13]D. Howse, *Greenwich Time*.

falls in the Rocky Mountain District, and hence is of no avail. But the third hour standard, or the time of the 120th Meridian, is very central and convenient for roads on the Pacific coast. Again the fifth hour eastward is adopted as the standard time of England, and is the basis of longitude on all marine charts.[14]

Saratoga Springs, N.Y.   C. F. Dowd
May 15, 1872.

Just as in England there was great debate on the change to Greenwich mean time, so there was great debate over Dowd's proposals. It took eleven years for this proposal of Dowd's to be adopted by the railways of Canada and the United States. Sunday, November 18, 1883, at or before noon, was the time chosen for all public clocks to be altered to the "new standard of time agreed upon, first by the railroads, for the sake of uniformity of the schedules, but since generally adopted by the community through the action of various official and corporate bodies as an obvious convenience in all social and business matters." The advantages of the new scheme were outlined by *Harper's Weekly:*

On Saturday, the 17th of November, when the Sun reached the meridian of the eastern border of Maine, clocks began their jangle for the hour of twelve, and this was kept up in a drift across the continent for four hours, like incoherent cowbells in a wild wood.

But on Monday, the 19th of November—supposing all to have changed to the new system on the 18th—no clock struck for this hour till the Sun reached the seventy-fifth meridian. Then all the clocks on the continent struck together, those in the Eastern Section striking twelve, those in the Central striking eleven, those in the Mountains ten and those in the Pacific striking nine.

The minute hands of all were in harmony with each other, and those of all travellers' watches. Time-balls everywhere became perfectly intelligible, and the bliss of ignorance was no longer at a premium.[15]

---

[14]D. Howse, *Greenwich Time.*
[15]*Harper's Weekly* (New York), December 29, 1883.

Prime Meridian for the World

The need for a prime meridian to encompass the whole world was already seen by a seventeen-year-old boy in 1847. In that year this boy posed "Where does the day begin?" in the *Rectory Umbrella*, which was a paper he edited for his brothers and sisters. In his article he said:

Half of the world, or nearly so, is always in the light of the Sun: as the world turns round, this hemisphere of light shifts round too, and passes over each part of it in succession.

Supposing on Tuesday, it is morning at London; in another hour it would be Tuesday morning at the west of England; if the whole world were land we might go on tracing Tuesday morning, Tuesday morning all round, till, in twenty four hours we get to London again. But we know that at London twenty-four hours after Tuesday morning it is Wednesday morning. Where, then, in its passage round Earth, does the day change its name? Where does it lose its identity?[16]

This was no ordinary boy. His name was Charles Lutwidge Dodgson, and, on the face of it, he became a dull, mediocre lecturer in mathematics at the Oxford College of Christ Church; but in reality he was to become world famous as Lewis Carroll, the author of *Alice in Wonderland*. Now that we have a system of longitude and time covering the whole world, we can answer the question that he posed. It is on the international date line that the day changes its identity.

In the early 1880s there was no single meridian for the whole world. The sea charts of most of the major countries used the meridian of Greenwich. The exceptions were France and Algeria (who used the Paris meridian), Portugal, who used the one through Lisbon, and Spain, who used the one through Cádiz. For land maps, most countries did not use the Greenwich meridian. The

[16]Reprinted in *The Magic of Lewis Carroll*, edited by J. Fisher, Nelson, 1973.

exceptions were the United Kingdom and colonies, the United States, and Japan. Many international meetings and discussions took place in an attempt to rectify this situation, but, for the most part, no workable decision was reached until the International Meridian Conference was held in Washington, D.C., in October 1884.

This conference agreed on a number of resolutions, of which the first three are the most important, since these were the ones that led to the acceptance of the Greenwich meridian as prime meridian of the world. The first three resolutions stated:

I. That it is the opinion of this Congress it is desirable to adopt a single prime meridian for all nations, in place of the multiplicity of initial meridians which now exist.
II. That the conference proposes to the Governments here represented the adoption of the meridian passing through the centre of the transit instrument at the Observatory of Greenwich as the initial meridian for longitude.
III. That from this meridian longitude shall be counted in two directions up to 180 degrees, east longitude being plus and west longitude minus.[17]

These were the decisions that placed Greenwich not only at the center of the longitude system, but also at the center of the time zone system which encircles the globe. It also made the name Greenwich a household name. The main consequence of this conference is well summarized by Derek Howse, former head of Navigation and Astronomy at the National Maritime Museum, Greenwich:

The principal impact of the Washington conference on the man-in-the-street was the adoption, country by country, of a time-zone system based upon the world's new prime meridian, Greenwich—

[17]International Conference held in Washington for the purposes of fixing a Prime Meridian and a Universal Day, October 1884; Protocols of Proceedings.

The Greenwich Meridian. (*Trustees of the National Maritime Museum*)

and this despite the fact that the time-zone system, though discussed, was not specifically recommended by the conference.[18]

In our day, with hundreds of international flights daily from one country to another, with innumerable intercontinental telephone calls, it is absolutely necessary to use a time zone system when drawing up schedules involving more than one country. It would be difficult to conceive of a world without the meridian at Greenwich.

The Greenwich Time Signals via Radio

The invention of radio telegraphy, and the subsequent development of radio as a means of communicating sounds and signals over very large distances, added a new dimension to Greenwich time. From about 1904 Greenwich time could now be made available to ships at sea. The familiar time pips were introduced into the domestic radio service by the British Broadcasting Company in 1924. In that year the astronomer royal, Frank Dyson, suggested to the director general of the company that a "six-pip" time signal be broadcast on the last six seconds of each hour. This new service was inaugurated by Dyson himself in a broadcast to the nation on February 5, 1924.

The Scheduling of Space Probes

The launching from Earth of space probes that can successfully rendezvous with the Moon or planets requires scheduling on a grand scale. Just as man-made satellites are like artificial Moons moving within the gravitational field of Earth, so space probes are like artificial planets moving in the gravitational field of the Sun. Usually a space probe is first put into orbit around Earth. Then the rocket motors give it an extra boost in speed to put it into orbit around the Sun. This orbit is usually much more elliptical than those of the planets, and it is so chosen that the path of the probe will take it close to the orbit of another planet. The probe must

[18]D. Howse, *Greenwich Time*.

be launched at the right time, so that the planet will actually meet the probe where their orbits cross. It is rather like running to catch a bus—you must be at the bus stop at the same time as the bus if you want to catch it. Obviously this analogy is not quite right, because you can get there before the bus arrives, and then wait for it, whereas in the case of planets and space probes, neither the probe nor the planets can wait at any point along their respective orbits.

Some space probes have visited more than one planet in the Solar System, and on such occasions their launch dates and their orbits have to be very carefully planned so that they rendezvous with each planet in turn, at the right moment. For example the NASA *Mariner 10* space probe went to visit Venus and Mercury, while *Voyager 2* was launched so that it could rendezvous with Jupiter, Saturn, Uranus, and Neptune in turn. At each encounter the space probe gets a gravitational tug from the planet it is encountering, which gives its speed a boost, and thus hurls it on to the next planet. This procedure is called "gravity assist," because the extra energy is supplied by the gravitational field of the planet.

This very sophisticated type of scheduling on a Solar System scale has only been possible because we know the schedules of the planets with such great accuracy, and we know the rules that govern the motion of space probes. All this has come about because of the ancient astronomers and astrologers. As we will see in later chapters, astronomy as a scientific discipline arose out of the need for a calendar in the ancient world. The motions of the Sun, Moon, and stars could be used for this purpose. Later, people used the Sun and stars for timekeeping, direction finding, and navigational purposes. However, the irregularity of planetary motion meant that it could not be used for any of these purposes. The early interest in planetary motion was largely motivated by a conviction, held by some peoples in the ancient world, that the positions of the planets at the birth of an individual, and the subsequent motions of the planets, could affect the destiny of that individual. The case in support of this assertion has been argued by Prof. T. S. Kuhn in his book *The Copernican Revolution*, Princeton University Press, 1957. This led to a careful observational study of planetary motion. The long unbroken record of planetary motion resulting from these observations led to the realization that there were temporal patterns in these data. Mathematical techniques were then developed which enable astronomers and astrologers to predict the future motions of Sun, Moon, and planets from a knowledge of their past and present positions. This in turn gave rise, very much later, to Kepler's discovery of the traffic rules for celestial objects—Kepler's laws of planetary motion. In the hands of Sir Isaac Newton these data and Kepler's laws were developed into general laws of motion for all objects larger than molecules, and the law of gravitation. The laws enable us to understand the motions of cars along highways, ships across the sea, planes in the sky, space probes to the planets, and the stars in galaxies. Very little understanding of this regularity would have emerged from the study of just the Sun, Moon, and stars. It was the data on planetary motion that provided the key to the cosmos. This means that the highly developed celestial mechanics we have today, so necessary for astronautics, is our heritage from the long unbroken studies of planetary motion undertaken by astronomers in the ancient world for astrological purposes.

Conclusion

In this chapter we saw how the increasing complexity of our social structures has led to the need to adapt our own personal schedules to the needs of the society in which we live. The great advances that have taken place in the technology of travel and communications have meant that our systems of timekeeping have had to be changed to take into account the global nature of world society. Our exploration of the Solar System by space probes has led to the expansion of our framework of time to encompass planetary dimensions. In the next chapter we will look at the origin of one essential ingredient of all our schedules—our calendar.

2

Calendars—
Schedules of Light

The first concern of people's early interest in the apparent motions of Sun, Moon, and stars seems to have been connected to the making of calendars. Calendars were also a necessary prerequisite for the development of a systematic approach to astrology. In this chapter we will concentrate on the origins and development of the calendar, from ancient to modern times. We will briefly look at the different types of evidence available on the origins of the calendar, then at a variety of different solutions to calendar problems worked out by different cultures at different times, and then we will consider the origins of our own calendar. However, to set the scene, let us see why calendars were needed in prehistoric times, and the general nature of problems connected with the construction of calendars.

Why Calendars?

In order to survive in the harsh conditions that gave rise to the predecessors of modern man, it was necessary to find food, and to avoid falling prey to larger animals. People in very early times depended for their food either on hunting or gathering food from trees and plants. They knew that animals, birds, and plants were not available all the time, but they had no calendar to help plan their hunting and gathering to coincide with times when food was available. However, they soon realized that the night sky was constantly changing with the seasons of the year.

These early hunter-gatherers would have noticed, for example, that when certain patterns of stars were on the eastern horizon immediately after sunset, it was always at a time of year when certain berries were ripe for eating. They may also have noticed that some birds and animals would disappear from the landscape for a period, only to reappear when other patterns of stars were appearing on the western horizon just before sunrise. In this way they developed the use of the sky as a calendar. It may well have been during these times that there arose the notion, in the legends and myths of these cultures, that the divisions of time, and the development of the calendar, was the work of celestial deities. The "tables of fate" of ancient Babylonian mythology were the work of the god Nebo, who wrote the destinies of the coming year on these. In Egypt this task was performed by Thoth—the divine scribe. In South America the ancient Maya attributed the invention of their calendar to the bird-serpent deity, Quetzalcoatl.[1] Subsequent development of agricultural civilizations made greater demands of the calendar makers, and the whole problem required a series of astronomical observations spanning a long period of time.

The Calendar and Agriculture

Agricultural communities developed in many different parts of the world, but all the great ones had one feature in common: They started along plains surrounding great rivers.

In Egypt the Nile, in Mesopotamia the Euphrates, and in China the Hwang provided water for these great early civilizations. The organization of smaller groups of people into larger settled cultures, and later on into states, arose initially from the need to centralize the regulation of water. The silt brought down by the rivers was extremely fertile, and it yielded very good crops, but the manage-

---

[1]See "The History of the Calendar in Astronomy and Space," by A. A. Dickson, *Astronomy and Space*, 1, 4, 1972. According to Webster's Family Encyclopedia, Quetzalcoatl was associated with Venus during the Aztec period. It does not claim that the god was exclusively Aztec.

ment of the water and the silt demanded some organizational skills. The people who had these skills developed into a separate class of officials and rulers. In order to control this water, rivers had to be deepened, dikes needed to be built and canals dug. This was an ongoing process and only a strong central authority could ensure that the general interests of the state could be successfully linked to more local interests. A powerful central authority was also needed to organize the defense of the fertile plains against aggressive neighbors from the surrounding deserts and mountains.[2]

The amount of water available in the great rivers had a seasonal flow, and so more accurate calendars were needed to predict when the rivers were likely to flood. Yet, large fluctuations in weather conditions at the same time of different years would have been well known to the farmers; so why was such precision necessary? The answer is that in all ancient cultures and civilizations agricultural activities were accompanied by religious rites, ceremonies, and festivals. The gods in whom people believed represented the dominant natural forces, which imposed some regularity on the social structures of the day. When one was in the service of the gods, carelessness could not be allowed. There had to be an exact observance of ritual, and the calendar was essential to the chronological ordering of various rituals. Thus, the calendar became an object of continual care, looked after by the acting officials, who then became, as a result of their special knowledge, socially powerful. This view of the evolution of social classes may well be an oversimplification of the facts, but it does not alter the conclusion, which is consistent with the evidence, that the construction of a practical calendar was an important and vital task, and it gave some status to those who sought workable solutions to the problems it raised.

The Calendar Problem

The complexity of the calendar problem arises from the fact that the basic periods involved are not simple fractions of each other.

[2]See *A History of Astronomy* by A. Pennekoek, Interscience, New York, 1961. The scenario he proposes is an attempt at synthesizing the available data.

The average period of the Moon is 29.53059 days; the solar year is 365.24220 days. This means that twelve lunar periods amounts to 354.3671 days, which is eleven days short of one year, and so after three years a calendar based on the Moon would be thirty-three days short of three seasonal cycles. To bring such a lunar calendar back in step with the seasons, it would have been necessary to include an extra month of thirty-three days every three years. The calendar problem really consists of finding a larger period after which the Sun and the Moon will return to their same mutual positions. Later in this chapter we will consider how some cultures found workable solutions to this problem, but first we will look at the evidence available for studying the history of the calendar problem.

Sources on the History of the Calendar

The sources on the history of the calendar take a variety of forms. They take the form of cave paintings from many different parts of the world, papyri from ancient Egypt, clay and stone tablets from early Babylon, and stone rows and circles, temples, and other monuments spread across the world, from the islands of Polynesia, right through the Far and Near East, across western Europe and early America. In this section we will briefly review some of this evidence.

(1) Ancient Egyptian Sources

Inside some coffin lids, and in some graves, which date from as early as 2000 B.C., there are to be found pictures of an astronomical method of finding time. Some of these show a row of seated men; over each one of these are twelve lines representing the twelve parts of night. The positions of the stars are marked on the vertical lines and in each line a star that can be seen in this position at a certain time is mentioned. Although this was really a star clock, as we will see in the next chapter, its construction is very much related to the Egyptian calendar in use at this time, and so it has been sometimes referred to as the diagonal calendar.

There are also about eighty monuments, some of which are concerned with astronomy in one way or another. Mostly these are in the form of ceilings, the majority of which are in tombs, but there are also some in temples. One of the most famous of the ceilings is the one from Dendra, which was originally part of the ceiling of a chapel on the roof of a temple, but is now preserved in the Louvre in Paris. All twelve signs of the zodiac are depicted in the central part of this ceiling, and around the circumference are to be found the decans, which formed the time-telling stars of the Egyptian star clock mentioned above.

(2) Babylonian Astronomical Documents

Our knowledge of Babylonian astronomy is based largely on various clay tablets covered with the cuneiform script used in ancient Mesopotamia for about three thousand years, until the first century of our own era. The cuneiform clay tablets which contain records of serious astronomical observations can be divided into two groups of documents. The first group is really one long document, which is the Babylonian calendar, and it lists the appearances of Venus as an evening or a morning star during the reign of King Ammisadaqa. The second group records astronomical observations which come from the ancient capital city Babylon, in what is now southern Iraq. These are really in the form of astronomical diaries. There are about 1,200 fragments of these diaries, and these texts are now in the British Museum.

(3) Stone Circles and Rows

The Stone Age monument at Stonehenge, in Wiltshire, in the south of England is one of the most famous stone circles that have been credited with some astronomical significance. However, there are many other circle and stone rows to be found in western Europe. In the absence of any documentary evidence that can support the various theories concerned with the use of such sites for astronomical observations, we can only surmise how they might have been used in this way. It seems very likely that they might have been used for solar observations, marking the points on the horizon at which the Sun rose and set at the solstices. They might have also been used for some observations on the rising and setting of the Moon. However, the most controversial aspect of the astronomical importance of Stonehenge, in particular, relates to its use as an eclipse predictor—which was able to predict the likelihood of eclipses, although it would have been unable to predict which eclipses would have been visible from the site. It is extremely difficult to decide if this computer aspect ever was a reality, or whether it is the result of modern surveyors and astronomers endowing these stones with a significance which they never actually had in the culture of their Stone Age builders.

(4) An Aztec Calendar Stone

The Stone of the Sun is perhaps the most magnificent of all the monuments of Aztec art. This great block of basalt is 3.6 meters in diameter and weighs twenty-five tons. In the center of this stone is the face of the sun god of the Aztecs, and the four squares around the head of the ruler probably represent the four seasons. This monument was completed in 1479, after more than fifty years of work.

(5) Maya Manuscripts

The highlands of Guatemala, the western edges of Honduras and El Salvador, the eastern Chiapas, and the whole of the Yucatán Peninsula formed the region occupied by the Maya. Most of our knowledge of Maya astronomy comes from part of the Codex Dresdenis, which is a manuscript preserved in the Saxon Regional Library in Dresden, Germany. This work originates from the twelfth or thirteenth century, but it is believed to be a copy of older originals. It consists of a number of different astronomical tables on a variety of subjects. For example, the "Venus Table" contains data on the appearance of Venus as a morning and evening star for about three centuries. This particular planet was of major importance to the Maya.

Early Egyptian Calendars

All of those early communities, for which we have evidence regarding their astronomical practices, used the Moon for calendarmaking purposes. The Egyptians were no exception to this general rule. However, unlike some of their nearest neighbors, they began their lunar month not with the first appearance of the new crescent in the west at sunset, but with the morning when the old crescent of the waning Moon could be seen no longer just before sunrise in the eastern sky. They divided their lunar year into three seasons, each consisting of four lunar months. There were four months of inundation, during which the Nile overflowed and covered the valley, then there were four months of planting and growing, and this was followed by four months of harvest and low water. In order to keep this lunar year in step with the seasons, a thirteenth intercalary month was introduced every three years. Later on they used the bright star Sirius to regulate the inclusion of this extra month. The early Egyptian astronomers—usually known as hourwatchers—noticed that just as the Nile was about to rise, the star Sirius could be seen rising in the east, just a short while before the Sun itself rose. Such a rising is called a heliacal rising, and it follows a period of invisibility, when Sirius is virtually rising and setting with the Sun and so could not be seen. To the Egyptians, Sirius was the goddess Sopdet or Sothis, and the reappearance of this goddess heralded the inundation for the Egyptians.

In pagan Egypt this calendar was used for centuries. Early in the third millennium B.C. a new calendar was introduced, probably for administrative purposes. This calendar consisted of three seasons of four thirty-day months each, with five additional "epagomenal days" or "days upon the year," which were considered to be festival days, thus giving 365 days in all.[3] The Egyptians were also aware, soon after the introduction of this calendar, that the real year was longer by about one quarter of a day than their civil year, but they never bothered to do anything about it. However,

[3]See R. A. Parker, "Ancient Egyptian Astronomy" in *The Place of Astronomy in the Ancient World*, edited by F. R. Hobsen, Oxford University Press, Oxford, 1974.

it is to their credit that they had determined the length of the natural year, and that they had invented one of the most sensible and practical calendars of the ancient world.

Babylonian Numerical Astronomy

The Babylonians invented a very sophisticated form of numerical astronomy, which was able to predict the motions of Sun, Moon, and planets with some precision and was also able to forecast the likelihood of eclipses occurring.

Their approach to astronomy was extremely important in the subsequent development of mathematical astronomy in many parts of the Western world. Professor A. Aaboe, a leading authority on ancient astronomy from Yale University, had this to say about their particular approach to theoretical astronomy:

Thus the astronomical tradition in the West is linked to Babylonian astronomy. Mathematical astronomy was, however, not only the principal carrier and generator of certain mathematical techniques, but it became the model for the new exact sciences which learned from it their principal goal: to give a mathematical description of a particular class of natural phenomena capable of yielding numerical predictions that can be tested against observations. It is in this sense that I claim that Babylonian mathematical astronomy was the origin of all subsequent serious endeavour in the exact sciences.

Initially this type of Babylonian astronomy was invented to cope with the fact that they had a strict adherence to a lunar calendar, and the problems raised by this demanded the development of numerical techniques, which could later be applied to the movements of other celestial bodies. In the next section we deal with the problems posed by their calendar.

The Babylonian Lunar Calendar

In Babylon they started their month on the first day they saw the thin crescent of the Moon in the west just after sunset, so their calendar was more in keeping with those of their neighbors than with that of the Egyptians. The inconvenience of starting the month with the actual sighting of the thin crescent is obvious, since it is so dependent on conditions in our atmosphere. It was for this reason that the Babylonians wanted to develop a theoretical astronomy, so they could predict when, in principle, they should be able to see the crescent Moon, and they could then start the month on this day without having to wait for an actual sighting. There were, however, some problems they had to overcome before they could achieve this.

We know that as the Earth goes around the Sun we would see the Sun (if we could see the Sun and stars at the same time) against a different constellation of the zodiac every month, so the Sun does have an apparent motion against the background stars. This apparent pathway is called the ecliptic. The Moon is going around our Earth, so it too has a pathway against the stars, which is different from that of the Sun. The apparent speeds with which the Sun and Moon move are different; the Sun moves through about one degree per day, whereas the Moon moves through about thirteen degrees per day. In addition to this the speeds of both bodies vary slightly as they move against the background stars. All this is very relevant to calculating when one should be able to see the crescent Moon.

First of all the Moon must be a certain distance from the Sun in the sky for the crescent to be seen in the sunset glow. Also important is the angle that the line joining the Sun and Moon makes with the horizon. If this angle is very small the Moon will be too close to the sunset glow on the horizon to be seen. This meant that the Babylonian astronomers had to make a careful study of the movements of both the Sun and Moon. In order to do this they had to invent a method of describing the positions of both bodies against the stars, which formed a natural map against which these objects, and the planets, moved. Just as the postman needs an address before he can deliver a letter to a given house, so astronomers have to define addresses for the Sun and Moon in the sky. This was normally done by giving the number of degrees that each body had moved into a given constellation of the zodiac.

To describe the motion of, say, the Moon, it was necessary to give the number of degrees by which it had moved into a given constellation on a number of different dates. In order to predict where the Moon would be at some time in the future it was necessary to be able to predict these numbers for future dates. The Babylonians did this by noticing patterns in these sets of numbers, and then trying to reproduce these patterns using sequences of numbers, for example, 4, 8, 12, 16, 20, etc., to try to reproduce these observed sets. Their theoretical astronomy was purely arithmetical, and at no time did they seek to picture how the celestial objects were arranged in space. This numerical approach did in fact allow them to work out a predictable lunar calendar, and it also helped them to predict at least some of the eclipses that they observed.

The Julian Calendar

On his military campaigns to Egypt, Julius Caesar became acquainted with the civil and administrative advantages of the Egyptian calendar. He also found out that the Egyptians had discovered that the natural year was much closer to 365.25 days, but that this fact was not incorporated into their calendar in any systematic way. He decided to correct their calendar, and introduce the resulting new calendar into the Roman world. As a result he decreed that the Julian calendar should consist of three "common years" of 365 days each, and a fourth year of 366 days. Unfortunately, for thirty-six years his decree was misinterpreted, and every third year was made a leap year. It was left to Augustus Caesar to realize that an error had been made, and he took the necessary steps to correct this mistake.

The Sky as an Agricultural Calendar

The poet Virgil wrote the Georgics between 39 and 29 B.C. In this poem he uses the signs of the zodiac to give practical advice to farmers about tasks associated with the farming year. However, Seneca's verdict on the poem seems to indicate that he did not achieve what he set out to do. He says that Virgil "wished not to teach farmers, but to delight readers." However accurate that may be, the poem nevertheless does contain some delightful passages linking astronomical phenomena with agricultural tasks. For example:

*When the Scales make the hours of daytime and sleeptime
balance
Dividing the globe into equal hemispheres—light and
darkness,
Then set your bulls to work, farmers, and sow our barley.*

Further along we have:

*But if for a wheat harvest or crop of hardy spelt
You work your land, and are keen on bearded corn alone,
Let first the Atlantid Pleiads come to their morning setting
And the blazing star of the Cretan Crown sink in the sky,
Before you commit to the furrows the seed you owe them,
before
You entrust the hope of the year to an earth that is still
reluctant.*[4]

The Aztec Calendar

The Aztecs ruled an empire in central and south Mexico before their defeat by Hernán Cortés in the sixteenth century. Theirs was a rich, elaborate, and advanced culture. They were great builders of palaces and temples. They worshiped many gods, but especially one called Huitzilopochtli, to whom they made human sacrifices on one of the sacrificial days of their calendar.

In some respects the Aztec calendar resembled the Egyptian calendar. Both calendars consisted of a total of 365 days, and both ended with five sacrificial or festival days. However, the way the rest of the year was divided up differed a great deal in the two cases. Whereas the Egyptians had twelve months, each consisting of thirty days, the Aztecs had eighteen months, each consisting of twenty days.

[4]Virgil, "The E clogues," "The Georgics" Translated by C. Day Lewis, 1940, Reprinted by Oxford University Press, Oxford, 1983.

The Mayan Calendar

The Mayan calendar was a complex mixture of three concurrent ways of marking the passage of days. The first consisted of 365 days, the second of 360 days, and the third was a sacred almanac of 260 days. They made a careful study of certain periods connected with the planet Venus, and they could successfully predict eclipses, although they did not know which eclipses would be visible to them from their part of the world. J. E. S. Thompson, an acknowledged authority on the astronomy of the Maya, had this to say about their achievements:

In conclusion, I believe that Maya calendrical and astronomical achievements were made independently of the Old World, except that giving animal names to constellations, in the Maya 'zodiac' and in other parts of the heavens, as well as some days in Middle American calendars, may have been a custom surviving from very simple systems of counting of hunter-gatherers brought by immigrants to the New World by way of the Bering Strait, perhaps as early as 10,000 B.C.[5]

Islam and Astronomy

The Islamic religion made a great deal of use of celestial phenomena, so the study of astronomy became a major concern of Islamic science. First, the Islamic religious calendar has always been based on the Moon, just as the Babylonian calendar was at an earlier stage in history. As a result of this the astronomers of Islam had to make a careful study of the positions and movements of the Moon. In particular the appearance of the crescent Moon marked the end of the month of Ramadan, which was the ninth month of the Islamic year, when a fast was observed during the hours of daylight. Second, their religion required them to offer daily prayers at specific times of the day. Third, when these prayers were performed, they had to face in the direction of their holy city of Mecca.

[5]J. E. S. Thompson, "Maya Astronomy" in *The Place of Astronomy in the Ancient World.* Edited by F. R. Hobson, Oxford University Press, Oxford, 1974.

The Islamic astronomers built special observatories for carrying out the necessary observations; they developed mathematical techniques that would enable them to draw up lunar almanacs; and they worked out methods for finding the direction of Mecca from various parts of the Islamic world.

Many of the followers of Islam had a nomadic life-style, and so it was also necessary to develop portable astronomical instruments to help them to find time and the direction of Mecca wherever they found themselves. The first such instrument was the astrolabe, which was a combination of two separate devices. The first part was an instrument that enabled one to measure the height of the Sun, or particular stars, above the horizon, and the second part was a combined star map and calculator that could be used to work out the time from measurements made with the first part. They also invented a device, called the qibla indicator, which would enable them to make observations on celestial objects and then calculate the direction of Mecca.

The Gregorian Calendar

Over the years astronomers have measured the length of the year with ever-increasing accuracy. It is now known that the natural year is 365.2422 days long. This meant that even the Roman calendar was slightly inaccurate. By the year 1582 an error of ten days had accumulated as a result of this inaccuracy. A decree was issued by Pope Gregory XIII in that year to correct this situation. This decree stated that the day following October 4 would be called October 15. It was also decreed that leap years falling at the end of a century would not be counted as leap, unless the first two figures were divisible by four. This was how the Julian calendar, which itself was of Egyptian origin, gave rise to the Gregorian calendar.

Differences between Protestants and Catholics, and divisions of the Eastern and Western Christian Churches, meant that the positive advantages of the Gregorian calendar were not accepted straightaway in many countries. France, Italy, Luxembourg, Spain, and Portugal adopted the new calendar in 1582. The Catholic states of Germany, the Netherlands, and Belgium followed in 1584. Although the changeover was started in Switzerland in 1583, it was not completed until 1812. In the United Kingdom and its colonies the change was made in 1752.

The Calendar of the Christian Church

The calendar used by most Christian churches, in the Western world, is a mixture of the Hebrew lunar calendar and the Gregorian solar calendar. Easter Day is a movable feast in the Christian calendar, and all the other movable feasts, for example, Rogation and Ascension, follow in a fixed sequence from that. The rules to be used for the calculation of Easter Day are to be found in the Book of Common Prayer. Here we find the following statement: "it [Easter Day] is always the first Sunday after the full Moon which happened upon or is next after the twenty-first day of March; and if the full Moon happens upon a Sunday, Easter Day is the Sunday after."

When the Gregorian calendar was introduced, there was a lot of debate over the date of Easter, and it was decided at this stage to lay down these rules from which it would be possible to calculate the date of Easter for years to come. The approach completely dispensed with the need to undertake any astronomical observations in order to fix Easter. From the point of view of the astronomer, however, these rules are not as simple as they may at first seem. The Moon which is used to fix the date of Easter is an idealized "ecclesiastical Moon" defined by sets of tables, and it does not correspond precisely to the position of the real Moon in the sky. The vernal equinox does not always fall exactly on March 21—it can vary by a day on either side—so once again it is an idealized equinox that is used in the calculation. In 1923 the Congress of the Eastern Orthodox Churches decided not to follow these rules, but to determine the date of Easter by the real Moon at the meridian of Jerusalem.

Christmas Day

Christmas Day is a fixed feast, determined solely by reference to the Gregorian calendar. The use of December 25 was really based on a pagan festival that also had its roots in an astronomical phenomenon. As we move from the northern summer toward winter, the Sun sets closer and closer to the southwestern part of the horizon and the days get shorter. On December 21, the Sun sets farther to the southwest than on any other day of the year, and we have the shortest day in the Northern Hemisphere. This is called the winter solstice. On December 25 there is a noticeable lengthening of the day, and the point on the horizon at which the Sun sets seems to be moving back from its westerly-most setting. Many people who worshiped the Sun as a god saw this day as that on which the sun god returned from the south, and hence for them is was a festival day. Although spring and the warmer weather were still a few months away, the days were beginning to increase in length, and this heralded the rebirth that would occur near the vernal equinox. The early Christian Church adopted this day as the day on which Christ was born. The evidence that is available on the possible dates for the birth of Christ do not substantiate this point of view.

The Star of Bethlehem

Most of the attempts to pinpoint the birth of Jesus are based on the nature of the Star of Bethlehem and astronomical records or calculations which then follow from the particular celestial sighting to which various scholars give their support. The whole subject is discussed in my book *Astrology: The Evidence of Science*,[6] in the chapter on "The Gift of the Magi." Here I will just quote a few short extracts from this book and add some additional material that has come to hand since the book was first published.

The wise men, or Magi, are referred to as astrologers in the New English Bible. This is really the only sensible way of seeing these men, because astrologers were, and are, the only people who associate births with celestial events. It is not part of any purely astronomical or religious custom to link the birth of any individual with celestial phenomena, but it is very much part of a centuries-

[6]Percy Seymour, *Astrology: The Evidence of Science*, Penguin, London, 1990.

old astrological tradition. It is necessary to accept the fact that the wise men were astrologers, if one is to understand the fundamental importance of the Star of Bethlehem." . . . Further along in this chapter I said: "Jupiter was the Star of Bethlehem— as it rose at sunset on Tuesday, 15 September 7 B.C." . . . I went on to say "Jupiter rises at the same time of every day, although, if it is too close to the Sun in the sky as seen from Earth, we do not always see it rise. This means the rising of Jupiter is in itself not unusual. What made the rising of 15 September 7 B.C., of such great interest to the Magi-astrologers were the associated astronomical events. Jupiter was very close to the planet Saturn at the time of rising, and both planets were in the constellation of Pisces. The appearance of two planets very close together in the sky is called a conjunction. Conjunctions of Saturn and Jupiter take place roughly every 20 years, so this too is not unusual.

The circumstances that start to make the year 7 B.C. of special interest are that in that year conjunctions of Saturn and Jupiter took place three times. Such a series of conjunctions is called a triple conjunction, and for Saturn and Jupiter it takes place only once every 139 years. A triple conjunction in the constellation of Pisces takes place only once every 900 years, and Pisces also had a special significance for the astrologers.

Jupiter, in ancient astrology, was identified as the planet of kings. Saturn was the planet that ruled over Saturday, the Jewish Sabbath, so it became known as the protector of the Jews. The world known to the ancients was divided up into geographical regions, each of which was associated with a sign of the zodiac. The geographical region around Palestine was associated with Pisces.

In December 1984 I set up these astronomical events in the William Day Planetarium, of which I am director. On December 18, 1984, there was a report on this demonstration on the front page of *The Times*, and as a result the event made world news.

Another Possibility for the Star

In December 1987 *The Times* carried a report concerning another suggestion about the Christmas Star. This was based on an article written by Dr. Richard Stephenson that had appeared in the December issue of *Physics Bulletin*.[7] In this article Stephenson suggested that the Star was a supernova explosion, since two such events had been recorded by Chinese astronomers in 4 and 5 B.C. Supernovas are not really new stars, as the Latin word nova would imply; they are stars that for physical reasons suddenly greatly increase their brightness over a period of days.

I wrote a letter to *The Times*, stating my objections to Stephenson's proposal. The letter was not published. However, an expanded version of the letter was published a few months later in the *Physics Bulletin*. I now quote the entire letter, just as it appeared.

I would like to comment on Richard Stephenson's views on the "Star of Bethlehem" (see *Physics Bulletin* December 1987 p. 454)

Firstly he points out that the Saturn-Jupiter conjunction of 7 B.C. was not an impressive one, since Jupiter and Saturn were always more than one degree apart. This is a red herring, since Matthew does not say that the 'Star' was spectacular or that it came as a surprise to the Magi. The event was unimpressive enough to be missed by Herod's advisors, but significant enough for the Magi ("astrologers," in the New English Bible). To ignore the fact that astrology was an important part of the world view of antiquity is to try to fit ancient astronomical observations into the procrustian bed of our own cosmologies.

The Saturn-Jupiter conjunction was important to these astrologers because it occurred three times in 7 B.C. Such an event, in the constellation of Pisces (also important to the astrologers) only occurs once every 900 years. The 'Star' was not simply an association of a celestial event with the birth of Christ by the people of the place in which he was born; it actually caused three men to journey to Bethlehem in search of him.

[7]Richard Stephenson, *Physics Bulletin*, p. 454, December 1987.

The nova hypothesis ignores the world view of antiquity. This saw the sphere of the stars as the region of perfection, thus stars could not vary their brightness with time and so novae could not exist. Consequently there are hardly any recordings of novae, and this is why Stephenson and his colleagues had to search Chinese and Korean records to find one. Not even the nova of the Crab Nebula was recorded in the west, several centuries later. It was Tycho Brahe's discovery of a supernova in 1572 which shattered this world view!

Also, in the ancient world comets were associated with catastrophes and the death of kings, not with good tidings. Hence I still believe that the triple conjunction of 7 B.C. is the most likely event to herald the birth of Christ, and that 15 September is the most likely date for that birth.

P. A. H. Seymour   February 1988
William Day Planetarium,
Plymouth Polytechnic[8]

Astrology and the Calendar

This brings us to the question of the origins of astrology. In a later chapter I will argue that human beings did have a more highly developed awareness of cosmic cycles that evolved with life and that gave us an evolutionary advantage in coping with rhythms in the local environment that were linked to these cycles. However, when we talk about astrology in the West, we normally have in mind natal astrology—which links personality traits with the positions of the Sun, Moon, and planets in the sky, at the time of birth. This type of astrology is a systematic development of our earlier cosmic awareness, and before such an enterprise could be undertaken, certain astronomical discoveries had to be made. This means that astronomy as a systematic science had to precede the development of western natal astrology.

Although the claim has often been made that astrology was responsible for the origin of astronomy, there is very little evidence to substantiate this assertion. This point is made by Professor Otto Neugebauer, in the following quotation:

[8]P. A. H. Seymour, *Physics Bulletin*, Bristol, March 1988, p. 138.

Few statements are more deeply rooted in the public mind or more often repeated than the assertion that the origin of astronomy is to be found in astrology. Not only is historical evidence lacking for this statement but all well documented facts are in sharp contradiction to it. All the above mentioned facts from Egypt and Babylon (and as we will presently see, also from Greece) show that calendaric problems directed the first steps of astronomy.[9]

It is likely that some early association between celestial phenomena and a wide variety of terrestrial events was made, but the systematic development of astrology required several ingredients. Among these were a system of constellations, a reasonable calendar, astronomical methods of timekeeping, and a means of calculating the positions of the planets in the sky, even when they were not directly visible. In later chapters we will discuss these matters in more detail.

Conclusion

In this chapter we considered the development of calendars in general and our calendar in particular. All modern schedules, personal, local, national, and global, have as their basis a calendar for specifying the dates of various events. However, most interactions in the modern world also require precise specifications of time. In the next chapter we will consider the development of various methods of timekeeping.

[9]From O. Neugebauer, *Astronomy and History—Selected Essays*, Springer-Verlag, Heidelberg, 1983.

3

Timekeeping Schedules
of Light

In the center of Plymouth there now stands an enormous sundial. When the erection of this dial was first proposed, the idea gave rise to a great deal of debate. Some people pointed out that it was entirely unnecessary to have such a sundial, because in our own day and age digital clocks and watches could give us the time much more accurately, and in any case one could not tell the time on the sundial when the sky was overcast. My own view is that this dial is not only artistically pleasing, but that it stands as a permanent monument and reminder, as do sundials old and new all over the world, of the fact that the spinning of Earth on its own axis in relationship to the Sun is the very basis of our timekeeping systems.

In this chapter I will discuss the evolution of timekeepers, from ancient to modern times, and will also discuss various mechanical devices which are used to simulate the motions of the Sun, Moon, and planets.

Egyptian Star and Shadow Clocks

In order to tell time at night, the Egyptians introduced a sequence of thirty-six stars—called the decans or the decanal stars—more or less evenly spread across that part of the sky called the ecliptic, which can be defined as the apparent pathway of the Sun against

The Sundial in Plymouth. (*Mr. Harry Patikas*)

the background stars. On a particular night the first star seen rising after dusk would mark the end of the first hour of the night, and the second decanal star rising in the east would mark the end of the second hour of the night, and so on. About ten days later the star that marked the end of the first hour would be rising about forty minutes earlier, so it would not be seen in the dusk. The star that marked the end of the second hour of the night ten days earlier would now mark the end of the first hour, and this was how one would progress through the year. During the equinoxes, when we have equal day and night, eighteen of the decanal stars would already be above the horizon at dusk, so only eighteen would be seen rising in the course of the night. However, during the summer, only twelve decans could be seen rising at night, because the nights were shorter. The Egyptians decided to settle for twelve hours to the night for the whole of the year.

The Egyptians also realized that the shadows of objects cast by the Sun moved with some regularity, and they invented the shadow clock to take advantage of this fact. This shadow clock had a shape that resembled that of a modern bed with a headboard, but no footboard. In the morning the "head" of this clock would be pointed toward the east, and the time would be marked by the position of the shadow of the headboard on the graduated base—the bed part. After midday the clock would be turned around, with the "head" toward the west. Using this clock the Egyptians developed a system of daylight hours, which had four hours to the morning and four hours to the afternoon. There were also about two hours at dawn, when the Sun had not yet risen, during which it was too light to use the star clock, and there were another similar two hours at dusk, which, with the eight already mentioned, gave a total of twelve hours to the day. They thus decided to settle for twelve hours to the day, as well as twelve hours to the night, giving a total of twenty-four hours in all.

This then is the origin of our own twenty-four hour day and night. It will be apparent that the lengths of the hours varied from one season to the next. This was not uncommon in many time-keeping systems. Although equal hours were used in Greek theoretical astronomy, they really only became generally accepted after the invention of mechanical timekeepers.

Sundial

Sundials are, in effect, a development of the shadow clocks of the ancient Egyptians. Most sundials consist of two parts: some form of indicator, called the gnomon, which casts a shadow on a graduated surface, called the dial face. In many dials the gnomon is arranged so that it is parallel to the axis of Earth. In the simple cylindrical-type sundial the gnomon is so placed, and it is arranged to also form the axis of a semicylinder, which is graduated on the inside. Since the Sun moves through fifteen degrees per hour the shadow cast by the gnomon on the inside of the semicylinder will also move through fifteen degrees per hour. Thus, in this case, the graduations on the dial face will be equally spaced.

Several sundials have flat dial faces, either vertically or horizontally mounted. In these cases the dial markings on the dial are not equally spaced and these have to be carefully calculated for the specific geometry of the sundial.

Sundials come in a large variety of shapes and sizes, and the basic simplicity of the concepts involved provide the designers of dials with a great deal of scope to show their artistic flair. Sundials reached the peak of their popularity between 1500 and 1800. During this period they were used as checks on mechanical clocks, which eventually replaced them as the major method of social timekeeping. Not all dials were fixed. Several different types of portable sundials were invented, which allowed travelers to tell time at locations limited to a narrow range of latitudes. These portable dials usually incorporated a small magnetic compass, since the main axis of the dial had to be aligned with the north-south direction before it could be used to tell time. Watches superseded these portable dials.

The Nocturnal

It is generally known that in the Northern Hemisphere the North Star (also called the Pole Star) can be treated as being fixed immediately above the north cardinal point, and that the stars close to it go around this star in circles. The stars and the constellations that do so are called the circumpolar stars and constellations. One of the best known of the circumpolar constellations is the Great Bear. There are seven stars in this constellation that are much brighter than the rest, and these have been given a variety of different names in different countries. These seven stars are called the Big Dipper in North America and the Plough or Charles Wain (wain being an earlier form of the word wagon) in England. If we drew an imaginary straight line through the two stars known as the pointers of this constellation, that line would lead to the North Star. This line moves through about fifteen degrees per hour, so it can be used as the basis of a timekeeping system. At first seamen and shepherds used to memorize the position of the pointers, at midnight, for each fortnight of the year, and by comparing the appropriate midnight position with the observed position on a given night, at an unknown time, they could deduce the time to within about a half hour. The nocturnal was invented to enable people to carry out this task with great accuracy and without having to remember the midnight positions.

This instrument was made out of a thin sheet of wood, usually about a tenth of an inch thick. It consisted of three discs with extensions of various sizes, all held together by a large rivet with a hole of about a quarter of an inch in diameter through the center. The three discs were able to move independently of each other. The largest disc was about four and a half inches in diameter, and had an extension in the form of a handle by which the observer could hold the device. On top of this was a smaller disc, about three inches in diameter, to which was attached a small pointer able to point to the dates marked on the circumference of the first disc. On the circumference of this small disc were marked the hours of the day and night. The third disc was about one inch in diameter, and it had an extension in the form of an arm which was about seven to eight inches in length.

To use the nocturnal, the sailor would first ensure that the pointer on the inner dial pointed to the correct date on the outer dial. This would be the date on which he was trying to find the time. Holding the nocturnal vertically, he would face north, and by looking through the hole in the rivet he would locate the North Star. He

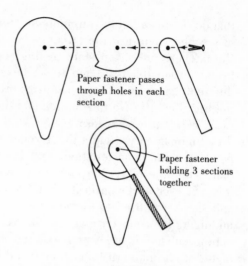

Paper fastener passes through holes in each section

Paper fastener holding 3 sections together

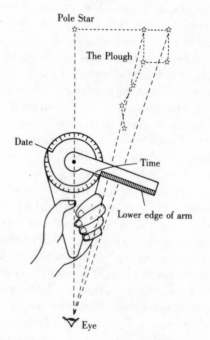

Pole Star

The Plough

Date

Time

Lower edge of arm

Eye

The assembly and use of a Nocturnal made of transparent acetate; designed by the author. (*Dr. P. Seymour*)

then would move the arm of the nocturnal until the pointers of the Plough were just level with the edge of the arm. The time of night could then be read against this edge on the time dial.

Mechanical Time

Even in the time of the ancient Egyptians attempts were made to divorce the general methods of keeping time from actual astronomical observations. To this end they invented the water clock, known later by the Greeks as the clepsydra. There were two main types of water clock. In one type, water from a fairly large reservoir flowed into a graduated cylinder, and the time that had elapsed could be read by the position of the water with respect to the graduations. In the other (outflow) type, a vessel containing water was in the form of a conical funnel with a small neck. This was necessary to ensure that the water level would fall at a constant rate. When the water level is high the pressure at the neck is great, so the outflow will be greater. As the level drops the pressure is less, so the outflow is also less. However, in a conical vessel there is less water to shift as the level drops, so the level will change by equal amounts in equal intervals of time. The time was read by noting the level of water with respect to the graduations on the cone.

It took several centuries before accurate mechanical timekeepers were developed, but there is some evidence now available that the first steps in this development were laid in the ancient world of the Greeks. Why did the Greek scholars want to invent mechanical devices to represent celestial motions?

The Stimulus from Astrology

When we talk about astrology in the Western world, we usually have in mind natal astrology, which links the personality and destiny of the individual with the positions of the planets at birth and the subsequent motions of these planets with respect to the birth chart. In order to lay the foundations of this type of astrology, the ancient astrologers needed three things. First, they needed a reliable calendar; second, they needed star maps showing the constellations to act as a referencing system; third, they needed methods of telling time during day and night. The apparent motions of the Sun, Moon, and planets against the background stars served to define a set of constellations that is called the zodiac. To cast a personal horoscope it was and still is necessary to know the positions of the planets, Sun, and Moon along the zodiac at birth, and the zodiac constellation on the horizon at the time of birth. This meant knowing the positions of the planets at this time even if they could not be seen in the sky during the night. It was necessary to be able to predict the positions of the planets against the background zodiac stars. As we saw earlier, Babylonian arithmetical or theoretical astronomy enabled such calculations to be carried out.

Although the Babylonian methods were reasonably accurate, what was needed was a more detailed geometrical model which could explain how the heavenly bodies were arranged in space and a method for calculating future movements of the planets from such a model. These requirements were supplied by the geometrical models of Greek astronomy.

Greek Models of the Heavens

One of the first models proposed in ancient Greece to account for the motions of the stars, Sun, Moon, and planets was that of the philosopher Aristotle. He proposed that Earth was a sphere fixed at the center of the universe. Concentric with Earth was a very much larger sphere, which enclosed all things, called the celestial sphere. The stars were fixed to the celestial sphere, and since this sphere was spinning on its own axis once every twenty-three hours, fifty-six minutes, each star would also take this time to go once around the Sun. The space between the sphere of Earth and the celestial sphere was filled up with seven other clear concentric crystalline spheres, and to each of these was attached one of the planets, the Sun, and the Moon.

The motion of the outer sphere was transmitted downward by means of friction between neighboring spheres. Thus, the sphere of Saturn moved the least with respect to the background stars, because it was touching the celestial sphere, and the sphere of the

Moon moved the most, because the friction drive was least effective in this case, and the lunar sphere was in contact with the fixed Earth, which further reduced the effectiveness of the drive. Most other Greek models were a development of this scheme. This also provided the philosophical basis of cosmology which was to underlie religious, cultural, and scientific thinking in the Western world for centuries.

Eudoxus and Ptolemy

Aristotle's simple scheme could not explain the complexities of planetary motion. It was well known that the planets moved through the zodiac constellations, all with different speeds, and not always in the same direction. Venus and Mercury never moved very far from the Sun in the sky, and they were never seen at midnight. Mars, Jupiter, and Saturn would, most of the time, move from west to east against the background stars, but sometimes they would change this direction, and move from east to west. These motions were, of course, in addition to the east-west motion of the whole sky.

In order to overcome the problems associated with these movements Aristotle made use of a system of spheres invented by the astronomer Eudoxus. Eudoxus had devised for each planet a set of spheres, nestling one within the other, and pivoting about independent axes, rather like the gimbals of a ship's compass. By giving each sphere an appropriate independent movement about its own axis, Eudoxus was able to simulate the movement of the planets. One great disadvantage of this scheme was that the planets were always on spheres that were concentric with Earth, so they did not change their distances from us, yet it was known that the planets varied their brightness as they moved against the background stars.

Ptolemy was well aware of the problems of the scheme proposed by Aristotle, and because he wanted to make accurate planetary predictions, for astrological purposes, he introduced various geometrical devices to overcome these problems. He proposed that each planet moved about its own little circle—called the epicycle—the center of which orbited Earth in a circle called the deferent.

These geometrical schemes not only provided greater accuracy with regard to predicting planetary positions, they also opened up the exciting possibility of representing these models in mechanical form, and in so doing helped in the development of the concepts necessary to build mechanical timepieces.

Early Mechanical Models of Celestial Movements

According to Dr. Henry King, who wrote the book *Geared to the Stars*, the earliest known reference to a mechanical model of the Sun, Moon, and planets is contained in *De Republica*, written by Cicero around 60 B.C. Here we quote from King's book:

In one of the discussions (recorded in Cicero's book), Philus informs his companions that after Marcus Claudius Marcellus captures the opulent city of Syracuse in 212 B.C. he carried off along with much booty two spherae made by Archimedes. One of these, a solid and compact globe, had stars marked on its surface and was placed in the Temple of Vesta. The other, not in solid form, showed the motions of the Sun, Moon, and planets, and was the only item of the spoils of war kept by Marcellus for his own use.[1]

No copy or parts of these devices have been found, and no detailed descriptions or plans have survived, so we do not know how Archimedes accomplished what he was supposed to have made. However, the mechanical difficulties presented by the construction of such devices leads one to suspect that they could only have demonstrated the basic ideas involved, and that they did not faithfully represent the subtleties of the system of Eudoxus and Aristotle.

The Antikythera Mechanism

We do have some positive evidence that the Greeks knew about gearing, and that they used it to construct at least one device

[1] H. C. King, *Geared to the Stars*, University of Toronto Press, Toronto, 1978.

connected with celestial motion. This evidence comes from the discovery, in 1900, of such a mechanism in the wreck of a Greek ship off the south coast of Greece, near the barren islet of Antikythera; hence the fragments of this instrument has been called the Antikythera mechanism. The corroded remains of this mechanism, which was made of bronze, were investigated using X rays and radioacative gamma rays. D. J. de Solla Price presented the results of this investigation in 1974. He concluded that the original was capable of carrying out calculations connected with the calendar, so it seems that it also represents one of the earliest mechanical calculators. Professor G. J. Whitrow said of this mechanism, "According to our present knowledge, this machine was the nearest the artificers of antiquity came to inventing a truly mechanical clock."[2]

From Astronomical Models to Mechanical Clocks

Up to the present time we have found no definite links between the earlier geared astronomical models and the first mechanical clocks, but, to quote from Professor Whitrow, "the way in which a surviving late fourteenth-century clock such as that of Wells Cathedral displays the phases of the Moon and figures which emerge at successive hours suggests that such clocks were the product of a continuing tradition from the distant past." Although there exists some documentary evidence to support this thesis, the true origin of mechanical clocks still represents an unsolved mystery. On the basis of the evidence that we do have, it now seems likely that the mechanical clock was invented between 1280 and 1300.

The invention of the "verge-and-foliot" escapement mechanism was an important invention that made such clocks possible. This consisted of a horizontal bar—called the foliot—which was pivoted at its center to a vertical rod—called the verge—to which were attached two pallets. These pallets engaged the teeth on a vertical wheel. The toothed wheel was driven by a weight suspended from a drum, and it pushed the verge first one way and then the other way, thus causing the oscillation of the foliot. The toothed wheel

[2]G. J. Whitrow, *Time in History*, Oxford University Press, Oxford, 1989.

advanced through the distance of one tooth for each to-and-fro movement of the foliot. The speed of oscillation of the foliot could be altered by changing the distance between the weights that it carried near its ends. The clock at Salisbury Cathedral, which is supposed to be the oldest surviving clock in England, has a verge-and-foliot escapement. However, it does not have hands to show the time, but, instead, it strikes the hours. The fact that this escapement did not have a well-defined natural frequency, combined with the effects of friction, meant that the early mechanical clocks were not very accurate. Nevertheless, they provided a useful social function.[3]

The Astrarium of Giovanni de Dondi

One of the most remarked of all astronomical clocks was invented and built by Giovanni de Dondi in the middle of the fourteenth century. The construction of this mechanical model of the universe took him sixteen years. Unfortunately the original did not survive, but de Dondi left clear instructions on how to build one, and from these instructions two replicas have been built. One is housed in the Smithsonian Institution in Washington, D.C., and the other in the Science Museum in London.

These clocks have seven faces, one showing the movement of the Sun, another showing the movement of the Moon, and five showing the movements of the naked eye planets known to the ancients. These movements are depicted according to Ptolemy's conception of the motions of Sun, Moon, and planets. Thus, for the Sun and Moon dials the motions are shown as circular around Earth, but for the five planets de Dondi used gearing to simulate the epicycles and deferents of Ptolemy.

In his assessment of this clock, Dr. Jacob Bronowski in his book *The Ascent of Man* had this to say: "But more than the mechanical marvel is the intellectual conception, which comes from Aristotle and Ptolemy and the Greeks. De Dondi's clock is their view of the planets as seen from Earth."[4] Further along he says: "It is a mar-

[3]H. C. King, *Geared to the Stars*, University of Toronto Press, Toronto, 1978.
[4]J. Bronowski, *The Ascent of Man*, BBC, London, 1973.

vellous intellectual conception; very complex—but that only makes it more marvellous that in A.D. 150, not long after the birth of Christ, the Greeks should have been able to conceive and put into mathematics this superb construction."

Although I agree with Bronowski to some extent, I think that he underestimates to some degree the greatness of de Dondi's intellectual contribution. I once attended a lecture at the Science Museum, London, given by the horologist who had just completed a replica of this clock. He pointed out the many problems that he had to solve because they were not clearly specified in the plans of de Dondi. One of the most interesting, at least from my point of view, concerned the difficulty of cutting oval-shaped, or elliptical, gears, which de Dondi had introduced to cope with the irregularities of Mercury's orbit.

Ptolemy had been aware of these difficulties concerning Mercury and he coped with them in the following way. He still used epicycles and deferents, but Earth was no longer placed at the center of Mercury's deferent, but slightly to one side of the center. On the other side of the center was another point about which the center of the epicycle moved with constant speed. In order to reproduce these movements mechanically de Dondi had to use elliptical gears. Dr. King points out "that the oval figure is not equivalent to Mercury's elliptical orbit" which has since been determined with great accuracy. Be that as it may, the fact remains that de Dondi introduced the mathematical concept of elliptical gearing to represent the motions of Mercury two hundred years before the birth of Kepler, who made the discovery that all the planets go around the Sun in elliptical orbits.

The Development of Pendulum Clocks

The accuracy of mechanical clocks improved by more than a factor of ten with the invention of the pendulum clock. This clock started with the work of the great Italian astronomer and scientist, Galileo Galilei. The story goes that Galileo made his important discovery while attending a service in Pisa Cathedral. While watching the swinging of the cathedral chandeliers, he noticed, using his own pulse as a timekeeper, that the period taken to complete one swing was independent of the amplitude of the swing. In other words, when the chandeliers were swinging through large arcs, they took the same time to complete one swing as they did when they were swinging in smaller arcs.

In 1637, Galileo devised a series of gear wheels which were controlled by a toothed wheel regulated by a pendulum, with the pendulum itself, operated by hand. This device could be used to count oscillations. Although Galileo made many great contribution to physics and astronomy, including the application of the telescope to astronomical observations, he did not succeed in inventing a clock that could be regulated by a pendulum. This great leap forward was taken by the Dutch physicist and astronomer Christian Huygens, in 1673. Huygens used the swinging of a pendulum to regulate the speed of a driven toothed wheel, in much the same way as the verge-and-foliot was used to regulate such a wheel in the earlier clocks. However, because the pendulum had such a stable and well-defined period of oscillation, the accuracy of his clock was much greater than that of earlier clocks. Later refinements to the escapement mechanism by other horologists improved the accuracy of such clocks still further. Despite the greater precision offered by the pendulum clock, the simple pendulum had limitations of its own.

Problems with Pendulums

The pendulum works on the following principle. Any length of string, with a weight on its one end, will come to rest vertically, if it is held at the other end. This is as a result of the force of gravity acting on the mass attached to its lower end. This force tries to keep the mass at the lowest possible point. If the pendulum is pushed away from this vertical position, then gravity will try to pull it back to its original position, but in doing so the mass will gain speed which will allow it to go in the opposite direction, after it has passed through the equilibrium point. The process is then repeated. It is friction with the air that eventually slows it down. The period of swing of a simple pendulum depends on two factors: the length of the pendulum and the force of gravitation at the point on Earth where the pendulum is being used. Near the poles the force of gravitation is stronger than it is at the equator. To compensate for changes in the force of gravitation as a pendulum clock is moved from one location to the next, one can adjust the length of the pendulum.

Most pendulums are made of metal, and this means that even at a fixed location, the period of the pendulum will change as the temperature changes and the length of the pendulum changes as a consequence. The problem of how to compensate for this was first solved by George Graham. In 1726 he made a special pendulum in which he used mercury in the blob to counteract the expansion of the metallic pendulum rod, in such a way that the period of swing of the pendulum was unaltered. Other technical refinements led to further improvements in the accuracy of the pendulum clock. When it was first invented, it had an error of about ten seconds per day, but before the middle of the nineteenth century this had been reduced to one-tenth of a second per day—giving an improvement factor of one hundred!

Quartz Clocks and Atomic Time

Another great step forward in the accuracy of time measurements was taken by the invention of quartz clocks. These clocks depend for their accuracy on the very stable mechanical oscillations of the crystalline mineral known as quartz. Thus, they completely dispense with the oscillations of a pendulum in the gravitational field of Earth. Such clocks were introduced into the Royal Observatory in 1942. They turned out to be accurate to about two milliseconds per day.

The introduction of mechanical methods of timekeeping did not dispense with the necessity of checking our clocks and watches against the spinning of Earth, which still provides the ultimate standard of time. However, the invention of more accurate clocks showed that the rotating Earth is not a sufficiently accurate timekeeper for the modern world, because it is subject to small variations. The solid body of Earth is surrounded by air and water, and there are seasonal changes in the way these fluids are distributed with respect to the land masses. For example, the freezing and melting of the ice caps at the poles depends on the seasons, and this in turn affects the rate of rotation of Earth, and hence the length of the day. There are also small irregular changes caused by processes in the interior of Earth. The tides in shallow seas also absorb energy from the rotating Earth, thus slowing it down by about 1.5 milliseconds per century. Although these changes are all extremely small they do mean that Earth cannot be used as a standard. It is these considerations that led eventually to the adoption of international atomic time.

Atomic time is based on atomic clocks. The standard in such a clock is given by the frequency of vibration of a particular atom. The second of the new International System of Measurement is defined formally as the duration of 9,192,631,770 periods of radiation corresponding to the transition between two hyperfine levels of the cesium-133 atom. In this transition the spin of the outermost electron of the atom flips over with respect to the spin of the nucleus. The frequencies concerned are in the radio region, and hence they are fairly easy to measure—this is why the cesium atom was chosen. Astronomical time is still used for practical purposes, but it has to be checked against atomic time.

Conclusion

In this chapter we saw that originally our timekeeping systems were based on direct observations of the Sun or the stars. The development of mechanical timekeepers changed our direct reliance on such observations. However, since our social systems are based on the actual motions of our Earth, it was still necessary to keep a check on the relationship between mechanical and astronomical time. This was done at the observatories set up specifically to aid the mariner in his attempts to navigate out of sight of land. As we saw in an earlier chapter, the time signals originating from these observatories were then distributed first on a local, then on a national, and finally on a global scale. In the next chapter we will look at the close association between navigation and time.

4

The Haven-finding Art

The use of the stars for direction finding and position fixing on Earth seems to be almost as old as their use in making calendars and timekeeping. Some people have argued that the stars were first linked together to form the constellations known to us in the west by the Minoan navigators who sailed the islands of the Aegean around 1600 to 1400 B.C. Using the information in a poem called the *Phenomenon* by Artus, written about 200 B.C., Professor Michael Ovenden and his colleague, Professor Archie Roy, both from Glasgow University, came to the conclusion that the Minoans used the points on the horizon at which certain stars rose and set to marked compass directions (long before the invention of the magnetic compass), so that they could sail easily from one of the Aegean islands to the next. Ovenden and Roy surmised that in order to memorize the most important stars that could be used in this way, the Minoans linked the stars together to form useful and recognizable stellar patterns.[1, 2] There is other evidence that suggests that it was the Greeks who realized that in order to make good maps of Earth they first had to make good maps of the sky, but

[1]M. W. Ovenden, "The Origins of the Constellation," *Philosophical Journal*, vol. 3, Glasgow Philosophical Society, Glasgow, 1966.
[2]A. E. Roy, "The Lamps of Atlantis," lecture delivered on the island of Somas in Greece, 1980, private communication.

the methods they used to relate celestial and terrestrial maps were not very accurate. In this chapter we look at the use of the Sun, Moon, and stars for finding direction and fixing position at sea and on the land, from the early beginnings in the ancient world right up to modern-day practices.

Direction Finding

Most of the evidence on the use of Sun and stars for finding direction is largely circumstantial. With regard to the Minoans it consists of a detailed scientific analysis of the poem already mentioned, which was written more than one thousand years after the supposed formulation of the stars into constellations. We also have rather uncertain evidence from Egypt. Some Egyptian astronomical monuments and papyri seem to show that the pharaohs were assisted by astronomers when laying the foundations of the pyramids, but such sources contain very little detail and no other sources have been discovered that could fill in such detail. From the available evidence it now seems as if the astronomers could mark out the compass directions using the points on the horizon at which the Sun (or some bright stars) rose and set, and these markings could be used to lay the foundations of the pyramids, many of which point to the cardinal points with an accuracy of about two minutes of arc. There is also no documentary evidence to support the claim that the many stone circles, for example Stonehenge, were actually astronomical observatories, although some surveys of these sites do seem to indicate that they mark points on the horizon at which the Sun rose and set at the solstices and the equinoxes.

Phoenician Navigation

Homer's epic poem, *The Odyssey*, which describes the travels and adventures of the mythical hero Odysseus, provides some evidence that the stars were used for navigational purposes by the ancient Phoenician seamen before the time in which Homer wrote this work. Although we do not have exact dates for this poet, classical scholars date the poem between the twelfth and seventh centuries B.C.

The Odyssey describes, in Book Five, how Calypso gives Odysseus sailing instructions, after helping the hero to build a craft. We quote from Alexander Pope's translation:

There viewed the Pleiads, and the Northern Team,
And great Orion's more refulgent beam;
To which, around the axle of the sky,
The Bear revolving, points his golden eye,
Who shines exalted on th' ethereal plain,
Nor bathes his exalted forehead in the main.

Here Calypso is referring to the Great Bear, and she is telling Odysseus to keep this constellation on his port side as he crosses the sea. Not much else is recorded with regard to navigation until about 610 B.C. We are then told by Herodotus that Necho, king of Egypt, ordered some Phoenician ships to sail down the Red Sea and, after rounding the African continent, to enter the Mediterranean through the Pillars of Hercules after a voyage lasting three years. However, after the time of Necho, navigation along the west coast of Africa seems to have been neglected until the fifteenth century, when it was revived by the Portuguese under the able guidance of Prince Henry the Navigator.

The Problem of Finding Latitude

The first problem that had to be solved by the Portuguese navigators was how to find latitude using the Sun and stars. In the Northern Hemisphere, this was not too difficult, as one could get a good estimate of one's latitude, at sea, by measuring the height of the Pole Star, or North Star, above the horizon in degrees. This star is almost directly overhead at the North Pole, so here it will have a height above the horizon of 90 degrees, and this is the latitude of the Pole, or its distance from the equator in degrees. At any other latitude, north of the equator, the latitude of the observer is to a first approximation, very nearly equal to the altitude of the Pole Star. The fact that this star is not quite at the pole of the sky, the point about which the whole sky seems to move, can be corrected for by the use of Pole Star tables. These were drawn up by the Portuguese, and they gave the "error" that one had to subtract from, or add to, the measured altitude of the Pole Star in order to get the correct latitude. It was also necessary to develop instruments that could measure the altitude of the Pole Star from the deck of a ship.

Altitude-measuring Devices

The first devices used for measuring altitude cannot really be called instruments, because they did not actually measure the altitude of Polaris (another name for the Pole Star) in degrees. What they did do was to allow the navigator to sail north or south until he was at the required latitude of his port of destination, by making a continuous series of observations, repeated at regular intervals, and these observations would satisfy a particular requirement when this latitude was arrived at. An early device of this kind was the kamal, which was invented by Arabic navigators.[3]

The word kamal is the Arabic version of the word guide. The most basic version of this device consists of a wooden board in the shape of a rectangle, to which is attached, at its midpoint, a thin cord. The cord is knotted at various points, and these knots correspond to the latitudes of ports along the route of the navigator. If, when biting on a particular knot, and holding the board in such a way that the cord is taut, the navigator can just see the Pole Star above the upper edge while the lower edge seems to touch the horizon, he will know that he is at the latitude corresponding to that knot. Although first used by the Arab seamen of the Red Sea and the Indian Ocean, this device became known to European navigators through Vasco da Gama, after he rounded what became known as the Cape of Good Hope in southern Africa, in 1497. Apparently a modified version of the kamal is still used by Arab navigators in the Red Sea and off the East African coast.

The cross-staff is another device for finding the altitude of Polaris, which works on basically the same principle as the kamal. This device seems to have been invented by Levi ben Gerson, a Jew from Provence, who lived from 1288 to 1344. The earliest

[3]C. H. Cotter, *A History of Nautical Astronomy*, Hollis and Carter, 1978.

version of this device, as described by Gerson, consisted of a graduated staff with a square cross-section, with a cross-piece, set at right angles to the main staff, along which it was free to slide. One end of the staff was held at the eye, and the two ends of the cross-piece, when correctly set, would exactly fit between the horizon and Polaris, when the navigator was at the required latitude. The mariner's astrolabe and Gunter's quadrant were two other devices which could be used to find the height of Polaris, and hence latitude.

Using the Sun for Navigation

Since the Pole Star was not visible when sailing south of the equator, and since there was no equivalent star near the south pole of the sky, the Portuguese had to develop methods for using the Sun for navigating the southern seas. On one of the days of the equinox the Sun would be directly overhead, at the zenith, when it was midway between the east and west cardinal points. At any other place on Earth, on one of these days, the distance of the Sun from the zenith, in degrees, close to noon, would be equal to the latitude of this place. On any other day of the year one had to take into account the fact that the Sun had a certain distance from the celestial equator—the celestial equivalent of the terrestrial equator—in degrees, and this had to be added or subtracted from the measured zenith distance, in order to find latitude. To facilitate this method, the Portuguese astronomers drew up tables, giving this distance for different days of the year.

Most of the altitude-measuring devices, mentioned in connection with finding latitude using Polaris, could not be used for taking altitudes on the Sun because they would involve looking directly into the Sun, which obviously would result in damage to the eye. One exception was the mariner's astrolabe, described by Martin Cortes in *Arte de Navegar*. This device consisted of a heavy open ring made of metal, so that it would hang steadily in a vertical plane. It was usually only a few inches in diameter so that it offered little resistance to the wind, when it was in use. It was held vertically by means of a metal ring fitted to the top of the instrument. An alidade, pivoted through its center, having two sights, was fitted diametrically across the ring. One of the quadrants was graduated in degrees of altitude. Each of the sighting vanes carried two holes. One was a relatively large hole for use when observing the Pole Star; the other, smaller hole was used when observing the Sun. When used with the Sun the ring was held lined up with the plane of the vertical through the Sun. The alidade was then turned until a beam of sunlight passed through the hole in the upper sighting vane and fell near the corresponding hole in the lower vane. Another device, specifically invented for use with the Sun, and working on a similar principle to the astrolabe, was the backstaff, which seems to have been first made by John Davis toward the end of the sixteenth century. It consisted of two wooden quadrants of different radii, joined together along two of their radii. Attached to these quadrants was a fixed horizon vane, at right angles to the plane of the quadrants, which had a slit in it, through which the horizon could be seen. The sight vane was able to slide along the curved part of the larger quadrant. It had a hole in it through which the observer could look, and he would line this hole up with the slit in the horizon vane and the sea horizon. The shade vane was able to slide freely over the curved part of the smaller quadrant. This shade vane was adjusted until its shadow, cast by the Sun, which was behind the observer, fell on the slit of the horizon vane. The altitude of the Sun was then the angle between the shade vane and the horizon vane, which was obtained by adding the two angles given on the graduated curved sections of the quadrant.

The Longitude Problem

Although seamen could use the methods described above to find how far north or south they were of the equator, they had no idea of how far east or west they were of any reference line of longitude. Indeed, no such reference line existed at this time. This made sea voyages hazardous undertakings, and over the years many ships and men were lost because the navigator did not know how far east or west they were of islands or continents. The need to solve the longitude problem was thus a pressing social concern for all seafaring nations.

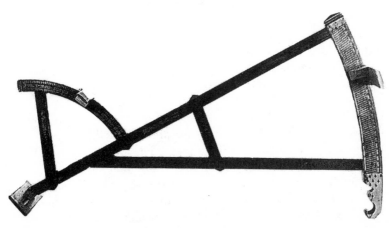

The Backstaff, a nautical instrument for finding latitude using the midday Sun (about 1740). (*Dr. P. Seymour*)

The Founding of the Paris Observatory

It was in 1667 that King Louis XIV set up the Paris Observatory. The main reason for founding this institution was to improve our understanding of the shape of Earth, and to prepare more accurate maps and sea charts, largely for the use of the mariner. In order to carry out this ambitious task, the astronomers had first of all to develop a method of finding longitude. In principle, it is easy to find longitude if one can find time by two independent astronomical methods. In an earlier chapter we saw that it is possible to find time by using the positions of the stars. However, another method of finding time had to be developed before the longitude of different places could be determined.

Galileo had suggested just such a method. Soon after he had made a telescope of his own, Galileo turned this telescope on to the planet Jupiter, and discovered that this body was orbited by four moons—now known as the Galilean moons. Galileo realized that these moons constituted another clock in the sky, so they could be used to find longitude. If an observatory were set up to record the positions of Jupiter's moons with respect to the planet, according to the observatory's local time, it would then be possible to work out the positions of these moons for some future time, and thus produce a set of tables that could be used to find longitude. An observer at some other location could find his own local time using the stars, and then by observing the Galilean moons through a telescope, he could, after consulting the tables, find the time at the observatory to which the tables applied. The difference between the two times—the observatory time and his local time—could be converted to a longitude difference. Each fifteen degrees of longitude would give a time difference of one hour.

Jean Dominique Cassini, the first director of the Paris Observatory, decided to develop this method. Once the latitude and longitude of the observatory had been established, Cassini started a survey of the whole of France. This was done by setting up portable observatories along the coastline of the country, and its borders with other countries, from which it was possible to observe the moons of Jupiter, and hence, by using the Paris tables, to find the time in Paris and compare it with the local times of the portable observatories. By 1681 the whole map of France had been redrawn, but the king was not entirely pleased, because it turned out that France was smaller than it was shown on previous maps, which, of course, were less accurate. It is said that Louis XIV accused the astronomers of diminishing his kingdom.

Galileo's method, as developed by Cassini, could not be used to determine longitude at sea, because it required a telescope on a suitable mounting to observe the satellites of Jupiter, and this was impossible on board a ship.

The Founding of the Greenwich Observatory

Because of the impracticality of using the Galileo-Paris method at sea, other methods had to be investigated. Sieur de St. Pierre, a young Frenchman, suggested to King Charles II of England that our Moon moving against the background stars could serve as a clock for finding longitude. This method demanded much more accurate knowledge of the positions of the stars, and more accurate methods for calculating the movements of the Moon against these stars. The committee set up to examine the claims of Sieur de St. Pierre advised the king that in order to obtain this knowledge, an observatory would have to be built. It was as a result of this advice that the king decided to set up an observatory in Greenwich Park. The royal warrant issued to establish the observatory was very carefully worded. This warrant, issued on June 22, 1675, stated:

Whereas, in order to the finding out of the longitude of places for perfecting navigation and astronomy, we have resolved to build a small observatory within our park at Greenwich, upon the highest ground, at or near where the castle stood, with lodging-rooms for our astronomical observator and assistant.[4]

An earlier warrant, issued on March 4, 1675, concerned the appointment of the first astronomer royal, the Reverend John Flamsteed:

Whereas, we have appointed our trusty and well-beloved John Flamsteed, master of arts, our astronomical observator, forthwith to apply himself with the most care and diligence to rectifying the tables of motions of the heavens, and the places of the fixed stars, so as to find out the so much-desired longitude of places for perfecting the art of navigation.[5]

In both royal warrants it was made quite clear that the main purpose of setting up the observatory, and appointing an astronomer royal, was to perfect those aspects of astronomy that could be applied to navigation. This became the guiding light of all the subsequent holders of this important post.

The Work of the Greenwich Observatory

The method of using the position of the Moon against the stellar background became known as the method of lunar distances, and it made greater demands of astronomy than any of its other previous

[4] D. Howse, *Greenwich Time*, Oxford University Press, Oxford, 1980.
[5] Ibid.

social uses. John Flamsteed set about equipping the Royal Observatory with telescopes fitted to accurately engraved circles, and with precision timekeepers, so that he could measure the positions of the stars with as much precision as was possible at that time. From these observations it was eventually possible to produce the first British catalog of the stars. Flamsteed was astronomer royal from 1675 to 1719, and during this time he was able to lay the foundations of the high-precision positional astronomy for which Greenwich became so famous. Also during his period of office, important developments were taking place elsewhere in other branches of science. As a result of Olaus Roemer's observations on the moons of Jupiter, it was shown for the first time that light had a finite speed of propagation, that it did not travel infinitely fast, as some scientists believed. It was also during this period that Sir Isaac Newton published two of his great books, *The Principia* in 1687 and *Opticks* in 1704. Edmund Halley, who was to become the second astronomer royal, published his book *Synopsis of Cometary Astronomy* in 1705, and in Holland, Christian Huygens published an equally important treatise on light. The improved observations made by Flamsteed were very useful to Newton, since he could use these data to test his theories in celestial mechanics with far greater accuracy than was possible with previous information. On the other hand, Newton's improved mathematical techniques provided a framework for calculating the position and motions of the Moon. However, it soon became obvious that a great deal of other work had to be undertaken before the method of lunar distances could be put to practical use at sea.

The problem of the Moon's motion was one of the most difficult problems in astronomy at that time. The Moon could, to a first approximation, be considered to be going around Earth. However, astronomers could not totally ignore the gravitational attraction of the Sun on the Moon and Earth, if they were to make accurate predictions of the Moon's future positions.

The state of mathematics at this time was not up to this difficult task, and the problem turned out to be too difficult even for the genius of Isaac Newton. The problem of the mathematics of the Moon's motion was eventually tackled by the Swiss mathematician Leonard Euler, whose mathematical career started in the year of

Newton's death. Here we quote from E. T. Bell's book *Men of Mathematics*, first published in 1937: "Euler did not solve it, but his method of approximate calculation (superseded today by better methods) was sufficiently practical to enable an English computer to calculate the lunar tables for the British Admiralty."[6]

Actually the first *Nautical Almanac* was produced by the fifth astronomer royal, Neville Maskelyne, who based the earliest almanacs on the tables of the Moon's motion produced in Germany by the astronomer Tobias Mayer, who had used Euler's method of calculation. Later almanacs were based on tables produced in England.

These almanacs proved to be invaluable to seamen. Armed with the *Nautical Almanac*, the navigator could measure the height of a star and the Moon above the horizon and the angular distance between these bodies, and combine this information with the data in the almanac; and, after a mathematical calculation which took three hours to complete, he would know his latitude and longitude to an accuracy of slightly less than one degree, or about thirty to forty miles. Greater accuracy was only achieved after the invention of the marine chronometer by John Harrison.

John Harrison and the Marine Chronometer

The importance of John Harrison in the history of the longitude problem is well stated by Richard van de Riet Woolley, eleventh astronomer royal, in the forward to the book *John Harrison* by Humphrey Quill:

John Harrison is an important figure in the history of navigation, and one of the finest representatives of English inventors and mechanics who caused this country to lead the world in the mechanical arts of the eighteenth century. It is perhaps not too much to say that the development of navigation in England led to the creation of a British Fleet which dominated the oceans of the world, and therefore to the creation of the British Empire itself,

[6]E. T. Bell, *Men of Mathematics*, Victor Gollancz, London, 1937.

which had such an important influence on the entire world in the nineteenth century.[7]

Harrison set out to make a timepiece that could be used at sea to accurately keep the time of some reference meridian during the entire voyage of a ship, which could last for several months. In order to achieve this, Harrison had to overcome several important problems. To prepare himself adequately for the task, he and his brother James set about making clocks that could keep time very accurately on land. In an earlier chapter we saw that the period of the pendulum, used to regulate accurate clocks, depended on its length. If the pendulum were made of a single metal rod, then this rod would expand and contract with changes in temperature. John Harrison overcame this problem by inventing the gridiron pendulum. This consisted of a series of parallel rods, with alternating rods made of two different types of metal, joined together at their ends. The lengths of the rods were so chosen, that the rods made of the one metal would cause an increase in the length of the pendulum, but the other rods would compensate for this increase, and thus the overall length of the pendulum would remain unchanged, thus giving rise to a stable period that would be independent of temperature.

He was also aware that a pendulum clock would not work well at sea, not only because of the rolling and pitching of the ship, but also because the force of gravity would vary with latitude, and this too would cause variations in the period of the pendulum. To overcome these problems Harrison decided that his first marine chronometer should have two dumbbell-shaped pendulums, working in opposition to each other, so as to counter the effects of the ship's motion, and the oscillatory motion of the pendulums would be caused by four helical springs, rather than by the force of gravitation. This arrangement introduced problems of its own, which Harrison also had to overcome.

In the first place, the dumbbell-like pendulums were very heavy, and as a result there was a great deal of friction between their central pivots and their bearings. Harrison overcame this by in-

[7]H. Quill, *John Harrison*, John Baker, 1966.

troducing a novel type of roller bearing. Furthermore, the tensions in the helical springs were temperature dependent, in that they increased with decreasing temperature. Harrison used a modified form of the gridiron pendulum principle to correct this. By placing the alternative rods in reverse order, he arranged for any temperature changes to be magnified rather than reduced, so the gridiron (which was not being used as a pendulum at all) could act like a temperature-controlled motor, which, through a system of levers, changed the spacing between the ends of the springs, and hence altered their tensions.

In all, Harrison made a series of four marine chronometers, each one incorporating further improvements and thus giving greater precision of timekeeping. It was, however, his fourth marine chronometer that was eventually tested at sea.

The Marine Chronometer and Greenwich

The Royal Observatory at Greenwich also played a part in the testing of the chronometer, to see whether it fulfilled the requirements for the prize of twenty thousand pounds that was offered by the British government to anyone who could solve the longitude problem with sufficient accuracy. The story of the first testing of Harrison's fourth chronometer (sometimes referred to as H4 or just No. 4) is related by Rupert Gould in his book *Marine Chronometer*. Since John Harrison was sixty-seven at the time, the test was conducted by his son William Harrison. Here we quote from Gould's book:

The "Deptford" sailed from Spithead with a convoy on November 18th, 1761, and after touching at Portland and Plymouth set sail for Madeira. On the ninth day after losing sight of land, the ship's longitude, by dead reckoning, was 13 degrees and 50 minutes west of Greenwich, but by No. 4 it was 15 degrees 19 minutes west. Digges was inclined to prefer the dead reckoning, but William Harrison maintained very forcibly that the timekeeper was correct, and that if Madeira was correctly marked on the chart they would sight it the following day. Accordingly, although Digges offered to bet him five to one he was wrong, he held his course, and was rewarded by sighting Porto Santo, the *N.E. island* of the Madeira group, at 6 a.m. the next morning. This greatly relieved the ship's company, who were afraid of missing Madeira altogether, "the consequence of which," as a contemporary put it, "would have been Inconvenient, as they were in Want of Beer."[8]

The Royal Observatory was involved in the final trial of No. 4, which took place on a voyage to Barbados in 1764. Here we quote from *The Royal Greenwich Observatory* by W. H. McCrea:

In the final test on a voyage to Barbados in 1764, the Observatory assistant Charles Green was official in charge, but Maskelyne (having no idea that he was soon to become Astronomer Royal) had accompanied him in the capacity of chaplain to HMS Princess Louisa in which they both made the trip. Indeed, Maskelyne had been commissioned to test Mayer's tables by observing lunar distances on the voyage, for these tables had also been submitted for the prize originally through Bradley. Harrison No. 4 made the voyage in HMS Tartar and it achieved brilliant success.

Very much later, in 1833, the sixth astronomer royal, John Pond, installed a time ball on the roof of the Royal Observatory which is there to this day. At five minutes to one this ball goes halfway up its supporting mast, at two minutes to one it goes all the way up, and at one o'clock precisely it drops. This was the first visual time signal in England, and ships going up and down the Thames could set their chronometers by the falling of this ball.[9]

Conclusions

In the last three chapters we have seen the gradual changes that have taken place in astronomical methods of calendar making, timekeeping, direction finding, and position fixing on land and at sea. Calendar making initially started with direct astronomical

[8]R. T. Gould, *Marine Chronometer*, Holland Press, London, 1973.
[9]"The Royal Greenwich Observatory" by W. H. McCrea, Her Majesty's Stationery Office, London, 1975.

observations on the Sun, Moon, and stars, but gradually a calendar was evolved which made it unnecessary to make such observations, because the cycles were known with sufficient accuracy for astronomers to calculate future calendars with a very high degree of accuracy. A similar course was followed with methods of time-keeping. At first it was necessary to use devices that depended directly on some type of simple astronomical observations, but then gradually mechanical clocks were developed, which made it unnecessary to make continuous observations on the Sun and stars. However, these mechanical timekeepers have to be occasionally checked and synchronized against other standard timekeepers, and these in turn have to be checked at observatories by making astronomical observations. The frequency with which this checking procedure needs to be carried out decreases as the accuracy of timepieces increases, but because of the vagaries of Earth's own rotation, by which we ultimately regulate our lives, we cannot dispense entirely with such checks, although the corrections that have to be made as a result are extremely small. In order to find latitude it was necessary to make observations on the Sun or Polaris, and until the rather recent development of radio and satellite navigational aids, this remained an important method. In order to find longitude at sea sailors needed to use two astronomical methods of finding time. This involved making actual observations on the sky and then combining these, by means of mathematical calculations, with the data contained in the nautical almanac. The nautical almanac in effect contained information that gave the time at some convenient meridian, usually Greenwich, at the local time when the observations were made.

The development of the marine chronometer allowed sailors to "transport" the time from a convenient reference meridian to sea, but it was still necessary to make direct observations on the Sun, Moon, stars, or planets to find their latitude and longitude. This is now unnecessary because of the development of radio and satellite navigational aids, although astronavigation is still used as an additional check. The nautical almanac is a sophisticated type of schedule, calculated on the basis of the known laws of celestial mechanics that govern the apparent motions of the Sun, Moon, and planets as seen from Earth. This schedule, when used in conjunction with a marine chronometer and a sextant to make observations on the Sun, Moon, planets, and stars, can still be used by amateur sailors to find their positions when out of sight of land. In the following chapters we will see how biological evolution has seemed to follow a pattern which is not dissimilar to the conscious development of calendars, clocks, and navigational aids to develop biological calendars, clocks, and navigational aids. It will also be argued that over the aeons of time we have evolved sophisticated internal biological almanacs and diaries that contain basic information on the motions of the Sun, Moon, and planets, and into which our own personal diairies have been programmed.

5

Biological Clocks Linked to Light

There is a variety of examples of internal biological clocks in plants and animals that are linked to the natural cycles of light which are an integral part of our environment. Over aeons of time the processes of evolution have bestowed on certain species of organisms a selective advantage for survival if they possess such clocks. Light interacts with matter in a variety of ways and at many different levels. Since a great deal of modern biology is concerned with attempts to explain biological functions, forms, and processes in terms of the basic properties of matter, in particular the interactions between atoms, molecules, and radiation, we will start this chapter with a brief look at some of the ways in which matter responds to light. The rest of the chapter will be concerned with several examples of biological responses to cycles of light and darkness—a subject generally known as photoperiodism.

Material Responses to Light

Before we can begin to understand the responses of atoms and molecules to light we have to have some idea of what atoms are like, that is, need a simple model of atomic structure. It is this structure that determines the properties of atoms, and hence the properties of elements composed of these atoms, and it is also this structure that gives information on how these atoms and elements will react to light. The simplest model of the atom is that proposed by the physicist Ernest Rutherford and further developed by another physicist, Niels Bohr. Their combined model of the hydrogen atom supposes that the atom is rather like a Solar System with just one planet. Most of the mass of the atom is concentrated in the central nucleus, which in our Solar System model resembles the Sun. In the case of the hydrogen atom this nucleus has just one particle in it—a proton—which carries a positive electric charge. Orbiting the nucleus is one electron that has a negative electric charge equal in magnitude to that of the charge on the nucleus, but its mass is only about one two-thousandth of the proton mass. The electron is only "allowed" to orbit the nucleus at certain distances from it, so it seems as if there are a set number of invisible independent tracks around the nucleus, and the electron has to be in one of these. This is because subatomic particles obey different traffic rules from the planets.

Newton's laws of motion determine the traffic rules of planets, but the traffic rules of electrons going around nuclei are determined by the laws of a branch of modern physics called quantum mechanics. Normally the electron will be in the track closest to the nucleus, but if the hydrogen atom absorbs a packet of light energy of just the right amount, then it can move from this track to one farther from the nucleus. Subsequently it will return to the track closer to the nucleus, and this time it will emit a packet of energy. The size of the packet of energy is in both cases determined by the laws of quantum mechanics. Although this is a simplified model of the atom it can nevertheless predict the behavior of the hydrogen atom with very reasonable accuracy. More complex atoms of the other elements have more protons in their nuclei, plus as many electrons going around this nucleus; in addition, they have neutrons in the nucleus which have no electric charges and a mass almost equal to that of the proton. The atom of each element will only emit a certain fixed range of packets of light energy, and from a full rainbow of light it will also only absorb the same fixed range of packets of light energy. This fixed range or pattern of energy packets is called the spectrum of that type of atom. Since each type of atom has its own unique spectral pattern, the spectrum can be used to identify the atom. It is the orbiting electrons that determine this pattern, and it is the same cloak of electrons that determine how the atom will react chemically with the atoms of other chemical elements to form the molecules of chemical compounds. The molecules of compounds have their own distinctive way of interacting with and emitting light, which can also be used to identify the compound. Atoms and molecules thus have the ability to store light energy for varying amounts of time, and this stored energy can be used to promote certain chemical reactions. Some of these reactions are important in biology.

Photosynthesis

The chemical process by which green plants synthesize organic compounds from carbon dioxide and water in the presence of solar energy is known as photosynthesis. This process occurs in the chloroplasts which are normally found in the green levels of plants. These chloroplasts contain a chemical called chlorophyll; they are usually lens shaped and made up of stacks of membranes enclosed in a gel-like matrix. There are two series of reactions, one known as the light reactions and one known as the dark reactions. In the light reactions energy from sunlight is absorbed by chlorophyll and converted into chemical energy. These reactions take place in the membranes of the chloroplasts. In the dark reactions, which can take place in light or darkness, this chemical energy is used in the production of simple organic compounds from water and carbon dioxide. These reactions take place in the matrix of the chloroplasts.

All forms of life are directly or indirectly dependent on plants for food, and thus photosynthesis is the basis for all life on Earth. Most of the oxygen in our atmosphere originates from the release of oxygen which accompanies the process of photosynthesis.

Other Responses of Plants to Light

Most multicellular plants have roots that secure them to Earth so they cannot change their locations. However, some do have bending and torsion movements as part of their response to light. It is possible to distinguish between two different kinds of response. The first type is known as photonasty, in which the light triggers the movement; the second type is known as phototropism, in which the light determines the direction of movement. The most important example of this latter type is that of bending toward the light. (This is called positive phototropism.) This particuar response occurs among photosynthesizing plants for which strong illumination is necessary for their survival. Since it is the leaves of the plants that contain the chloroplasts, it is these parts of the plants that exhibit positive phototropism. The roots of plants, on the other hand, have to bury themselves in Earth, so they exhibit negative phototropism (i.e., they move away from the light.) Nastic movements of plants differ from phototropism in that these movements are independent of the direction from which the light is coming. The opening of the evening primrose at night is an example of photonasty. However, nastic movements can be triggered by other stimuli. For example, tulip and crocus flowers open in response to a rise in temperature—this is known as thermonasty; the folding up and drooping of the leaves of the sensitive plant mimosa pudica when lightly touched is an example of seismonasty. Some plants also show sleep movements. For example, the clover plant folds together its leaflets at night. This type of nastic movement is usually referred to as nyctinasty.

Some plants seem to have a more complex response to the position of the Sun in the sky, which seems to indicate that they might have an internal biological clock that is somehow synchronized to the solar day. For example, the spotted cat's ear opens at 6:00 A.M., the African marigold opens at 7:00 A.M., the scarlet pimpernel closes at 2:00 P.M., and the evening primrose at 6:00 P.M. The fact that plants have such leaf movements was first discovered by the astronomer Jean Jacques d'Ortous de Mairan in 1729. De Mairan also demonstrated that these leaf movements continued for a few days even after the plant was placed in continuous dark. This discovery pointed strongly to the existence of an internal biological clock and to the fact that the diurnal cycle of light and darkness was just the environmental synchronizer of this internal clock. This is a view to which many biologists now subscribe, for many similar examples have been noticed in plants and animals.

Photoperiodism in Animals

Although de Mairan seems to have been the first scientist to carry out an experiment that demonstrated the existence of an internal biological clock, the phenomenon of photoperiodism in animals goes back a long way. Some Greek scholars, including Aristotle, wrote of the breeding rhythms displayed by many animals and recorded seasonal changes in the appearance of reproductive organs. Hippocrates wrote, "whoever wishes to investigate medicine properly, should proceed thus; in the first place consider the seasons of the year, and what effect each of them produces, for they

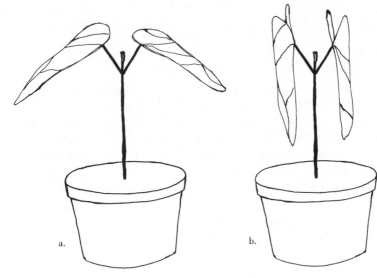

a. b.

The diurnal movement of the leaves of a bean plant; daytime position.

The diurnal movement of the leaves of a bean plant; night position. (*Dr. P. Seymour*)

are not all alike, but differ much from themselves in regard to these changes." Brian Lofts, in his book *Animal Photoperiodism*, goes so far as to suggest that:

There is no doubt, for example, that the saving of the Israelites from starvation during there wanderings in their wilderness by ". . . a wind from the Lord, that brought quails from the sea . . .", recorded in the Book of Numbers XI.31, refers to a flight of Coturnix blown off course during their annual migration.[1]

Evolution, by means of the process of natural selection, favors the survival of those individuals whose gene complexes allowed them to produce offspring at the most propitious season; progeny produced at other times suffers high mortality rates. Different survival rates will soon define the proper breeding season of a particular species, and in some vertebrates this has resulted in the establishment of annual cycles.

Two groups of factors have been identified which play a part in the establishing of such appropriate cycles. The first set is composed of "ultimate" factors, the second of "proximate" factors. Ultimate factors are those that promote breeding of populations at the optimal season. The most important ultimate factor is the availability of suitable food supplies. This determines the number of young that can be reared to an age at which they can begin to reproduce. But animals also have to, in a sense, "anticipate" the approach of a suitable season in which to breed. As a result they have evolved response mechanisms to environmental stimuli which enable them to do this. As pointed out by Lofts, "These are the proximate factors in response to which reproductive organs undergo their physiological development from a seasonally quiescent state to a functional breeding condition." The environmental synchronizer differs from one species to another, and in many cases more

[1]Brian Lofts, *Animal Photoperiodism*, Edward Arnold, London, 1970. Later on, evidence will be presented which seems to suggest that such flights are triggered by changing day length.

than one such synchronizer may be involved, and thus may differ in the strength of their biological action.

Photoperiodic mechanisms are the major environmental synchronizer for animals that live in temperate, subarctic, and arctic zones of the globe. It is now believed that these controlling mechanisms must have become important when living creatures moved from the oceans onto dry land. In the seas temperature is a reliable indicator of the changing seasons but on land temperature changes are much less reliable in this respect.

It was at the beginning of the twentieth century that Professor E. A. Schafer proposed a theory that seasonal variation in day length was the controlling factor for bird migration; for some of the time-dependent behavior connected with the preparation for migratory flights; and for the reproductive cycles found in a large variety of different species of birds. At this stage there was no experimental evidence to support this theory.

However, in the 1920s the Canadian zoologist William Rowan provided convincing evidence that day length does affect the reproductive behavior in vertebrates. Over a period of fourteen years Rowan made detailed observations of the species of bird known as the greater yellowleg. This bird breeds in Canada, migrates to Patagonia in the autumn, and returns to Canada to breed again in the early spring. The total distance covered in this round flight is about sixteen thousand miles. In spite of this enormously long journey the timing of the migration and the breeding is very precise. The eggs of this bird are hatched between May 26 and May 29 of each year. Rowan made a thorough analysis of the factors that could perhaps explain this remarkable regularity. Among the factors he considered were food, barometric pressure, temperature, intensity of sunlight, and day length. A series of detailed observations led him to conclude that the increasing day length after December 21 was the only factor precise enough to play the role of environmental synchronizer.

Rowan then set out to test his theory using the species *Junco hyemalis*, the slate-colored junco. He trapped some of this species of bird, which winters in Canada, and subjected them to artificially increased day lengths in a laboratory. Under these conditions the artificial photoperiods were increased gradually so that after a few weeks the birds experienced daylight conditions that were normally only present during late spring. The control specimens were kept under natural winter light conditions. When the two sets of specimens were examined the control birds had remained sexually underdeveloped with inactive reproductive organs, while those that had been exposed to unseasonally increased photoperiods were already in breeding condition. Later, Rowan released birds in various states of reproductive development and noted the effect on their migratory behavior. These experiments led him to conclude that the birds migrated when their sex organs were expanding, but not when they were inactive or in the full breeding state. This work established that the spring migration was, by means of the photoperiod, under the control of the environment.

Many different researchers in the field carried Rowan's work further using different species. These extended investigations revealed that although day length was the major proximate factor, it was not the only one, and the extent to which it affected sexual behavior and migration varied from one species to the next. In some species—for example the white crowned sparrow of North America—seasonal changes in the photoperiod seem to be in absolute control of the annual reproductive rhythm. In other species—for example equatorial weaver finches—there seemed to be an internal time schedule that was very little affected by variations in the photoperiod. It is now thought that internal rhythms like this are fairly widespread in birds, although it seems doubtful whether they ever exclusively control the annual cycle of migration and reproduction. It seems much more likely that environmental factors are necessary to synchronize internal rhythms to changes associated with the seasons. According to Lofts:

A. J. Marshall has likened such an endogenous rhythm to a clock in which the cogs seasonally engage various environmental "teeth" to which the species has evolved a response, and which have the capacity to accelerate or retard the timing. In other words, environmental factors such as photoperiodism serve to "set" the biological clock.

Photoperiodism in Birds

The most highly developed photoperiodic mechanisms among vertebrate animals occur in birds. We also know more about photoperiodism in these animals than we do for any other member of the vertebrate group. We have already seen that changes in day length affect the size and activity of the sex organs of birds. There are, however, other behavioral characteristics associated with migration that are also under the control of day length changes. One such activity is known as the zugunruhe. Normally birds show very little activity at night, but during the migratory period caged birds show a nocturnal restlessness which is the zugunruhe. This activity never occurs in nonmigratory species and in migratory species it only occurs during the migratory period.

Migratory birds also rapidly increase their weights just before they start on their long journeys. This weight increase is due to the laying down of large deposits of visceral and subcutaneous fat which is used as food reserves en route. However, the zugunruhe is not directly related to this buildup of fat. This has been demonstrated by feeding the birds special fat-free diets which prevent the buildup of fat; the birds still exhibited the zugunruhe. It now seems very likely that the migratory fat storage and the zugunruhe are controlled by mechanisms that use the same primary source of photoperiodic information.

Seasonally Dependent Sex Activity

One way of measuring sex activity in animals is to measure the sizes of their sex organs. In many cases it is the size of the gonads that is measured. Gonads are the paired organs in animals that produce reproductive cells. The most important gonads are the female ovary and the male testis. The gonads also produce hormones that control secondary sexual characteristics.

Throughout the year the gonads of birds show very large variations. The change in size can produce a weight increase of five hundred-fold. The gonads are largely inactive in the winter months and this is when they have their minimum size. The rate of growth increases as the day length increases. An investigation of size variations in three different species of British birds—the rock dove, the stock dove, and the wood pigeon—shows that the testis volume in these species reaches maximum sometime during August and September. The seasonal variation in the mean diameter of the largest ovarian follicle of the wood pigeon reaches a maximum in July and August and a minimum in December and January. This seasonal trend is not matched by that of populations of feral town pigeons; the mean diameter of the largest ovarian follicle for this species shows much less overall variation but there are slight maxima in March and September, and small minima between September and November.

The Molting of Birds

Many different species of birds show seasonally dependent molting. Since molting is rather a drain on the protein reserves of the bird, it is generally too much to accomplish at the same time as breeding. There are exceptions to this general rule in those cases where food supplies are abundant, as in wood pigeons, when the two processes can occur simultaneously. The need for a short breeding season which is followed by a quick molt is usually very important to migrant birds in high latitudes. This is because the replacement of the wing feathers must occur sufficiently early to enable the birds to undertake the southern migration, and it must also be achieved before the onset of poor autumn and winter feeding conditions puts restrictions on the intake of food. In those regions where environmental photoperiodic changes are very noticeable, as in intermediate and high latitudes, the molt may be dependent on seasonal day length changes. There is much evidence that molting cycles are photoperiodically controlled, at least to some extent, independently of breeding cycles.

Photoperiodism in Mammals

Less work has been done in the photoperiodic mechanisms of mammals, but what work that has been done has shown there are some important differences between mammals and birds. In the photoperiodic mechanisms of some birds the seasonal change in day length is entirely necessary for some cyclical activity such as spring gonadal recovery and the behavioral patterns associated with migration; but this is generally not so in most mammals. Mammalian photoperiodic controls are much less rigid and normally serve to time well-developed internal clocks which would result in the eventual development into a reproductive condition. This happens when the animal is experimentally isolated from its normal environmental cues. Most of the experiments on mammals have concentrated on studying the effects of photoperiodism on ovarian and estrous cycles (these are the cycles of reproductive activity shown by most sexually mature nonpregnant female mammals). Very little work has been done on male testicular cycles. Birds and mammals also differ in another important aspect. Whereas all birds so far shown to have photoperiodic mechanisms are activated by increasing day length, in mammals there exists evidence for both increasing and decreasing day length activation.

Long-Day and Short-Day Photoresponses

In higher latitudes there are many wild mammalian species which breed in response to increasing day length associated with spring. In such animals it is possible to induce them into a state of sexual activity by subjecting them, out of season, to artificially long days, such as occur in spring. Alternatively, it is possible to retard sexual activity by keeping such animals under a day length which is artificially reduced. Ferrets provide one example. Under normal natural conditions this animal has a sexually quiescent state that lasts from August or September until the following March. In the absence of experimental stimulation by light or hormone therapy, ferrets have never been known to breed during this period in intermediate and high northern latitudes. When female or male ferrets are subjected to prolonged photoperiods in midwinter they can be stimulated into sexual activity so that breeding takes place with births occurring in January.

Another example of a long-day response is provided by the reproductive activity of the mare. If sexually inactive mares are subjected to prolonged artificial photoperiods in January they show a resumption of ovarian follicular development within fifteen days of the commencement of the treatment. As is the case with the ferret, the cycle is not completely controlled by light, and animals kept in darkened stables will show a delay in the resumption of ovarian activity but not a complete inhibition. Similar responses to photostimulation have been shown in hedgehogs, hares, white-footed mice, and cats. The raccoon is very susceptible to such photostimulation, and can be induced to produce two litters in a year by the appropriate artificial photomanipulation.

As with birds, not all mammals have the same degree of sensitivity to seasonal photofluctuations, and some are apparently independent of seasonal light changes with regard to their reproductive rhythms. Domestic mammals and birds have shown trends of losing their dependence on photoperiodism, and many have evolved into continuous breeders in the absence of exposure to the selective influence of a seasonally limited food supply. The domesticated rabbit can breed virtually at any time of the year, but in the wild it is still strictly seasonal. However, even with domestication, mating and conception occur more frequently from March to July than at other times.

The sexual development and activity of short-day forms starts at the end of summer and early autumn. Many deer, sheep, and goats are of this type. A great deal of work has been done on sheep and goats, largely because of their commercial importance. These experiments have established the stimulatory effects of decreasing day length. In sheep the sexual season can be completely reversed by providing more light in the winter, and decreasing artificially the normal summer photoperiod. Out of season sexual behavior and reproduction can be induced by confining the animals to blacked-out pens for appropriate periods and replicating autumnal day lengths. In the Southern Hemisphere the sexual activity of such mammals is linked to the months of decreasing day lengths. When these animals are transferred to the Northern Hemisphere they soon become synchronized and respond to the northern autumn.

There is a relationship between latitude and the duration of breeding. This is not surprising, since the differences between day length and temperature in the summer and winter are much more marked the farther one gets from the equator. At the equator day length does not vary at all and the temperature is fairly constant throughout the year, but at the poles day length consists of six months of light and six of darkness. At intermediate latitudes the temperature and day length vary considerably between summer and winter. Sheep indigenous to countries in higher latitudes show a sexual season that is much shorter and more marked than that of a breed which has originated from parents indigenous to equatorial and tropical parts of the world. This can be understood by comparing, say, the reproductive cycles of the Suffolk and Merino ewes. Predecessors of the Merino sheep evolved in an environment where there were no strong seasonally occurring selective factors, and thus lambs born at any time of year had a reasonable chance of survival. The Suffolk ewes on the other hand are much more seasonally dependent, and thus only lambs born in the restricted period of the spring have a good chance of survival.

Photoperiodism in Other Species of Animals

Photoperiodic mechanisms also exist, at least to some extent, in lower vertebrates, but in these animals environmental controls which depend on light are far less highly developed than they are in birds and mammals.

Some species of fish possess such mechanisms. Keepers of home aquariums know that tropical guppies and swordtails can breed all year round, but they manifest a heightening of reproductive activity with increasing day length in the spring. It has also been shown that light can affect the state of the reproductive organs of several different species. Goldfish kept in the dark for a long time show a degeneration of their gonads.

Our present state of knowledge with regard to amphibians suggests that photoperiodic mechanisms which regulate annual reproductive cycles are absent in these animals. It now appears as if temperature and rainfall are the main environmental synchronizers for most amphibians.

Experiments on reptiles have not been very extensive, but although the information in this area is rather limited there is evidence that in some species reproductive processes can be influenced by light. The fringe-toed lizard, *uma notata*, is one species of desert lizard that has been studied in detail. This lizard lives in the deserts of Southern California and Arizona, where it inhabits areas of loose sand. When it is disturbed it burrows in the sand until it is hidden from view. In the winter the animals hibernate and remain underground for most of the day, only emerging for a short period near midday when it is warmer. In early spring they come out for longer periods of activity and hence experience an increasing number of daylight hours between January and the end of April. The increasing day length at this time stimulates the development of the gonads, and this gives rise to an increased sexual activity which culminates in breeding and egg laying in April. The photoperiodic behavior of this lizard has also been studied in the laboratory. Here it was shown that an unseasonal development into breeding condition in both sexes can be induced by using photostimulation (i.e., exposing winter lizards to an artificial photoperiod equal to that which they would experience in the summer months).

Conclusion

In this chapter we looked at several different responses to light. The simplest type of response was that involving a direct response to light. However, over the very long time scales associated with biological evolution, many organisms have evolved internal biological clocks and calendars that are fairly stable within themselves, but which require occasional checking against the daily and seasonal variations of light and darkness. This is not unlike the occasional checking we have to consciously undertake to ensure that our own mechanical or electronic clocks and watches are in step with the atomic time appropriate to our location on the surface of Earth. In recent years a European firm has brought out a quartz clock that automatically checks itself against radio time signals originating from radio transmitters situated in some European countries. It seems that nature has the prior claim to this invention, since the internal biological clocks of many different animals are constantly being checked against the natural modulation of light which is a part of our environment. This modulation is a direct result of the spinning of Earth on its own axis and its motion around the Sun. These movements are under the control of the laws of motion and the law of gravitation. In the next chapter we look at the role played by these laws in modulating the amount of radiation that we receive at a given location on Earth at a specific instant in time. We also look at biological tidal clocks that are linked by means of the oceans, the atmosphere, and the magnetic field of Earth to the periodic gravitational tug of our nearest natural neighbor in space—our own Moon.

PART TWO

6

Gravitation and the Cycles of Light

The daily and seasonal changes in the intensity of light that we receive from the Sun at a given place on the Earth's surface are controlled by the movements of Earth. These motions are in turn the result of a pattern of behavior exhibited by all bodies that are larger than atoms and which was first formulated in scientific terms by Isaac Newton in his laws of motion and his law of gravitation, so these laws enable us to understand the modulation of the light we receive from the Sun. We will see in this chapter how this all happens. We will also look at the cause of the oceanic tides, the variation of tidal height with lunar month, tides in the atmosphere, and terrestrial consequences of these tides. There are biological clocks in some sea creatures and in animals that inhabit the intertidal zone, which are linked to the tides; we will also look at some examples of these. In short this chapter will look at terrestrial and some biological consequences of gravitational linking between the Sun, Moon, and Earth.

The Motion of Sun and Moon as Seen from Earth

We all know that as seen from Earth the Sun seems to rise near the east and set somewhere near the west. We also know that this is due to the spinning of Earth on its own axis. The apparent pathway of the Sun across the sky during the day also changes as the year goes by. In summer in the Northern Hemisphere it will appear to rise north of east and set north of west. At midday in summer the Sun is also much higher in the sky than it is at midday during the spring and autumn, and it spends more hours above the horizon, so giving us more daylight. At midday in the winter the Sun is lower in the sky than it is at any other time of the year. It also has a much shorter apparent pathway across the sky and hence spends less time above the horizon. If we could see the Sun and stars at the same time, as one can do under the simulated sky of a planetarium, then the Sun will seem to move against the stellar background as the year goes by. This apparent pathway is called the ecliptic. If we project the equator of Earth onto the sky it will form what we call the celestial equator. The ecliptic is inclined to the celestial equator, so in the northern summer the Sun is north of the equator and in the northern winter it is south of the celestial equator.

The Moon goes around Earth and as seem from Earth it too has an apparent pathway against the background stars. This pathway is inclined to the ecliptic by about five degrees. We now know that the Moon is much smaller than the Sun and it is closer to Earth, so this means that the Moon can get between us and the Sun. This only happens when the Moon is at specific points of its apparent pathway against the stellar background. There are two points at which the Moon's apparent pathway crosses the ecliptic. These points are called the lunar nodes. If the Sun and Moon are at exactly this point at the same instant in time then the Moon is exactly between us and the Sun and we have an eclipse of the Sun. If the Moon completely overlaps the Sun we have a total solar eclipse, but if the overlap is not complete we have a partial eclipse. This happens because the Moon is a solid body having no light of its own, so it will blot out the light from the Sun, which is a very large and extremely hot sphere giving off a great deal of radiation. If the Sun is at one node and the Moon is at the other node, then Earth is exactly between the Sun and Moon, and the shadow of Earth will fall on the Moon. At such a time, called a lunar eclipse, the Moon does not just disappear from the sky—it will more often than not have a dull reddish color. This is because some of the red light from the Sun is bent around Earth by our atmosphere and so this light will reach the Moon. These apparent movements of Sun and Moon as seen from Earth can be explained in terms of the spinning of Earth on its own axis, the Moon's motion around Earth, and Earth's motion around the Sun.

The Motions of the Earth and Moon in Space

Earth is spinning on its own axis rather like a top, in that it will keep its axis oriented in the same direction in space. This behavior is best demonstrated by using a toy gyroscope. A well-balanced gyroscope will, once it is set spinning, keep its axis pointing in the same direction with respect to the distant stars no matter how it is moved about. All spinning bodies have this property. This fact is made use of in the gyroscopic compass, where an ordinary, but very precise, gyroscope is constrained by forces applied to its axis to spin in a horizontal plane, and which as a consequence will point in a north-south direction with its axis parallel to that of Earth.

Since Earth's axis can for very long periods of time be considered to point very nearly to the North Star, this means that it will stay like this no matter where it is along its orbit around the Sun. This also means that Earth's axis is inclined to the plane of its orbit, and as it goes around the Sun its axis will remain pointing toward the North Star. As a consequence of this kind of motion the North Pole of Earth will, during the northern winter, lean away from the Sun, but during the northern summer it will lean toward the Sun. It is this behavior of Earth's axis which causes a change in the apparent pathway of the Sun against the background stars.

The Moon's orbit around Earth is inclined to the plane of Earth's orbit around the Sun by about five degrees. This gives rise to the motion of the Moon as seen from Earth described in the previous section. Twice in its orbit around Earth, the Moon will pass through the orbital plane of Earth—these points are the lunar nodes that we discussed in the previous section.

The Moon and the Tides

Man has always known about the tides, and their association with the positions and phases of the Moon must have been known for centuries. But people argued whether the tides were influenced by the Sun, or Moon, or neither. Astrologers were in no doubt that such an influence did exist. However, Geoffrey Chaucer, the English poet, who lived in the thirteenth century, dismissed astrology, with particular reference to the tidal effect of the Moon, as an abominable superstition. The Italian scientist Galileo condemned the same suggestion as "occult nonsense." As we can see, there has always been a human tendency to decry new ideas as nonsense even by those scientists who suffered from such bigotry themselves! It was not until Isaac Newton had formulated the law of gravitation, and combined this with his laws of motion, that it became possible to understand the tides.

Astrologers in ancient Greece had argued that the influences of the planets (which then included the Sun and Moon) depended on the alignments of these bodies as seen from the fixed Earth. This was, to some extent, consistent with the fact that the tides varied with the phases of the Moon. The methods used for calculating tidal heights by astronomers were purely empirical, i.e. there was no underlying theory to the tides that involved long-range forces. Thus the astronomical methods of tidal prediction did not differ from those used by astrologers. This is the point being made by Chaucer in *The Franklin's Tale*, where the services of an astrologer are used to calculate the tides (see *Astrology: The Evidence of Science*). Galileo rejected the idea that the Moon could have a long-range influence on the waters of Earth. When Isaac Newton proposed his theory of gravitation, some of his contemporaries objected to his work because it involved instantaneous action at a distance (see Professor T. G. Cowling's pamphlet "Isaac Newton and Astrology," Leeds University Press, Leeds, 1977). Albert Einstein's theory of gravitation (The General Theory of Relativity) was at least partly inspired by the fact that Newton's instantaneous action at a distance did not fit into the field theory framework of physics, which came into vogue at the turn of the century. As we will see later, an important aspect of the theory explained in this book is that it places the influence of the Sun on Earth, and its correlation with planetary alignments, on a firm scientific basis.

Newton's law of gravitation tells us that every particle in the universe attracts every other particle by means of the force of gravitation, and that the force of attraction is related to the product of the masses of the particles. However, this force is weakened as we increase the distances between the particles. Since the Earth is very massive and we are so close to the Earth, we feel the attraction of Earth much more than we feel the attraction of other planets, or the stars, although such attractions do in fact exist. The waters that form the oceans of the world are being attracted by Earth—this is why they remain attached to Earth—but they are also attracted by the Sun and Moon. The Moon is much closer to the Earth than the Sun, so although its mass is very much less than that of the Sun, its tidal influence is stronger than that of the Sun.

The water on Earth immediately below the Moon is closer to the Moon than the rest, so it feels the attraction of the Moon more, and hence there is a slight piling up of the sea at the point just below the Moon. But there is also a bulge on the side of the Earth farthest from the Moon. This arises in the following way. The Moon does not really go around Earth; rather, both bodies go around their common center of mass. Another way of looking at it is to imagine a mobile of the Sun-Moon system. Because the Earth is more massive than the Moon, the point at which the two will be balanced would be almost one thousand miles below the surface of Earth, on the line joining the two bodies. This point is called the barycenter, and the Earth and Moon really go around this point. As Earth moves around this center the water on the Earth at the far side from the Moon has a tendency to be flung off into space and this gives rise to the second bulge. Between these two bulges are two shallows of water. When we pass through a bulge we say the tide has come in; when we pass through a shallow we say the tide has gone out. At first sight this would seem to show that the two high tides should be separated by twelve hours. But, during the interval between passing through the first bulge and passing through the second, the Moon has moved, so the interval becomes about twelve hours and twenty-four minutes.

111

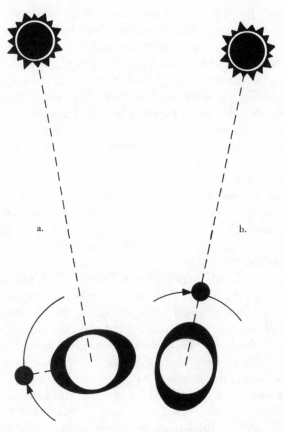

Positions of the Sun and the Moon at: a. Neap Tides, and b. Spring Tides. (*Dr. P. Seymour*)

Although the tide-rising force of the Sun is less than that of the Moon, it does nevertheless contribute to the overall performance of the tides. Just as there are two bulges associated with the Moon, so there are two associated with the Sun; one between the Earth and Sun and one on the other side of Earth from the Sun. When the bulges of the Sun coincide with the bulges of the Moon, as they do at new and full Moon, then there are higher tides than normal—the spring tides. When the bulges caused by the Sun are at right angles to those of the Moon, as they are at first and last quarters of the Moon, then we have lower tides than normal—the neap tides.

Newton's Laws of Motion and Planetary Orbits

Newton's law of gravitation is insufficient, by itself, to explain why the Moon moves around Earth and Earth moves around the Sun. In order to explain these motions we have to link gravitation with the laws of motion, but first we have to state these laws. They are as follows:

The first law. A body continues in a state of rest or uniform motion in a straight line unless it is acted on by a force that would tend to change that state of rest or uniform motion.

The second law. The rate at which a body changes its speed (if it is moving in a straight line) or the rate at which it changes direction (if it is moving at a constant speed) depends on the strength of the force exerted on it and on its mass.

The third law. If one body exerts a force on another body, the second body will exert a force on the first that is equal in strength but in the opposite direction.

We are all familiar with the consequences of the first law when we drive around a corner in a car. The car (and our bodies) really wish to continue in the straight line, but the force of the road on the wheels, and the wheels on the car, impel the car to change direction when we turn the steering wheel. A planet in the Solar System, like any other body, has a tendency to travel in a straight line. However, the force of gravitation acting between the planet and the Sun causes the planet to "fall" toward the Sun, and we say it orbits the Sun. Similarly, the Moon and all artificial satellites are really falling toward the Earth. However, orbiting bodies do not actuall fall and hit the surface of the body being orbited. This is because the body being orbited, that is, the Sun or the Earth, is spherical and the surface is constantly curving away from the orbiting body.

The Tides and Life in the Intertidal Zone

In his book *Supersense*, John Downer says:

The tidal rhythm makes the shoreline one of the harshest environments in the world. For part of the day it is pounded by water and for the rest of the time it is exposed to the desiccating heat of the Sun or the bitter cold of night. The creatures which live there manage to survive by being able to predict these violent changes.[1]

A large variety of living organisms are able to do this. On the north shore of Cape Cod there live microscopic plants known as diatoms. At low tide each day these golden brown algae come up through the sand in order to make use of the Sun's energy for photosynthesis. Since they come up together in large numbers they form a vast golden carpet along the line of the shore. A short while before the tide returns, this golden carpet disappears. All the diatoms move simultaneously back into the sand, just as if they were obeying a direct command from the Moon, which is about a quarter of a million miles away. If these plants are tested in a laboratory they behave in exactly the same way. In common with many other forms of marine life, diatoms have an accurate body clock tuned to the rhythms of the tides.

On the Brittany coast in France there lives a type of flatworm that has a rhythmic behavior similar to that of the diatoms. These organisms share their bodies with algae which they bring to the surface at low tides so that they can use the sunlight to manufacture food. The algae pay for their accommodation and transport by providing the flatworm with food.

Fishermen have for centuries held that the size of their catch can be related to the phases of the Moon. Research on herring and eel catches seems to support this suggestion; and in this

[1] J. Downer, *Supersense*, BBC, London, 1988.

case the causal connection might come for the response of these creatures to the amount of light available at night rather than the rising and falling of water levels due to the tides. The fishermen of the Mediterranean maintain that sea urchins taste best around the full Moon, which is what one would expect if they produce eggs at this time. There is also evidence to support this tale. In a small area around the Suez there lives a species of urchin which does ripen its eggs at full Moon, and an urchin living just off the coast of California also has a similar cycle linked to phases of the Moon.[2, 3]

Another living organism which has a reproductive cycle under the influence of the Moon is the coral polyp that lives off the northeast shore of Australia. The famous Great Barrier Reef is made up of the hardened skeletons of many millions of these dead polyps. The living polyps which are permanently attached to the reef reproduce sexually by releasing sperm into the sea. It has recently been discovered that the timing of their reproductive cycle is linked to a phase of the Moon, and to temperature. At either the first or last quarter of the Moon, which occurs roughly the same time each year, at a particular time of night, these polyps release their sex cells into the sea, turning it into a multicolored reproductive soup.

The aquatic larvae of a mayfly which lives on Lake Victoria in Uganda emerge and become adult two days after the full Moon, and the adult mayfly will subsequently lay eggs that follow the same cycle. However, when the mayfly is taken away from the equator it loses its lunar rhythm. On the Ascension Islands there lives the sooty tern, which also uses the Moon to synchronize its breeding. These terns return to the islands to nest every tenth lunar month. This means that their breeding cycle is in no way linked to the seasons. This is not very surprising since the Ascension Islands are very close to the equator and thus show only very slight weather changes during the year.

Many crabs also follow rhythms that are tidally linked. The shore crab prefers to forage under cover of water, which helps to hide

[2] R. R. Ward, *The Living Clocks*, Collins, London, 1972.
[3] J. Brady, *Biological Clocks*, Edward Arnold, London, 1979.

it from predatory birds. These crabs live higher up on the beach, and so they have timed their foraging activities to coincide with high tide. The fiddler crab has two sets of rhythms. It has an activity rhythm synchronized to the times of the local tides, and a daily rhythm of skin color change. Since the lunar day is twenty-four hours, fifty minutes, it means that the two rhythms will synchronize at two tides during a lunar month and these two tides will be separated by about a fortnight.[4]

Lunar-Annual Changes

An excellent example of a tidal-annual change is provided by the palolo sea worms of the South Pacific. These worms are about eighteen inches long and normally live in dim caverns in the seas of the South Pacific. The main sex cycle of these worms occurs once a year, during the last quarter of the Moon in November, which corresponds to spring in the south. The annual aspect of the swarming was recorded in *The Confessions of Lady Asanath* by Basil Thomson, who also described the effect of this behavior on the inhabitants of the islands of this region. According to Thomson: "The time of the annual swarming is a great occasion for the natives, as the palolo worm is regarded as a delicacy. . . . Cakes of the gelatinous mass are fried, and taste like oysters."[5] William Burrows, who was a commissioner on one of the islands in the 1940s, provided further details on this event. He noted that there were always two risings, a small one in October and a larger one in November. He recorded that "the main rising always occurs at dawn and, literally, the worm comes up with the Sun. It is, also, always at the time of high water."[6]

The swarming of the palolo worm represents a fairly complex type of cycle. The main rising occurs during a specific month of

[4]See also J. W. Hastings, H. G. Schweiger, *The Molecular Basis of Circadian Rhythms*, Dahlam Konfaranzen, Berlin, 1976.
[5]This is as quoted by R. R. Ward in *The Living Clocks*, Collins, London, 1972.
[6]Ibid.

the year (November), it occurs at the last quarter of the Moon, it occurs at dawn, and at high tide.

A still more spectacular example in precision timing of a lunar-annual cycle of a deep-sea creature is provided by the reproductive cycle of a biological family known as echinoderms, which lives off the coast of Japan. This creature liberates its sex cells just once a year in October at about three o'clock in the afternoon, on the day of one of the quarters of the Moon. In the years following the first release, there will be annual changes in the time of the lunar month at which the sex cells are released but it always alternates between first and last quarters of the Moon. Hence it alternates between first-last-first, getting earlier in October each year, until about the first of the month, whereupon it jumps abruptly to near the end of the month to start the same cycle again. The result is an eighteen-year cycle, called the Saros cycle, which is linked to the relative motions of the Sun and the Moon.

The Saros Cycle

This cycle is very close to eighteen years and eleven days. It is the period after which the relative positions of the Earth, Sun, and Moon repeat themselves. We already saw that the Moon does not have the same apparent pathway against the background stars as the Sun. We also saw that twice a lunar month the Moon crosses the apparent pathway of the Sun and that these points of crossing are called the lunar nodes. These nodes are, however, not fixed, and they gradually move along the apparent pathway of the Sun. The cause of this drift is the gravitational tug of the Earth's equatorial bulge on the Moon. If Earth were completely spherical then the Moon would have a fixed orbit with respect to the distant stars, but the gravitational effect of the bulge is to cause a small drift, and it is this drift which gives rise to the Saros cycle. According to Newton's third law of motion to every action there is an equal and opposite reaction so it is not surprising to find that the Moon also reacts back on this equatorial bulge of the Earth to give rise to a phenomenon known as the precession of the equinoxes.

117

The Precession of the Equinoxes

The Moon and the Sun both tug, gravitationally, on the equatorial bulge of our Earth. The Moon tries to get the bulge into the plane of its orbit around the Earth and the Sun tries to get this bulge into the plane of the Earth's orbit around the Sun. These forces have two effects on the Earth. First, they cause the precession of the Earth's axis. This is best explained using the analogy of a child's toy top. As a top begins to slow down its rate of spinning, because of friction with the atmosphere and with the surface on which it is spinning, the axis will lean over. The force of gravitation will try to pull the axis into the horizontal plane, but since it is still spinning it is trying hard to keep a fixed orientation in space. The combined result of these two tendencies is to cause the axis to describe a cone in space, with the apex corresponding to the point of contact with the surface on which it is spinning. This motion of the top's axis is called precession.

The axis of the Earth precesses as a result of the tug of Sun and Moon on its equatorial bulge, causing its axis to make a double cone in space centered on the center of Earth. It takes about twenty-six thousand years to completely describe the cone just once. Over the last few hundred years the northern end of its axis has been pointing towards Polaris—the Pole Star—but in about thirteen thousand years time the angle between the axis and the line joining the center of Earth to Polaris will be about forty-seven degrees. It is also this precession that causes the two points at which the celestial equator crosses the ecliptic to gradually move around the ecliptic. The point at which the Sun is during the northern spring is called the point of the vernal equinox, and the point at which the Sun is (as seen from Earth) during the northern autumn is called the point of the autumnal equinox. When the zodiac was first developed a few hundred years before the birth of Christ, the point of the vernal equinox was in the constellation of Aries—the Ram. About a hundred years before Christ was born, it moved into the constellation of Pisces—the Fish. A few years ago it moved into the constellation of Aquarius—the Water Carrier. The point of the vernal eqinox spends about two thousand years in each constellation.

The other effect of Sun and Moon on the equatorial bulge is called the nutation of the Earth's axis, and it takes the form a very slight nodding of the axis. This means that the double cone described before is a corrugated cone. The period of this nodding is very nearly equal to eighteen years, and it results from the fact that the lunar nodes are also moving around the ecliptic with a period of about eighteen years because of the Saros cycle. In the next chapter we will see that these movements of Earth's axis also have consequences for long-term trends in our climate.

The Nature of Tidal Clocks

In a previous chapter we saw that cycles of light and dark, and variations in day length, could be used to set internal biological clocks. We saw that the processes of evolution had given selective advantage to many species that had internal clocks that had periods close to the natural periods of the day and the seasons. Although these clocks could still keep time under conditions of constant light or darkness, their timekeeping abilities would die out after a while unless the clock was reset by occasional exposure to natural or artificial light cycles of the appropriate periods. It has also been discovered that in the case of organisms with tidal or lunar rhythms, these rhythms persist for a while even after the organisms are removed from their natural environment—the intertidal zone of a beach. These investigations gave rise to certain problems when the organisms were removed to laboratories far from the coast.

Professor Franck Brown reported on a particular set of findings that presents a specific problem concerning the physical energy which can reset the internal tidal clock of certain animals when they are removed from their natural habitat. We use his own words to describe these experiments:

Fifteen oysters shipped in a light-proof container by air from Milford, Connecticut, Fisheries Laboratory were placed in seawater in several large glass vessels. Threads were fastened to stainless steel saddles attached to their valve. The threads activated pen writers on a moving strip of paper. After analysing all the data for the first two weeks, two peaks in activity were noted in the lunar day, and these indicated maximum shell opening in the population of oysters at the times of the Connecticut high tides. When the data for the second two weeks were analysed in exactly the same manner, the double tidal cycles were seen to have moved about 3 hours later in the lunar day, a relationship which appeared to persist for the third fortnight of observation.

It was learned shortly afterwards that the peaks for the second two fortnights had drifted to, and become fixed at, the times of upper and lower transits of the Moon. Could this be fortuitous? Or perhaps the oysters were substituting the Moon-caused high tides of the atmosphere when away from the oceans for the stronger ocean tidal ones of their home seashore? This phenomenon was confirmed by M. F. Bennett in 1963 with crabs collected from two beaches with a 4-hour difference in tidal times. In the laboratory, in separate containers, the crabs synchronised their cycles to times of upper and lower lunar transits.

In the above quote Brown refers to the "tides of the upper atmosphere." The Sun and Moon give rise not only to tides in the oceans, but also to tides in the upper atmosphere, which manifest themselves as variations in the atmospheric pressure at ground level. For the most part these slight tidal pressure variations are masked by other pressure variations caused by changes in the weather. They can, however, be detected by subjecting a continuous pressure variation record to computer analysis. It is possible that a biological organism tuned to the tidal variation could resonantly detect the slight atmospheric tide even in the presence of the other variations in pressure, just as a radio receiver can pick up the one specific radio station to which it is tuned and ignore all other stations. However, another possibility exists which is revealed by some work of Franck Brown.

The results of these experiments are best described in his own words:

The first studies, with mudsnails, dealt with their response to altered directions of weak experimental horizontal magnetic fields. Not only were these animals responsive to fields very close in strength to the Earth's own field, but their responsiveness to these fields gradually altered with time of day, and with phase of Moon, or to the relationships between times of day and times of tides. These last were quite what one expected if the magnetic fields were, indeed, affecting daily and tidal rhythms of the organisms.

How can the magnetic field of Earth, which because of its long period steadiness can be used with a compass to find direction, give rise to fluctuations which vary with the time of day, with the position of the Moon in the sky, and with the phases of the Moon? These fluctuations arise in the following way. Just as overhead electric or telephone cables have a fixed general direction, but can be tugged about and set vibrating by the wind, so for the most part the magnetic lines of force, which start at the north magnetic pole, arch high above Earth's surface, and reenter Earth at the south magnetic pole, are steady over long periods of time, but can vibrate in ways that are linked to the position of the Sun and Moon in the sky. The vibrations linked to the Sun's position arise because of the effect of the solar wind on the whole magnetic field of Earth. This solar wind is a stream of very energetic fragments of atoms emitted by the Sun, which will force the magnetic lines closer to Earth on the sunward side and pull some of them out on the side facing away from the Sun. This means that the field will tend to be stronger on the side facing the Sun and weaker on the far side. Earth is spinning and a "magnetic wave" seems to go around Earth once a day. This is called the solar daily magnetic variation.

There is also another vibration called the lunar daily magnetic variation which arises from the tides in the upper atmosphere. The radiation from the Sun strips some of the electrons in the upper atmosphere of their outer cloak of electrons and as a result the gases here become electrically conducting. When an electrically conducting substance is moved across magnetic lines of force, then electric currents are set up in the conducting material. This is the principle of the electric generator. This means that as the Moon, because of its tidal tug, pulls the upper atmosphere around across the lines of force of Earth's field, so currents are set up in these gases. However, these electric currents generate their own magnetic field, which has to be added to the field already there. This is the cause of the lunar daily magnetic variation, which also changes with the phases of the Moon.

Conclusion

In this chapter we saw that it is possible to understand the motion of Earth around the Sun and the Moon around Earth in terms of the laws of motion and the law of gravitation. We also saw that these bodies, by their gravitational fields, attract the waters of the oceans and the gases of the atmosphere, thus giving rise to tides in these fluids. The tides of the upper atmosphere give rise to detectable changes in the magnetic field of Earth. All these environmental changes can act as the external synchronizers of internal biological clocks that have periods close to the average periods associated with the geophysical changes. Thus, there are some well-understood links among the Sun, the Moon, and life on Earth. In the next chapter we will look at the other environmental changes directly linked to the daily apparent motions of the Sun across the sky, and the seasonal changes associated with this motion. We will also briefly look at the importance of these changes for life on Earth.

7

Programming by Weather and Climate

The amount of radiation we receive from the Sun depends to some extent on where the Earth is on its orbit around the Sun. The presence of our atmosphere changes the way in which this radiation affects the temperature that is measured close to the surface of the Earth. This is one of the major ways in which seasonal changes occur in the short-period weather and long-period climate at any particular location on the Earth. An explanation of how this happens will be the main topic of discussion in this chapter. We will also look at the causes and consequences of more subtle variations in the basic seasonal changes. We will briefly discuss the biological consequences of these meteorological variations.

Seasonal Changes in the Weather

In order to understand seasonal changes that occur in the weather conditions at a given location on Earth's surface at a particular time of the year, we need to make a small diversion into some basic physical principles relevant to the propagation of light.

Consider a narrow beam of light consisting of a bundle of parallel rays. If this beam were projected onto a sheet of squared paper at right angles to its direction, it would form a circular spot of light on the squared paper. However, if the paper were not at right angles to the beam, the spot of light would no longer be circular,

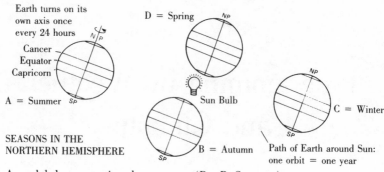

A model demonstrating the seasons. (*Dr. P. Seymour*)

but rather oval shaped. If we compared the area of the circular spot with that of the oval spot (found by counting the number of squares contained in each), it would be seen that the area of the oval spot was greater than that of the circular spot. This means that the energy falling on unit surface area of the circular spot is greater than that for the oval spot. In other words, the same amount of light is falling on each area but its surface density is more concentrated in the circular area than in the oval area. This is one reason why it is hotter at the equator than near the poles of the Earth. The rays from the Sun are at right angles to the surface at the equator, but not near the poles.

If we shine this same beam of light through a thick rectangular sheet of glass, with one face at right angles to the beam, it will be obvious that the path length through the glass will be shorter than it would be if the face were not at right angles to the glass and therefore the light had to go through a greater volume of glass. This brings us to the second reason why the amount of light received from the Sun changes with position on the surface of Earth. The radiant heat and light from the Sun passes at right angles through the "slab" of atmosphere immediately above the equator of Earth. However, the path length of the beam through the atmosphere increases toward the poles of Earth because there is more atmosphere to pass through. This means that more radiant heat and light is lost to the atmosphere the farther we get from the equator.

Hot gases at the equator rise, cool as they get to higher altitudes, move away from the equator toward the tropics, and then the now cooler gases sink back toward Earth at higher latitudes, before they move toward the equator. These movements are known as convection currents. These currents are in reality broken up into smaller convection cells, called Hadley cells, and they help to ensure that the temperature differences between the equator and higher latitudes are not too great. The spinning of the Earth on its own axis means that winds are directed, not along the meridians of longitude, but are deflected from this general direction by an effect known as the Coriolis effect, which is a direct result of the rotation of the Earth.

The Coriolis effect, named after the French physicist Gaspard de Coriolis, arises only when one is dealing with systems that are rotating. For example, consider a shot fired from a gun at the center of a rotating table. To an observer on the table it appears to travel in a curved path, but to an outside fixed observer it seems to travel in a straight line. It is the Coriolis effect that gives rise to the deflection of the trade winds that blow from the tropics to the equator. In the Northern Hemisphere these winds seem to come from the northeast, and in the Southern Hemisphere they seem to come from the southeast. In the northern summer rays from the Sun make an angle of ninety degrees with the surface near the Tropic of Cancer, but in the northern winter they make an angle of ninety degrees with the surface near the Tropic of Capricorn. This means that besides the days being longer in the northern summer, as we saw in an earlier chapter, the Northern Hemisphere will also receive much more radiant energy during the summer than it does in the winter. These factors together are thus able to explain the seasonal variations experienced on the surface of Earth. They also explain why these differences are greater as one gets farther from the equator.

Temperature Responses in Living Organisms

Chemical reaction rates are, on the whole, temperature dependent. The current approach in modern biology is to attempt to explain all biological processes in terms of biochemistry, and since reaction rates are temperature dependent it is not surprising that some biological processes are also dependent on the temperature of the environment. Most plants follow seasonal cycles that can be triggered by temperatures external to the organisms. Thus, it is not uncommon for plants that normally flower in the spring to form buds earlier in the year, if the winter has been mild and the temperature is high enough for them to do so. However, most forms of vegetable life follow a seasonal cycle that deviates only slightly from the norm, under suitable circumstances, when the external conditions are appropriate for them to do so. Many animals depend for their food supply on vegetable material, and thus evolutionary selection has favored those, as we have already seen, that produce offspring when the supply of food is plentiful.

Vertebrates can be divided into two main classes according to how they respond to temperature changes in the environment. Homoiothermic vertebrates, which include birds and mammals, are those that keep a constant body temperature independent of the temperature of the environment. They do so by using metabolic processes to counteract fluctuations in external temperatures. The hypothalamus in the brain is responsible for monitoring the temperature of blood and controlling the thermoregulation of the body by means of the nervous system and the hormonal control system. This can produce short-term responses, such as sweating in hot weather and shivering in cold, and longer-term adjustments to metabolism according to seasonal changes in climate—a process known as acclimatization. To assist in the maintenance of a temperature which is different from that of their surroundings, homoiothermic (warm-blooded) animals have insulated coatings in the form of fur, hair, or feathers. The relatively high internal temperatures of these species allow fast reactions on the part of nerves and muscles, and thus enable them to lead highly active lives even in cold weather. The internal biological clocks of many of these organisms show very little dependence on external temperature. It is as if these clocks are temperature-compensated, just like the chronometers of John Harrison.

In poikilothermic vertebrates the temperature of the body changes when the temperature of the environment changes. In such vetebrates the metabolic activities slow down proportionally to the ambient temperature. It is then not surprising that such animals are much more susceptible to seasonal fluctuations than homoiothermic species. The regulation of reproductive and other cycles by seasonal changes in environmental temperature, known as thermoperiodism, sometimes dominates over photoperiodism in these species of vertebrates. Although poikilothermic (cold-blooded) animals are not able to maintain a constant body temperature, they can respond in various ways to compensate for very high and very low temperatures. The tissue composition can change to regulate the blood flow to peripheral tissue and thus increase heat loss or heat absorption. Alternatively, the animal can actively seek sunlight or shade. Seasonal changes in metabolism are usually under the control of the hormonal system. In very hot climates poikilothermic animals may undergo estivation to escape heat. This is a state of inactivity that occurs in animals like lungfish during prolonged periods of drought and heat. In this state bodily activities such as feeding, respiration, and movement are considerably slowed down. Hibernation and dormancy are ways in which some animals cope with the low temperatures of winter.

Long-Term Changes in Climate

Sediments laid down over very long time periods contain information on past climate. This information often takes the form of the relative numbers of different species of microorganism that exist in sedimentary deposits laid down during different geological periods. The survival and reproduction rates of many of these microscopic life forms are very dependent on the temperature of the environment. Thus, the relative numbers of the bodies of these creatures found within deposits can be used as a record of temperatures that have existed in the past. These studies have revealed a complex record of climatic changes, on time scales lasting from several thousand years down to others lasting only several years. Some of these changes can be understood in terms of changes in the dynamics of Earth; others can be understood in terms of variations in the radiative output of the Sun. Let us look at a few of the possible causes of these climatic changes.

Climatic Changes Due to Gravitational Effects

If Earth were the only planet going around the Sun, then its elliptical orbit would be fixed in space, with respect to the distant stars. This, however, is not the case. Because there are other planets going around the Sun, and they also tug, by means of gravitation, on our Earth, so the long axis of Earth's orbit gradually moves around the Sun. The ratio of the long to the short axis of an ellipse is related to a quantity called the ellipticity. The ellipticity is large if these two axes are very different and small if the two axes are nearly equal in length. For example, in a circle the two axes are exactly equal, so the ellipticity is zero, whereas in a highly flattened oval it will be very high. Another effect of the gravitational tug of the planets on our Earth is to cause a small change in the ellipticity of its orbit over long periods of time. Jupiter is the main contributor to these effects, with Saturn playing a much smaller role, and the other planets playing only a very small part. The tug of the planets on the equatorial bulge of Earth also causes very slight long-period changes in the tilt of Earth's axis. All these changes, however minute, cause slight variations in the amount of radiation that we receive from the Sun, and this is reflected in slight changes in temperature on Earth's surface. This in turn gives rise to fluctuations in the annual populations of certain species of microorganisms.

More recently these indirect observations have been supplemented by more direct methods based on weather records covering relatively long periods of time that have come to us from China. In their book *Beyond the Jupiter Effect* John Gribbin and Stephen Plagemann discuss the link between planetary positions as seen from the Sun, and our weather.[1] This link was discovered in 1980 by two Chinese scientists, Ren Zhenqui, of the Peking Academy of Meteorological Science, and Li Zhisen, of the Peking Astronomical Observatory. These men found that when several of the planets were grouped within an angle of less than ninety degrees, which they called a synod, on one side of the Sun, and the Earth

[1] J. Gribbin, S. Plagemann, *Beyond the Jupiter Effect*, Fontana, London, 1977.

was on the opposite side of the Sun, then there were unusual weather conditions on Earth. They explained this in terms of changes in the actual orbit of Earth caused by the grouping of the other planets. The gravitational tug of the planets in this synod on Earth will cause changes in the length of time Earth will spend in the winter and summer parts of its orbit. This will cause slight changes in the actual lengths of the seasons, and this in turn will give rise to unusual weather conditions. Ren and Li made this discovery by studying ancient Chinese records that go back for more than three thousand years, which are available because China has the longest continuous civilization where such observations of the weather have been systematically recorded.

Solar Activity, Geomagnetism, Weather, and Climate

Sunspots were first seen with the aid of telescopes in about 1610, and ever since have been of intense interest to astronomers. Although they appear as dark regions on the visible disc of the Sun, this is entirely a contrast effect. The region of the sunspot is cooler than the surrounding areas of the Sun, so it emits less light and as a result it looks darker but of course it is extremely hot. The number of spots varies and reaches a maximum roughly every eleven years, but the period between successive maxima can be as short as seven or as long as seventeen years. It was in 1843 that a German astronomer named Heinrich Schwabe discovered the roughly eleven-year period of the sunspot cycle, and in 1852 a British scientist named Wallace Sabine found that the sunspot cycle was related to variations of the magnetic compass needle.

Several researchers have found correlations between solar activity, geomagnetism, long-term climate, and short-term weather. One such correlation shows a link between the twenty-two-year sunspot cycle and drought over the western United States. A convincing theory about a long-term climatic effect rests on the evidence for a link between the sunspot cycle and the rate of production of a radioactive form of carbon, known as carbon 14, in our atmosphere. The carbon 14 found in the annual rings of trees has been measured to show that solar activity was weaker in certain centuries than at other times. Using geophysical data on climatic conditions in the past seems to indicate that several periods of severe winters have corresponded to times when solar activity was much weaker. Professor Eugene Parker from the University of Chicago, a world authority on magnetic fields in astronomy, had this to say about this latter effect:

Whatever the connection between solar activity and terrestrial climate, it is difficult to avoid the fact that historical records of climate, and the geological indicators of climate, have kept in step with the general level of solar activity for 18 strides at irregular intervals of time. A simple coincidence of two unrelated phenomena is too improbable to consider. It appears, then, that magnetic activity has a longer arm and a heavier hand than anyone could have imagined.[2]

Another interesting discovery, this time concerning the link between weather and the geomagnetic field, was made by Goesta Wollin, formerly of the Lamont Geophysical Observatory in the United States. He showed that changes in the sea surface temperature were somehow linked to changes in the geomagnetic field, and he explained it as follows. The water of the oceans conducts electricity because of the salts dissolved in the water. Changes in the geomagnetic field cause currents to flow in the oceans, or affect currents already flowing. This causes changes in sea surface temperature patterns, which in turn affect the temperature above the ocean. Wollin showed that because of the relatively sluggish response of the oceans to changes in the geomagnetic field, changes in the weather lagged behind geomagnetic changes by about two years. More recently he was able to show that if the magnetic field changed very violently near a given observatory, then there would be unusual weather conditions in the vicinity of the observatory about five days later.[3, 4]

[2]E. N. Parker in *Cosmical Magnetic Fields* (Clarenden Press, Oxford, 1979) was drawing attention to the fact that irregularities in solar activity correlated with some indicators of climatic variations, e.g. mean temperatures.
[3]J. Gribbin, S. Plagemann, *Beyond the Jupiter Effect*, Fontana, London, 1977.
[4]See also Seymour, Percy, *Cosmic Magnetism*, Adam Hilger, Bristol, 1986.

Lunar Tides and the Wealth of Nations

The title of this section is the same as that of an article by Robert Currie of the Institute of Atmospheric Sciences at the State University of New York at Stony Brook, which appeared in *New Scientists* on November 5, 1988. In this article Currie points out that Theophratus, a former pupil of and successor to Aristotle, was the first person to suggest a connection between the Moon and climate, when he said, "The ends and beginnings of the lunar month are apt to be stormy." Currie adds that modern studies confirm the validity of this statement.

We have already seen that Sir Isaac Newton provided the basic theory of the tides. However, in his work Newton had investigated two particular models of how the Moon and Sun could give rise to the oceanic tides. In one model he assumed that the whole Earth was covered in water, and in the other model he assumed that the oceans were confined to a canal around the equator of Earth. It is obvious that neither of these corresponds to the real distribution of water on Earth. A more detailed theory of the tides, still making use of Newton's law of gravitation and the laws of motion, was developed in the nineteenth century by the great French mathematician the Marquis Pierre-Simon de Laplace. This mathematician was able to show that there should be tides in the atmosphere as well as the oceans. Although Laplace searched for the atmospheric tides in records of barometric pressure he failed to find them. In this century the tides were discovered by the British geophysicist Professor Sydney Chapman using improved instruments, better methods of extracting patterns out of "noisy" data, and records covering longer periods of time. Currie comments, "Chapman came closer than anyone to realising the potential importance of the tides."

Earlier on we saw that the lunar nodes move around the ecliptic with a period of about eighteen years. Currie was able to show, using more powerful methods of mathematical analysis on modern high-speed computers, that this cycle also manifested itself in the tidal record. He went on to show that this also caused modulation of the rainfall in the United States, and this in turn affected the crop production. He then proposed that the crop production was responsible for the "Kuznets long swing," cycles with a period of about twenty years in the American economy. These are named after the economist Simon Kuznets, who first noted them in 1930. Currie attributed the link between the Moon and rainfall directly to the atmospheric tides. It is, however, possible that some contribution may come from the magnetic disturbances induced in the magnetic field of Earth by the tides of the electrical conducting gases of the upper atmosphere. These in turn could affect the flow patterns in the oceans, and this can influence sea surface temperatures, according to the mechanism proposed by Goesta Wollin.

Mars and Terrestrial Temperature

At the First International Congress on Geo-Cosmic Relations, held in Amsterdam, the Netherlands, April 19–22, 1989, two meteorologists, J. V. M. Venker and N. C. Beeflink, presented evidence that terrestrial temperature seemed to be correlated to the positions of Mars in the sky as seen from the surface of Earth. They based these conclusions on a statistical study of the average daily temperature at De Bilt in the Netherlands, over a twenty-seven-year period from 1961 to 1988. In their paper they write:

The astronomical criterion in this study is the TROPICAL ZODIAC [eliptic] divided into 12 sectors of 30 degrees each. In other words, the ecliptic was used as a reference grid. In order to define the Mars-positions [angles], the main reference point was the Spring-Equinox or 0 degr. Aries-point.

In a remarkable percentage of cases it was found that when the planet MARS was passing the last degree of the noted sector a weather break was observed; likewise, when the geocentric position of this planet was a few degrees distance before the sector limits, the probability of such a weather break appeared to be low. Of the various elements that make up weather, temperature was singled out as the most suitable element for the statistical analyses.

Their results turned out to be statistically significant. This work is very important. It is the first positive indication that the geocentric position of a planet can directly affect a specific factor connected with weather, namely, temperature. It is possible to understand this result by combining the work of Currie, the theory of Goesta Wollin on geomagnetic changes and weather, and my own work on the magnetic tides of the planets.

I first proposed a theory for planetary magnetic tides in my book, *Astrology: The Evidence of Science,* to account for some positive evidence in favor of some aspects of astrology which were discovered by Michel Gauquelin.

Planetary Magnetic Tides and Weather

The magnetic field of Earth vibrates with a wide range of natural frequencies. According to my theory some of these frequencies are almost exactly the same as those associated with the weak tidal forces of the planets, and these tidal forces, though weak, are strong enough to make the natural frequencies keep in step with them: or, to use the normal langue of science, the natural frequencies become phase-locked to the tidal frequencies. In other words, some of the natural frequencies are tuned to periods associated with the tidal tug of the planets.

Detractors of my theory point out that the tidal effect of the Moon on the magnetic field of Earth is very much stronger than that of the planets, so the other planets could not possibly have an effect similar to that of the Moon. Let us look at the oceanic tides as a refutation of this argument. The calculation that critics of my theory use to show that the weakness of planetary tides is based on a particular theory of tidal effects: the so-called equilibrium theory of the tides. This assumes that the whole Earth is uniformly covered by water and that there are no land masses or atmosphere with which the water can interact. Scientists who work on tidal theory are quite aware that equilibrium theory on most occasions does not give us a good idea of the measured height of the tides—the tidal height is usually greater than that predicted by this theory. This is because the tides are amplified by the interaction with the geometry of the coastline, and they can also be magnified by weather conditions.

When applied to the oceans, this theory tells us that the tidal range, the average difference between high and low tides, can be between four and five feet. Yet, in many bays and estuaries the tidal range can be four or five times greater than this simple and naive theory predicts. In the Port of Bristol the range is about fifteen to twenty feet. In the Bay of Fundy in Canada the range is over fifty feet, and the Sun and Moon together move 100 billion tons of water in and out twice a day. This is in spite of the fact that their combined gravitational attraction on the waters of Earth is 1 million times weaker than the gravitational tug of Earth itself. The reason for these high tides is that the shape of the bay, and the way the bay shallows as it goes inland, amplify the weak tidal forces of the Sun and Moon. Scientists call this tidal resonance, and it occurs because the natural frequency associated with the movement of the water in the bay is very nearly equal to the tidal frequency associated with the Moon. Resonance can occur in many different situations in nature, whenever the fluctuations of an external force are in tune with the natural vibrations of a system, and as I will show, resonance is a vitally important though much misunderstood factor in understanding the effect of planetary gravitation.

How does the concept of resonance apply to the magnetic field of Earth? Earth's magnetic field extends into space in all directions. In the direction of the Sun it extends to about five times the radius of Earth, and in the opposite direction it extends to about twenty-five times Earth's radius. The sheer size of the magnetic field (usually referred to as the magnetosphere) serves to amplify the weak tidal forces of the planets and this can be explained even using the simple equilibrium theory of the tides. Since the magnetosphere, on magnetically quiet days, is at least ten times the size of Earth, the tidal range of a particular planet is ten thousand times greater in the outer parts of the magnetosphere than it is on the surface of Earth. Trapped in this extended magnetosphere are a number of charged particles which form what is known as a plasma. Near the surface of Earth the magnetic lines of force converge very rapidly before they enter the surface, and so they do form "bays" and "estuaries" which can amplify the weak tidal forces of the planets on the plasma. The situation is further enhanced by the fact that the magnetic field itself consists of lines of force which have a tension of their own, rather like the strings of a musical instrument, stretching out into space. These lines have their own natural frequencies, and some of these are in tune with the tidal tug of the planets. To use equilibrium tidal theory as applied to the surface of Earth to criticize a theory involving resonant tidal effects in the magnetosphere is not only intellectually dishonest, it is scientifically inappropriate, mathematically meaningless, and totally invalid.

There is, however, another factor affecting the tidal range—one which is overlooked by the simple equilibrium theory of the tides. In the case of the ocean tides of Earth there is also interaction between the sea and meteorological conditions. The height of the sea at a particular port can differ from that predicted on the basis of any theory, if the coming of the spring tides coincides with severe weather conditions, such as, for example, very strong gusts of wind. According to my theory, the influence of planetary tides on the magnetosphere can be considerably enhanced by magnetic storms. These storms are rather violent disruptions of the relatively quiet extended magnetic fields of Earth. During these disruptions the dimensions of the field change considerably, and there are measurable changes in the strength of the field at Earth's surface. Most of these storms have their origins on the Sun and they become more frequent as the cycle of sunspots builds up to a maximum, which it does roughly every eleven years.

The solar wind, which is a stream of particles coming from the Sun, distorts the magnetosphere, rather as an ordinary wind would distort a wind sock at an airfield. It is the gusting of the solar wind that gives rise to the magnetic storms of the extended magnetic field of Earth. According to my research there is evidence that the sunspot cycle is linked to the positions and motions of the planets as seen from the Sun. This part of my theory provides a further link with some ancient concepts in astrology. These matters will be discussed in a later chapter.

Conclusion

We have now seen, not only in this chapter, that temperature can affect the reproduction and survival rate of certain organisms, and since temperature is dependent on the climatic conditions which prevail at a given location on Earth, as well as on weather conditions that prevail at a given period of time, weather and climate can, by means of the processes of evolution, program some behavioral patterns in certain organisms. We also saw that long-term climate and short-term weather are both linked to the dynamics of the Solar System. The dynamics of the Solar System can be understood in terms of a mechanical model of the Solar System and the traffic rules for this model are described by Newton's laws of motion and his law of gravitation. This means that the ultimate factors controlling biological programming by weather and climate are the patterns of behavior which are evident in large-scale inanimate systems, such as our Solar System.

8

Animal Navigators

It is well known that many species of birds migrate over distances covering several hundred miles. But how do they find their way from one location to another? Only over the last few thousand years have humans developed scientific and technological means to consciously navigate accurately over large distances. Undoubtedly bird navigation is therefore an important problem for biologists. In 1963 Joel Carl Welty said, "Probably the knottiest problem in all ornithology is how a bird finds its way home." In this chapter we will consider two possible solutions to the problem of long-distance navigation in birds, namely the use of the Sun and the stars for this purpose. Over much shorter distances bees have to find their way from their hives to food sources and back again. How do they do this? We will look at a very convincing solution to this problem.

Solar Navigation of Birds

Gustav Kramer was a German biologist born in Mannheim in 1910. His first work concentrated on the physiology of lower vertebrates, but besides being a very able physiologist, he was also a keen naturalist. At the Max Planck Institute for Marine Biology at Wilhelmshaven, Germany, Kramer built up a school for orientation studies which carried on research in Europe and the United States. This institute looks out over the North Sea, being located on the

137

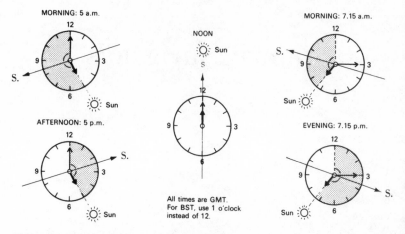

Using the Sun as a compass. (*Dr. P. Seymour*)

western shore of Jade Bay. One bird that particularly interested Kramer was the arctic tern. This bird nests within a hundred miles of the North Pole. In the fall it flies over Canada, across the Atlantic Ocean, down the west coast of the African continent, around the Cape of Good Hope, and finally ends up at its winter feeding grounds near Port Elizabeth, on the south coast of South Africa.

There are several other examples of birds flying over very great distances. We will just look at two of these. The bronzed cuckoo from New Zealand flies 1,200 miles from the Tasman Sea to small wintering areas in the Bismarck Archipelago and the Solomon Islands. Even more surprisingly the young cuckoos make the flight alone, their parents having preceded them by at least a month. Professor L. Richard Mehwald, who lived in San Jose, California, found that banded white-crowned sparrows returned not only to his garden but to the same bush in his garden, having flown 2,200 miles from their summer breeding grounds in Alaska.

In order to investigate the problem of bird navigation Kramer made use of a special type of behavior, well known in migrating birds. In an earlier chapter we mentioned the phenomenon of the zugunruhe, or the premigration restlessness of birds sometimes referred to as "flight fidgets." It was also known that during this period of restlessness caged birds tended to point repeatedly in a particular direction. Kramer set out to answer the question, Could this be the direction that they would eventually take if they were released from the laboratory cage that contained them?

Kramer decided to use European starlings for this purpose since they do well in cages, and the young birds are easy to collect. During the daylight hours of October, just before they normally start to migrate, he kept a constant watch on them. It was unnecessary to watch them at night since they were known to be diurnal migrators. The normal migration direction for starlings leaving Wilhelmshaven would be southwest. Kramer soon found out that with all their nervous fluttering, his captive birds tended to remain in the southwest corner of their cages, and to face to the southwest direction.

The next question he investigated was what environmental factors the birds were using as navigational cues. Were they perhaps using local landmarks? When he moved the cages to other locations with different landmarks, and also when he enclosed the lower part of the cage so that the birds could only see the sky, they still continued to favor the southwest direction. During the following spring, when the normal migratory direction would be to the northwest, as they headed back from the south, the caged birds pointed to the northwest. This then provided Kramer with the experimental method that he had sought for so long.

He designed a circular cage so that a bird inside it had no way of knowing which way it was facing, since the inner surface of the cage was perfectly symmetrical. From the perch at the center of the cage, a bird showing signs of zugunruhe would fly radially to the circumference of the cage and back again. The bottom of the cage was made of transparent plastic marked off into a number of sectors, so that Kramer could lie beneath the cage and record the bird's position at any time. An important environmental variable that he wanted to test was the direction from which the light fell on the cage. He was also interested in how varying the intensity of light would affect the direction preferred by the birds in the cage. In order to do this he built a six-sided pavilion in which to hang the observation cages. The sides of the pavilion each had a window provided with a shutter, and each window was also provided with a mirror so that light could be reflected into the cage at ninety degrees from its usual direction. Kramer arranged for the rotation of the cage itself, and for an opaque screen that could be placed around the whole pavilion. Just as his starlings had done in their cages in the open, the birds in the pavilion now pointed, during the spring, toward the northwest, when the windows of the pavilion were open on all sides. What amazed Kramer, as well as other scientists, was that the starlings changed their direction by ninety degrees when the light from the sky was changed by ninety degrees using the mirrors on the windows of the pavilion. This clearly indicated that they did not have any natural inherent tendency to point in their normal migratory direction. In the last century it had been proposed by some biologists that there was a natural instinct, based on unknown biological, rather than physical, agencies, which provided directional information. They also did not know what that direction was unless they could take bearings on the Sun. Thus the birds were responding to the radiation from the Sun.

In his later work he changed the experimental setup, by training the starlings under an open sky to seek food in a feeder to the west of the cage, no matter what time of day it was. He then erected a tent around the cage of the bird so that the real Sun was excluded, and then he placed an artificial "Sun" outside the cage but within the tent so that this "Sun" always shone from a fixed position in the west. The starlings behaved as if they were seeing the real Sun, and acted as though that "Sun" were moving as it ought to in the real sky. Since these starlings had been trained to seek food in the west feeder at any time of the day, they now sought food in the east at 6:00 A.M., in the north at noon, and in the west at 5:00 P.M.

These experiments clearly showed that the starlings were using their internal biological clocks, together with the position of the Sun in the sky, to find direction. Humans have also developed a method to find direction using the Sun in conjunction with an ordinary watch having a dial face. This can be done as follows. Place the watch on a level surface. Hold a matchstick at right angles to the surface and very close to the rim of the watch face. Keeping the matchstick steady, turn the watch until the shadow of the stick cast by the Sun lies along the hour hand of the watch. The tip of the hour hand should point to the place where the matchstick just touches the rim of the watch. At the center of the face an angle is formed by the shadow of the matchstick and the line joining 12 to the center. The line bisecting this angle is along the north-south line. At noon the south direction is the one pointing directly through the figure 12. In the morning, south is in the direction that is before 12 on the dial, and in the afternoon and early evening in the direction after 12.

In order to test this hypothesis still further, several other researchers in this area of ornithology carried out additional experiments on other birds that were known to be diurnal migrators (i.e., those that migrate by day rather than by night). One such experiment took the following form. Some birds were placed in artificial daylight conditions, in which the times of sunrise and sunset were changed by a specific number of hours. This had the effect of resetting their internal clocks by the same number of hours. When released under the real sky, the birds flew in the wrong direction by the number of degrees that the Sun would have moved in that time. These experiments provided strong support for Kramer's Sun compass hypothesis.

Birds that Navigate Using the Stars

If birds can orient themselves by the Sun during the day, is it not possible that they can do the same at night using the stars? The biologists E. G. Franz Sauer and Eleanore Sauer, his wife, of the University of Freiburg in Germany, decided to investigate this hypothesis. In their first experiments they used warblers in a cage with a glass window on top, so the birds could see some of the sky, but none of the surrounding landmarks. Just as Kramer had done with his starlings, the Sauers observed the direction that the warblers favored by observing from below the directions in which they fluttered during the zugunruhe. It turned out that these directions were, in every case, characteristic of the species of bird. The blackcaps, the whitethroats, and the garden warblers all pointed to the southwest in the autumn, this being their normal direction for the autumnal migration. These birds normally flew southwest from Freiburg to Spain, down to Gibraltar, and then across the Straits to Africa. On the other hand, the lesser whitethroats pointed in their cages toward the southeast. Their normal migratory flight path from Germany took them southeast across the Balkans and then south along the river valley of the Nile. It also turned out that it made no difference whether the birds had been hand-raised or had been trapped in the fields near Freiburg. In other words, their directional abilities were genetically programmed rather than learned.

The Sauers continued their investigations by looking at a wide range of natural conditions. They found that the birds were disturbed by moonlight and by very bright meteors (which are sometimes erroneously called shooting stars). If clouds began to form in the skies, the birds would initially show some hesitancy in deciding on direction, but as long as they could see the brightest of the stars, through the clouds, they pointed in the normal migratory direction associated with their particular species, for the appropriate time of year. However, if the cloud was so thick that no stars could be seen, the birds exhibited no directional preference and finally went to sleep.

We have already seen in a previous chapter how the sky changes as we change our latitude. Thus at the North Pole of Earth the Pole Star will be directly overhead, whereas at any other latitude in the Northern Hemisphere its height above the horizon in degrees will be very nearly equal to its latitude (or its distance from the equator in degrees). This effect of changing latitude can be simulated under the artificial night sky of a planetarium. Through the cooperation of Captain M. Berger and Dr. W. Stein of the Olbers Planetarium in Bremen, the Sauers were able to carry out some experiments with warblers and other birds in this planetarium, which has a twenty-foot dome. They used the same method for making observations as previously.[1]

Under diffuse lighting conditions within the planetarium warblers showed no preferential direction, but fluttered about in random directions. When a blackcap was shown a simulated spring sky, it pointed toward the northeast, as it would do under normal conditions. When the sky was changed to an autumn sky it pointed to the southwest, the direction it would take to get to Spain. The lesser whitethroat pointed to the southeast, the direction in which it would fly to get to the Balkans. The most interesting behavior within the planetarium came from one individual lesser whitethroat. We have already seen the migration course of this species—first southwest across the Balkans, and then due south toward the headwaters of the Nile. This particular whitethroat was one that they had raised from the egg; it had never been out in the wild and so it follows that it had never been on a migratory flight with other members of its species. Since a planetarium can simulate the sky as seen from different latitudes, this lesser whitethroat was first placed under the planetarium sky as it would have been seen from Freiburg. As expected, it faced toward the southeast. The planetarium sky was then shifted to simulate the sky as it would be seen from latitudes that were increasingly closer to the equator. The bird continued to point southeast, until a latitude of forty degrees was reached, eight degrees farther south than the latitude of Freiburg. At this simulated latitude it shifted its direction toward the south-southeast until, at a latitude of fifteen degrees, it bore due south. An important observation on these experiments was made by Donald Griffin, onetime professor of zoology at Harvard, who had been studying bird migration and navigation for many years:

Real advances in understanding a subject like bird migration almost always come as partial or complete surprises. A generation ago neither I nor any other scientist would have predicted with

[1] E. G. Franz Sauer, *Celestial Navigation by Birds*, Scientific American, August, 1958. See also *The Living Clocks*, R. R. Ward, Collins, London, 1972.

143

the slightest confidence several . . . [of these] discoveries about bird migration. . . . Future advances may be equally unexpected. If scientific progress were predictable, it would become a sort of engineering, useful perhaps, but much less fun.[2]

Celestial navigation by birds using starlight is important from the point of view of criticisms leveled against astrology. It is often pointed out that the gravitation tug of the planets is far less than that of the Moon and the Sun. It is also pointed out that the light we receive from the Sun is far greater than that which we receive from the planets, by a factor of 100 billion. We have already discussed how the tidal forces of the planets can be considerably enhanced by resonant amplification. As far as we are aware at the moment, no such methods of enhancement exist for nocturnal migrators. However, the Sun is obviously not in the sky at night, so these migrators have adapted their eyes to respond to the very much weaker light levels of the stars so that they can migrate at night. Smaller birds tend to migrate at night for two reasons. First, with their faster metabolism they exhaust their energy stores in flight faster than other birds do. They thus have to replace these stores quickly and efficiently, and this is best done during the daytime. Second, by migrating at night they are less likely to be distracted by their surroundings and are better able to concentrate on covering large distances; and they are safe from their predators. An additional advantage is that the air is in general more stable at night, so they are less likely to be pushed off course by wind and they expend less energy when flying in calm air. In a later chapter I will argue that early humans used the stars and naked eye planets for navigating at night, and this was how they developed an awareness of the movements of the stars, and the average periods of the naked eye planets.

The work of the Sauers on bird orientation under laboratory conditions and in the planetarium was further supplemented by experiments in the field. Birds released under clear skies tend to fly

---

[2]D. R. Griffin, *Bird Migration*, Doubleday, Natural History Press, Garden City, N.Y., 1964, as quoted by R. R. Ward in *The Living Clocks*.

in definite compass directions, whereas birds released under overcast skies fly in random directions. In one experiment two groups of birds were used. One group of birds were fitted with contact lenses that allowed them to see objects under normal conditions of daylight but fogged out starlight, while a second control group were not fitted with these lenses. When released under the night sky, the birds in the first group took longer to find their way home than those of the second group. In a variation of this experiment the birds were divided into three groups. The first group were fitted with contact lenses and had small magnets tied to their feet; the second group were fitted with contact lenses only; while the last group had neither contact lenses nor magnets. The birds of the first group never returned home, while those in the second group took longer to return home than those of the last group. This seems to indicate that birds can navigate either by the stars or by the magnetic field of Earth, although they seem to prefer to use the stars. We will return to this question in a later chapter, because this correlation between visual and magnetic navigational cues is important to the theory of how human biological clocks become synchronized to planetary cycles.

Navigation of Bees

Karl von Frisch is the world authority on the social life of bees. He also made one of the most dramatic discoveries of twentieth-century biology. This is described by Professor Archie Carr, graduate research professor of biology at the University of Florida, in the following words:

One of the most dramatic zoological events of this century was the discovery by Karl von Frisch of Germany, of the Sun compass in honey bees. . . . For ages men have wondered how bees could fly so straight to a source of nectar and back to the hive again. The brilliant work of von Frisch revealed that bees hold to their beelines by taking a bearing on the Sun, and take its apparent motion into account in plotting their beelines at different times of day. . . . This [is] called the Sun compass sense. Discovering it was one of the most important advances ever made in the study of animal orientation. That the discovery should have included finding bees communicating with each other in such an elaborate way is an almost incredible coincidence.[3]

The experiments of von Frisch showed that bees can find their way to food sources and back to the hive again using a Sun compass not unlike that used by diurnally migrating birds. Moreover, once a bee has found such a food source, it can pass on information concerning its distance from the hive and its direction with respect to the Sun at a given time. To do so it uses a dance language. To quote Professor Carr again:

In the dark, on the vertical wall of the hive, she [the bee] makes and reverses a small upright circle. Every so often she dances a diameter across it; and then circles some more. The angle the diameter makes with the vertical tells other bees which way to fly. The vertical is the Sun's azimuth position—its compass bearing from the hive—and the danced diameter shows the angle that the flight path to the food makes with the Sun's direction. All another bee has to do is mentally to lay the dance pattern out flat, with what was the vertical now pointing in the direction of the Sun, and then fly away in the direction the diameter shows.[4]

On those days that the Sun can be seen bees make use of the actual Sun, just as the birds do. However, on cloudy days they make use of the polarization of the sky, which depends on the position of the Sun in the sky. Since light consists of waves, with the waves vibrating at right angles to the direction of propagation, it is possible to produce waves that are vibrating preferentially in one direction only. This can be done by passing the waves, which are normally vibrating in all directions, through a special polarizing filter that will block most of the waves, but will allow through those that are vibrating in the chosen direction. As the light from the Sun passes through our atmosphere, some of it becomes polarized at right angles to the direction in which it is moving. This gives

[3]A. Carr, *Guideposts of Animal Navigation*, Biological Sciences Curriculum Study Pamphlet 1, Boston: D. C. Heath and Co., 1962.
[4]Ibid.

rise to a pattern of polarized light in the sky, and this moves around with the Sun and thus can be used to locate the Sun's position. The sky near the zenith is polarized at right angles to the direction of the Sun. This polarization can be detected by special elements, called ommatidia, that occur near the tops of the compound eyes of the bees. They use this polarization, in conjunction with their internal biological clocks, as a navigational aid.

The distance to food from the hive is also communicated by the dance of the bees. When the bee moves along the diameter of the circle it has danced, it waggles its body from side to side. The number of times it waggles its body is related to the distance to the food. The more it waggles, the farther the food is from the hive. The waggle distance code is slilghtly different for each race of honeybee.

Longitude, Time, Birds, and Bees

In an earlier chapter we saw the problems faced by human navigators and astronomers when they tried to solve the longitude problem. We also saw that the problem was only solved to a high degree of accuracy once Harrison had invented the chronometer, which could keep accurate time at sea. Do birds and bees have any knowledge of their longitude, and if they do, how do they find it? As far as birds are concerned the answer is far from clear.

A chronometer can be used to find longitude because it keeps accurately the time of some reference meridian, which in most cases is the Greenwich meridian. By comparing his own local time with that of the Greenwich meridian a seaman can deduce his longitude. Although birds have very accurate internal clocks, these will reset themselves to the local time of the terrestrial location in which the bird finds itself, so these clocks do not have the stable, location-independent property which is the essential feature of the chronometer. The Sauers, however, thought it possible that birds had some sort of starmap-clock programmed into their brains that would allow them to compare the sky of their northern territory with that of other locations along the route, and thus enable them to deduce their longitude. They investigated this possibility under the artificial sky of the planetarium in Bremen, but their findings were inconclusive.

Dr. Klaus Hoffmann of the Max-Planck-Institute for Behavioral Physiology had this to say about the problem:

To clarify the situation, and to get further insight into the clock mechanisms involved, more diversified experiments under planetarium conditions seem necessary, including experiments with birds whose clocks have been artificially shifted. As far as I am aware, no such experiments have been performed.

Since bees do not travel very great distance they do not really need to know their longitude. Nevertheless, it is interesting to see how they would cope with a change in time zones. Karl von Frisch was interested in this question before the Second World War. He decided to investigate the problem by training a group of bees to seek food at a specific hour of local German time, and then transporting them across the Atlantic Ocean to America. One of his students volunteered to undertake the crossing and make notes on all her observations as the crossing was under way. Unfortunately, she was seasick for the entire voyage and was unable to make a single note. The war came and von Frisch left off with these experiments until after the war, when planes were flying regularly from Paris to New York.[5]

It was Max Renner, one of von Frisch's collaborators, who actually carried out the experiment. In June 1955 Renner, in a special bee room in Paris, trained a group of forty bees to fly to a feeding dish between 8:15 and 10:15 A.M. French summer time. On June 13, Renner considered that the bees were adequately trained, and so he flew with the bees to New York. Professor T. Schneirla of the American Museum of Natural History in New York was at the airport to assist with speeding the passage of the bees through customs. Less than twenty-four hours after they left Paris the bees were in an identical room in the museum. With regard to their feeding time, two possibilities were open to the bees. Either they would wait the five-hour time difference between New York and

[5]R. R. Ward, *The Living Clocks*, Collins, London, 1972.

Paris to pick up some clue from an external factor geared to eastern daylight time, or they would start feeding just twenty-four hours after their last training in Paris.

Renner tells us:

At 3:15 Eastern Daylight Time, the first bees came out of the hive and started flying about the room, as if their location had not changed. . . . And the visits to the feeding place so numerous and thorough that it was difficult for the observer to note down each visitor correctly. The results of this experiment, as well as the reverse one (training in New York and testing in Paris), has answered the question as to the nature of the bees' orientation in time: the trained collector bees maintained their 24-hour rhythms independently of external influences that periodically recur during the day. Bees have an internal clock, governed by their organism.[6]

Fairly early in his investigations von Frisch had noted that there were small errors in the dance direction. The bees visiting a particular location would get the angle wrong by a very small amount. He also discovered that the error would change in the course of the day, but the overall pattern would be very similar from one day to the next. His first tentative hypothesis was that there was some built-in error in the system by which bees measured the force of gravitation. The problem was eventually solved by Martin Lindauer, a student of von Frisch. He found that the error vanished if coils of wire carrying electric current created a magnetic field in the hive that was just sufficient to cancel out Earth's own field. He also found that the exact magnitude of these errors was related to daily fluctuations of Earth's field. This means that bees were able to detect the extremely small daily fluctuation of the geomagnetic field called the solar daily magnetic variation.

Conclusion

In this chapter we have discussed some of the clues which birds use for navigational purposes when they undertake their long mi-

[6]M. Renner, *The Clock of the Bees*, Natural History, October 1959.

gratory flights. The evidence very strongly suggests that diurnal migrators make use of a Sun compass which combines actual observations of the Sun with a very stable internal biological clock. Those birds that are nocturnal migrators seem to use the movements of the night sky to find direction during migration.

We also saw that bees can use the position of the Sun in the sky, together with an internal biological clock, to find direction on days when the sky is clear and the Sun is visible. However, on cloudy days bees make use of the special properties of their compound eyes to deduce the position of the Sun from the polarization of the sky.

There is also some evidence that the magnetic field of Earth can be detected by birds and bees, and that this field may play a part in the navigational methods of these creatures. This possibility will be further explored in the next chapter.

9

The Magnetic Compasses of Life

Over the last few decades it has been discovered that many species of animals have the ability to respond to the directional properties of Earth's magnetic field. In other words, these animals seem to possess built-in magnetic compasses. In this chapter we will look at research that has been done on different biological organisms regarding biological compasses that are magnetic in origin. We will also look briefly at some attempts to clarify the nature of the compass mechanism, and its location in the organisms that do seem to have such abilities. However, let us start with a look at the historical roots of magnetism, the development of the magnetic compass, and some relevant aspects of Earth's magnetic field.

Magnetism and the Magnetic Compass

The Greek philosophers seemed to have been aware of two solid substances, the properties of which set them apart from all other substances. These substances were amber and lodestone. When amber was rubbed it mysteriously attracted small pieces of paper to it. Similarly, lodestone was found to attract iron to it in the same mysterious way. This power to attract without touching was very puzzling to the ancients, but they do not seem to have investigated the subject experimentally, and they made no practical use of these properties.

The evidence that we have to date seems to indicate that the Chinese were the first to discover the directional finding properties of lodestone, around the second century A.D. They did so in connection with a device called a diviner's board. This was a flat piece of nonmagnetic metal, about two inches square, on the perimeter of which were marked certain signs, including their own signs of the zodiac. At the center of this board was a very smooth circle, on which could be placed the bowl of a specially shaped spoon made of lodestone. This spoon could be set spinning on the board, and the particular sign on which it came to rest was used in a form of divination called geomancy.

The belief underlying Chinese geomancy was that the houses of the living and the tombs of the dead must be oriented in an appropriate direction if living people wished to enjoy wealth and happiness, and if they wanted to avoid evil influences. The shapes of the land and the direction of winds, waters, and streams were all considered to be important from the point of view of the geomancers' craft. Geomancy required a knowledge of compass direction at different places on the surface of Earth, and how these directions varied with time. The diviner's board was further developed for this purpose, and eventually gave rise to the geomancer's compass. Professor Joseph Needham, the great Cambridge scholar on Chinese science and civilization, said that geomancy was the true origin of the modern science of geomagnetism, much as astrology acted as a stimulus to astronomy, and alchemy foreshadowed chemistry.

In the twelfth century, knowledge of the compass had reached Europe. We know this to be the case because it was referred to by an English monk, Alexander Neckham, in a work that dates from this period. However, most people had no idea how or why the compass worked. Two theories were prevalent at this time. One suggested that the compass needle was responding to some celestial influence that originated from the Pole Star. Another theory proposed that the influence originated from large deposits of lodestone near the North Pole of Earth.

We can find true north using the Sun or the stars, but magnetic north is, of course, the point to which a compass needle points. The angle between true north and magnetic north is called the

The Geomancer's compass. (*Dr. P. Seymour*)

declination, and it varies from one point on Earth's surface to the next. If a magnetic needle is placed in a horizontal pivot, and this axis is at right angles to a line pointing to magnetic north, then the needle will make an certain angle with the horizontal plane. This is called the inclination of the compass, and this is not equal to zero except at some places close to the equator of Earth. Information about the variation of declination and inclination with position on Earth's surface was collected by seamen as they undertook their voyages of discovery. This was used to great effect by William Gilbert, physician to Queen Elizabeth I. He was able to show that the magnetic field of a sphere made of lodestone was very similar to that of our Earth, and thus he went on to propose that the seat of Earth's magnetic action was not the heavens, but Earth itself.

History of Earth's Magnetic Field

The Earth's magnetic field changes with time. Three different methods have been used to investigate these changes. Actual measurements of the strength, inclination, and declination covering a long period of time are the most direct method of investigating long period changes. This technique is limited to the period for which accurate observations have been recorded, and systematic observations which can be used for this purpose only started in 1635. Accurate observations cover an even shorter period—from 1830 to the present day. These observations show not only that there have been changes in the strength of the field, but that the positions of the geomagnetic poles have also changed.

Two other methods can be used to investigate longer-term changes: One is known as the archaeological method and the other is known as the geological method. Before we can describe these in any great detail we need to make a small excursion into the magnetic properties of materials in general.

If a bar magnet were broken into very small pieces, and each piece tested with a compass, it would be found that each piece behaved as if it were a complete magnet itself. It is now known that a magnet consists of a large number of very tiny regions, called domains, each of which is like a little magnet. In an unmagnetized piece of iron these domains are randomly orientated, but in a magnetized piece of iron the domains are aligned so that they all point in the same direction. If a magnet is heated above a certain temperature, known as the Curie temperature, it will cease to exhibit magnetic properties, and it can only be remagnetized once it has cooled below the Curie temperature. This can be explained in terms of the domain theory of magnetism. As the magnet is heated up the domains tend to move about more violently, and the violence of the movements will increase with temperature. Eventually a temperature will be reached where the domains move about so violently that they can no longer sustain their original alignment, and the magnetism of the iron bar is lost. If the bar is allowed to cool in a magnetic field, for example the Earth's field, then at least some of the domains will become aligned in the field and the iron will become slightly magnetized in the direction of the field. The number of domains that will become magnetized in the direction of the external field will depend on the strength of the field, hence the strength of the resulting magnet will be a measure of the strength of the field in which it was magnetized. These facts have been useful in the investigation of long-term changes in the direction and strength of Earth's magnetic field.

Many civilizations in various parts of the world had kilns which had been baked to very high temperatures, and the tiny fragments of magnetic materials in the floors and walls of these kilns would have been heated above the Curie temperature. This would mean that any magnetism present in the fragments would have been destroyed. As the kilns cooled the tiny particles would be remagnetized in the direction of Earth's field as it was when the kiln was last fired. The number of magnetic particles aligned by the field is related to the strength of Earth's field at that time, so we can obtain information about the strength and direction of the field at various times by studying the magnetic particles in kilns from various ancient civilizations that can be archaeologically dated in some other ways. This method is useful for investigating the field over the last few hundred years, and it shows that the field has varied in a wavelike fashion, about the average strength, over the last eight thousand years. The period of this "wave" is seven thousand years, with a minimum in about 4000 B.C. and a maximum just before A.D. 1000.

The last method is based on geological data and provides information on changes in the field covering a period of about 5 million years. The method is based on the fact that almost all rock contains small quantities of iron compounds and when a rock is formed it becomes magnetized in the direction of Earth's field as it was at the time of formation. Once again the strength of the magnetism is related to the strength of the field at that particular time. The age of the rock can be found by geological methods. The measurements made using this method produced the surprising result that the direction of the Earth's field has reversed several times during the last 4.5 million years. The long-term variations of the strength and direction of the field led scientists to ask questions about the origin of the field.

Electricity, Magnetism, and the Magnetic Field of Earth

Several scientists have, over the last few centuries, contributed to our understanding of the very close relationship between magnetism and electricity, but the man who made the largest contribution was Michael Faraday. The work of his predecessors had shown that an electric current can generate a magnetic field. Faraday was able to show that if a coil of wire was moved with respect to a magnet, then an electric current would be generated in the wire. This is the principle behind the large electric generators that are used to generate electricity in our power stations. It can now be said, quite generally, that an electric current has associated with it a magnetic field, and that a changing magnetic field will give rise to an electric field.

A great deal of information on the internal structure of Earth is obtained by studying seismic waves, originating during earthquakes, as they arrive at different geophysical observatories. These data have been combined with other data on the average density of Earth, compared with the density of the surface rock, to construct a picture of the internal structure of Earth. The outer core probably consists of an iron-nickel alloy in liquid form, which has certain fluid and electrical properties.

One of the most convincing theories of geomagnetism attributes Earth's magnetic field to a self-sustaining dynamo operating in the molten parts of the outer iron-nickel core. If Earth had some intrinsic magnetism to start with, then the motions of this part of the core would give rise to electric currents. These currents would give rise to a magnetic field and this field would in turn sustain its own current, provided there were a source of energy to sustain the motions of the core.

There are three possible mechanisms that could give rise to the motions of the outer core which are necessary for this self-sustaining dynamo theory to be applicable to Earth. The first is similar to the thermal convection currents seen when, for example, heating soup in an open pan. The soup in contact with the bottom of the pan will rise to the surface since, being hotter, it is less dense than the rest of the soup, and the cooler parts of the soup will sink toward the bottom, setting up convection currents. These currents are maintained by the heat below the pan. In the case of Earth, the nuclei of atoms of radioactive substances such as uranium, thorium, and plutonium are continually breaking up into smaller atoms and subatomic particles. This process is called radioactive decay, and heat is produced as a result of the process. The decay of these substances in the core of Earth could provide the source of the heat necessary to maintain the thermal convection of Earth's dynamo.

We have already seen that Earth's axis precesses due to the gravitational pull of the Sun and Moon on the equatorial bulge of Earth. This provides a second possible source of energy to sustain motion in the outer core. Because the outer core of Earth is fluid it does not immediately take up the changes in motion of the solid parts of Earth, and the different rates of precession between core and mantle could give rise to complicated motions that could sustain a dynamo.

The third mechanism is associated with the separating out of dense materials from less dense materials in the outer core, due to the growth of the inner core. The dense material will move downward and the less dense material will move upward. This movement will mean a change in the gravitational energy of the outer core and this energy will thus be available to generate currents which could give rise to the magnetic field of Earth. Several geophysicists favor this particular mechanism, which at present seems the most likely explanation of the source of energy for powering the generation of the Earth's magnetic field.

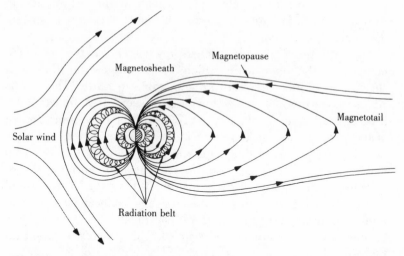

The Magnetosphere of the Earth. (*Dr. P. Seymour*)

The Magnetosphere of Earth

Over the last two decades the use of magnetic measuring instruments on board Earth satellites has greatly increased our knowledge of Earth's magnetic field far above the surface. These satellite measurements have shown that the field is contained within a region—called the magnetosphere—which is compressed on the sunward side and drawn out into a long tail on the opposite side. The Sun emits a continuous stream of very energetic particles known as the solar wind. These particles consist mainly of electrons and protons with traces of other ions and the nuclei of atoms, and they are quite often referred to as solar cosmic rays. As they are electrically charged they cannot cross the lines of force of Earth's field, but stream past it, making a bow shock wave very similar in structure to the bow wave of a ship as it passes through the water. Somewhere behind Earth the various strands of the solar wind meet again, thus enclosing Earth's field within a pear-shaped region called the magnetosphere. The region behind Earth is called the magnetotail. Also trapped in the magnetosphere are the charged particles of the Van Allen radiation belts. Near the magnetic poles of Earth the magnetic field becomes much stronger and the particles get "reflected" at these points, and hence they tend to bounce back and forth between the poles and along the field lines. However, as these particles follow tighter curves in a strong field than they do in a weak field, and as the field gets weaker with distance from Earth's surface, the particles will also have an east-west drift around Earth. The combination of the north-south motion and the east-west drift will cause the particles to move within the Van Allen radiation belts, each belt corresponding to a different average energy of the charged particles contained within them.

Magnetic Bacteria

In 1975 Dr. Richard Blakemore, a biologist working in the United States at the University of New Hampshire, discovered that certain bacteria were influenced by Earth's magnetic field in that under the microscope they would be observed to swim consistently toward magnetic north. This discovery was confirmed by placing bar magnets close to the microscope slide on which the bacteria were placed. The magnetic field of these magnets would override the weaker field of Earth, and the direction of swim of the bacteria could be changed by altering the positions and orientations of the magnets. Further experiments showed that the bacteria were moving toward the north because they wanted to swim downward. This was confirmed by an experiment in which the bacteria were taken to the Southern Hemisphere. Here they swam south, once again because they want to move downward toward the sediments and away from the surface of the water where the concentration of oxygen, which is toxic to them, is much higher. When these bacteria were studied under the electron microscope they were seen to contain a string of "beads," each bead consisting of a magnetic substance called magnetite—the principal ingredient of lodestone. These discoveries brought a new respectability to the frequently made suggestion that many organisms can detect and respond to the magnetic field of Earth.

The work of Blakemore also offered a possible explanation for another series of experiments. These experiments were concerned with studying the effect of reversals of Earth's field on microscopic life forms. By studying the fossilized remains of such forms of life found in sediments laid down a very long time ago, it became apparent that certain species that had existed for hundreds of thousands of years suddenly became extinct. Some of the scientists working in this field showed that these extinctions seem to be closely linked with reversals of Earth's magnetic field, and they suggested that these organisms might actually have needed to use the field for some purpose. This suggestion was made before Blakemore made his discovery. If these organisms (known as radiolaria) were using the field for the same purpose as Blakemore's bacteria, then the reversal of the field would have led them to the higher toxic levels of oxygen in the water and thus to extinction.

Magnetic Marine Navigators

We have already seen that if an electric conductor moves across a magnetic field then a current is generated in the conducting material. If a fish is swimming across the lines of force of Earth's magnetic field, it will be like the coils of wire in a dynamo, in that small electric currents will flow in its body. If the fish is swimming along the lines of force, then no currents will flow. Thus, if a fish were sensitive enough to electricity to pick up any currents induced in its body, this response would allow it to use Earth's field for directional guidance. Several marine organisms have electric sensors sensitive enough to detect these induced currents and they do indeed use these to orient themselves.

It is not unknown for large groups of whales to swim ashore and then to find themselves stranded on the beach, unable to move their huge bulks back into the sea. Reports of such mass beachings of whales go back for several centuries. People making such observations had no explanation for this unusual behavior, although it was sometimes suggested that it was probably due to a breakdown of some unknown navigation system. However, when the recorded positions of these strandings in the United States and Britain were plotted on maps on which were also marked contours showing the behavior of the geomagnetic field, some pattern seemed to emerge. Detailed magnetic maps show not only the very large scale structure of the field, they also show variations in the intensity of the field caused by differences in the magnetic properties of the underlying rocks. Just as one can draw smooth curves through points on maps that represent locations having the same height above sea level (contour lines), so one can draw lines through those points that have equal intensity of magnetism. On ordinary contour maps, valleys will have contours that show smaller heights above sea level than hills and mountains. On magnetic contour maps, areas of high magnetic intensity will be like "magnetic hills," and areas of low intensity will resemble "valleys." The pattern that emerged when the strandings were plotted on magnetic contour maps was that the majority of strandings occurred where magnetic valleys ran directly from the sea to the shore. This research does seem to indicate that whales navigate by using magnetic maps of the sea floor. In the dark depths of the ocean, landmarks are not plentiful, so it seems as if the whales "see" the magnetic contours as sub-marine highways. This explanation, however, does give rise to some problems, one of which is why dolphins and porpoises seldom run into these difficulties. A possible reason is that whereas whales sometimes migrate over great distances, dolphins and porpoises stay closer to home; thus, they become more familiar with the magnetic anomalies of their local environment and so build up a much more detailed map of the region that they inhabit.

Magnetic Navigation by Birds

In an earlier chapter we already hinted at the possibility that birds use magnetic information on their migratory flights. Here we will look at this possibility in more detail. It now seems likely that migrating birds respond less to the direction of the magnetic field at a given point than they do to the inclination of the field—the angle the field lines make with the horizontal. In other words, migrating birds find compass direction by sensing the angle that the magnetic lines of force make with its body as it passes through the field. The lines of force are angled toward the birds as they fly south and away from them as they fly north. When the birds cross the equator these lines are horizontal and parallel to their line of flight. Flamingos and other birds that fly over this area as they migrate can no longer use magnetic directional cues, and have to rely on Sun or celestial navigation instead.

But how do birds detect this magnetism? Some researchers in the United States found evidence for magnetite in the heads of certain migrators, and suggested that this was the basis of a simple compass mechanism. If this were the cause then the "compass needle" could be demagnetized by putting the head of the bird in the center of coil of wire through which was passing a rapidly changing electric current. The magnetic field caused by the current would destroy the alignment of the magnetic domains. However, this experiment showed that the bird's ability to find direction from Earth's field was unaffected by this attempt at demagnetization. Other mechanisms for magnetoreception have been proposed, which do not require a specific magnetoreceptor organ. According to one of these proposals, the body of the bird is a weak electrical conductor, and as it moves through the lines of Earth's field so, like an electric generator, an electric current is set up between its two ends. An alternative explanation involves electrostatic forces generated by friction between the bird's wings and the air, and the subsequent interaction between the separation of electrical charges in its wings and the magnetic field of Earth. It has also been suggested that Earth's field could influence the movement of lymph in the lymph tubes. All these suggestions present some problems, one of which is that they require detection of rather small effects against a lot of background noise.

Magnetic Bees and Butterflies

In the last chapter we also briefly mentioned evidence that bees have some response to daily changes in the magnetic field of Earth. Further experiments suggest that they also use this magnetic sensitivity in the way they build their combs. It has been discovered that when a swarm of bees leave to found a new colony, the vertical parallel combs in the new hive have the same orientation as do combs in the hive that they have left. However, by applying an artificial external field to the hive, it is possible to get the bees to change this orientation.

One of the longest migrations in the insect world is that undertaken by the monarch butterflies in North America. These insects fly south for up to four thousand kilometers. The butterflies from the eastern side of the continent overwinter in a small area of central Mexico, while those on the western side travel to California. The southern migrators are several generations removed from those that flew north during the previous spring. They must thus inherit their knowledge of the migratory route. In common with many other butterflies, they appear to use the Sun as a direction aid. It has been suggested that this is insufficient, on its own, to explain the accuracy with which they fly. Once again these butterflies were tested for traces of magnetite, and it turns out that of all butterflies so far tested, monarchs contain the greatest amount of magnetite. The difficulties of carrying out other tests on these insects are enormous, so we only have the circumstantial evidence of the magnetite to go on, but it may well be that these creatures also use the geomagnetic field to find direction.

A Magnetic Compass in Humans

There are some experiments which seem to indicate that humans also have the ability to subconsciously find direction directly from Earth's magnetic field, although some people seem to have that faculty more highly developed than others. The first experiments in this area were carried out by Dr. Robin Baker, a zoologist from Manchester University. Baker, in one of his early experiments, drove blindfolded students via winding routes to distances up to fifty kilometers from the university. He found that students gave good estimates of the direction of the university while still blindfolded, but when their blindfolds were removed they became disoriented.

In a second series of experiments, Baker used a busload of blindfolded schoolchildren. He divided the children into two groups; one group had bar magnets attached to their heads while the second group had magnetized pieces of metal similar in shape and size to the bar magnets attached to their heads. The second group was much better at finding the direction of north than the first group.

John Downer in his book *Supersense* had this to say about the experiments of Robin Baker:

This suggested that the artificial magnets were interfering with a natural magnetic sense. Other experiments led to similar conclusions but, unfortunately, tests performed elsewhere have failed to confirm these findings. So, although it seems likely that we too have a magnetic sense, this is as yet unproven.

Downer's book, which accompanied the television series of the same name, produced by himself, was published in 1988, so presumably he must have finished writing it in 1987, and perhaps ended his literature search sometime before that. He quotes no references for his statement, so it is unclear which experiments he is referring to in this statement. However he seems to have missed a paper, written by R. Robin Baker, entitled *Human Navigation and Magnetoreception: The Manchester Experiments Do Replicate* (see *Animal Behaviour* 1987, 35, 691–704), in which Baker analyzed and discussed all the relevant experiments that had been carried out in other parts of the world by researchers other than himself. In this paper he said:

These experiments have produced results with a conservative probability of occurring by chance that is less than 0.001 [one in a thousand] with respect to non-visual orientation and less than 0.005 [one in two hundred] with respect to magnetoreception. As evidence for the existence of a non-visual ability to orient and navigate based, at least in part, on megnetoreception, the results obtained by other workers now rival those obtained at Manchester. Despite this, other workers continue not to offer support for the view that humans possess magnetoreception ability. This stark contrast between positive results and negative interpretations remains an unexplained feature of the literature on human magnetoreception.

The evidence in favor of such a human magnetic sensitivity was taken a stage further in 1989, at a conference in Cardiff, in Wales, organized by the Royal Institute of Navigation, and entitled *Ori-*

entation and Navigation: Birds, Humans and Other Animals. At this conference Dr. Robin Baker reiterated some of the points made above. He was, however, not the only contributor to address the question of magnetoreception in humans. R. Gai Murphy, in her paper called *The Development of Compass Orientation in Children,* discussed her experiments carried out with children and young people. The results of these experiments suggest that magnetoreception ability in children between four and eleven years of age is very weak. For teenage boys this ability increases only marginally, but for females the ability increases noticeably after the age of nine and reaches a plateau of performance around eighteen years. She concluded her paper with these words: "The magnetic manipulation experiments proved that magnetism was indeed involved in the ability to judge direction and that some children are able to judge direction using the magnetic field of the earth."

The matter has been discussed more recently by Mary Campion in her paper "Do Humans Possess a Latent Sense of Orientation?" (*The Journal of Navigation*, 44,1,76–84, January 1991). She concluded from her own experiments at the University of Keele that humans do have the ability to find direction using the Earth's field, but this ability only manifests itself when dealing with large samples, suggesting that not everyone has this ability to the same extent. Further experiments carried out by her also suggests that it is a latent ability, because the ability to judge direction was better on later experiments with the same group of people than it was initially.

Conclusion

In this chapter we have looked at the basic properties of Earth's magnetic field, its long-term variations, its extension in space, and its origin. We also looked at how a variety of different species of animal respond to the direction that this field takes at different points on the surface of Earth, and how they use this response for navigational purposes. There now exists some evidence that humans also have the ability to find direction using the geomagnetic field. We will leave the last word to Dr Robin Baker, the discoverer of this human magnetic sensitivity, who said in his book *Human Navigation and the Sixth Sense:* "At first, the possibility that humans have a magnetic sense seems incredible. Throughout this book I have discussed the evidence for humans side by side with the evidence for other animals. I maintain that, when placed in this wider perspective, it would be incredible if Man did not have a magnetic sense."

10

Magnetic Programming of Biological Clocks

Research into geomagnetic records covering several decades has revealed that the magnetic lines of force of the Earth's field are rather like the strings of a musical instrument in that although they have a general direction they can and do vibrate about this average alignment. Some of these vibrations seem to have no pattern to them, but others have detectable patterns connected with the positions of the Sun and the Moon, and to the sunspot cycle of about eleven years. In recent years it has also become clear that many biological organisms can detect and respond to systematic changes of the geomagnetic field, especially those connected with the apparent movements of the Sun and Moon, as seen from the surface of Earth. This has led some scientists to suggest that the geomagnetic field may be second only to the Sun and sky in giving organisms information on time, location, and direction. Other scientists have suggested that over aeons of time many different species have become locked in step with specific fluctuations of the geomagnetic field.

In this chapter we will look at the short-term systematic changes of the geomagnetic field, and some of the known causes of these changes.[1] I will explain my theory relating geomagnetic activity to

---

[1] Further details on the magnetic field of Earth can be found in *Cosmic Magnetism*, Percy Seymour, Adam Hilger, Bristol, 1986.

planetary alignments as seen from the Sun. We will then look at the evidence for links between these vibrations of the magnetic field of Earth with biological clocks and some aspects of animal behavior.

Some Short-Term Changes in the Geomagnetic Field

The magnetic field of Earth is vibrating with a large number of different frequencies, some consisting of several cycles per minute, some of several cycles per day, some with one or two cycles per lunar day, others with a few cycles per year, and yet others with cycles related to the sunspot cycle. In this respect the magnetic field is rather similar to the many radio and television waves surrounding our Earth. As we tune a radio receiver with the volume turned to its maximum, we will pick up loud signals every time the tuning pointer reaches the frequency at which a given radio station is transmitting, but between stations there is a continuous hiss. This hiss we can call the continuous spectrum, and it arises from a variety of natural causes and high-technology equipment. Each radio station broadcasts at a very narrow frequency. If one had to plot a graph of the volume of sound coming out of the speaker against the frequency at which the tuner is set, then the continuous hiss will be a very uneven horizontal line, but each time we tune a radio station we will get a loud response at a very precise frequency, and this we can represent on our graph as a vertical "spike" which is normally called a spectral line.

The vibrations of the geomagnetic field can also be represented by such a spectrum, with a continuous background hiss and a number of sharp lines related to fairly specific frequencies at which Earth's field is broadcasting much more energetically.

The solar daily magnetic variation is a prominent feature of spectrum, with a period of one solar day, but this line also has present the harmonics of the solar day, with periods of twelve, eight, and six hours in many places. There is also evidence, as one would expect, for lines consisting of the lunar day and its harmonics. Near twenty-seven days there is another line, which may be due to some effect associated with the lunar month or it may be due to the effects connected with the rotation of the Sun on its axis. There is a line at one year and another at six months. It is also now known that the amplitudes of these lines all vary with the sunspot cycle. We will now look at some of these lines in more detail.

(i) The Solar Daily Magnetic Variation

This variation in the magnetic field has already been mentioned in a previous chapter, so here we will fill in some of its more subtle points. This variation results from the distortion of the geomagnetic field by the solar wind. The daily rotation of the Earth on its axis means that we are rotating within this distortion. This distortion is not symmetrical with respect to the center of Earth. The field is considerably compressed on the sunward side and drawn out into the long magnetotail on the side of Earth away from the Sun. It is this asymmetry which gives rise to variations that are shorter period harmonics of the solar day—those of twelve, eight, and six hours. The distortion of the magnetosphere is caused by, as we have already seen, the stream of very energetic subatomic particles coming from the Sun, called the solar wind. This means that the distortion is related to the strength of the solar wind, which is itself modulated by the sunspot cycle. The field of study concerned with the complex connections between Sun and Earth is known as solar-terrestrial relationships, and it started in the last century.

(ii) Solar-Terrestrial Relationships

Earlier we saw that the Royal Observatory at Greenwich was established to provide astronomical data that was useful to the navigation of ships. Since the position and motion of the Sun were important to the navigator, it would have been natural for the detailed study of the physical conditions of the Sun to develop out of the other work of the observatory. However, the stimulus for setting up a solar department at Greenwich came from a different and unexpected direction. Heinrich Schwabe, a German astronomer, had in 1843 discovered that there exists a cycle in the number of sunspots observed on the Sun at different times, and that about every eleven years the number of spots reached a maximum. In 1852 Wallace Sabine, a British scientist, discovered that this cycle was related to variations in the compass needle. This provided the astronomers at Greenwich with a reason for setting up a solar department at Greenwich. It was argued that as the main purpose of the observatory was to serve the interests of mariners, and as Greenwich had a magnetic observatory for this purpose, it was the obvious place to investigate the links between events on the Sun and the terrestrial magnetic field. Two other phenomena, the aurora and magnetospheric storms, also display links between sunspot activity and Earth's magnetic field.

Auroras and Magnetospheric Substorms

In high latitudes in the Northern and Southern hemispheres of Earth, it is not uncommon to see moving curtains of light in the night sky. Mostly these curtains of light, called auroras, are greenish blue, but red auroras are also seen on some occasions. These are known as the northern and southern lights, and the general technical name for this class of phenomena is the aurorae polaris. The use of fast jet planes carrying all-sky cameras, combined with satellite observations, has helped scientists to determine the region in which the maximum number of auroras occur. This region is called the auroral oval and it is actually the intersection of the outer shell of the Van Allen radiation belts with Earth's atmosphere. The auroral light is emitted by atoms and molecules of different gases in the upper atmosphere, which have been excited by collisions with the energetic particles in this belt. The interaction of the solar wind with the magnetic field of Earth distorts the auroral oval. This distortion accounts for the fact that the auroral oval is seen at higher altitudes on the dayside and lower latitudes on the nightside of Earth. With increasing solar activity the auroral oval becomes wider and its lower boundary moves noticeably closer to the equator. The occurence of auroras and the width of the auroral oval are related to events on the Sun by means of phenomena called magnetospheric substorms.

The solar wind carries with it strands of the magnetic field of the Sun, and these magnetic lines of force splay out into interplanetary space to form the interplanetary magnetic field. A substorm is the process whereby some of the increase of energy in the solar wind, and changes in the interplanetary magnetic field, are fed into the auroras.

The substorms are part of longer-lasting and more extensive changes in the magnetosphere, and consequent variations in the field strength at ground level, which are called the magnetic storm. The "sudden storm commencement" is marked by a sudden increase in the strength of the field. This increase in field lasts for a few hours, after which there is a more gradual decrease to a magnitude below that expected during quiet times. The decrease is the main phase of the storm and it lasts for one or two days. Thereafter there is a gradual recovery to the "quiet" magnitude. One or more substorms occur during the main phase.

The Annual Variation in the Geomagnetic Field

The strength of the geomagnetic field also has a slower variation of one year. In an earlier chapter we saw that the axis of Earth is inclined to the plane of its orbit around the Sun, and that this inclination remains in the same direction for long periods of time. The magnetic axis is inclined to the rotation axis by 11.5 degrees. This means that the magnetic axis rotates about the rotation axis once a day. In the northern summer the rotation axis leans toward the Sun, making an angle of 23.5 degrees with the vertical to the plane of Earth's orbit. This means that in the course of one day the angle that the magnetic axis will make with this vertical will vary between twelve degrees and thirty-five degrees, but at both these limits it will still be leaning toward the Sun. The situation will be very different in the winter when the rotation axis is leaning away from the Sun. The limits between which the magnetic axis changes are still the same, and at both limits the axis is leaning away from the Sun. This means that the distortion of the magnetosphere by the solar wind is different in the winter from what it is during the summer. It is this change that is responsible for the annual variation in the strength of the field at ground level. The annual variation is also evident in the amplitudes of the solar daily magnetic variation, and the lunar daily magnetic variation.

Changes in the Lunar Daily Magnetic Variation

Although, as we have already seen, the lunar daily magnetic variation is the result of the tides in the upper atmosphere of Earth, and one would expect it to show effects similar to the spring and neap tides of the oceans, the actual observed effect of the Sun on lunar daily magnetic variation is much more complicated than expected by analogy with the ocean tides. This is because the Sun not only affects the upper atmosphere by means of simple gravitation tidal effects, but also by means of its radiation, and it distorts the magnetosphere via the solar wind. The ability of the upper atmosphere to generate magnetic fields depends on its electrical properties. The lower atmosphere cannot generate such a field because it is electrically neutral. The solar wind and radiation from the Sun create ions in the upper atmosphere, that is, they strip some of the electrons off atoms, and thus the upper atomsphere becomes an electrically conducting medium. When this medium is dragged around by tidal forces it generates the lunar daily magnetic variation. Its effectiveness in doing so depends on the number of ions and electrons within itself, and this in turn depends on the strength of the solar wind and the Sun's radiation. These ionizing agencies are more effective when sunspot activity is high than when we are experiencing a solar minimum. It is thus not surprising that the amplitudes of the solar and the lunar daily magnetic variations should be increased at the times of high sunspot activity. The phase and amplitude of both these variations varies with position on the surface of Earth. This is because the actual geometry of the field changes from place to place. Although the geometrical configuration of the field at ground level cannot change on time

172

scales less than several months, the field above the ground does change as a result of increases in solar activity. This gives rise to another way in which energy from the solar wind can be fed into increases and phase changes in the magnetic variations at ground level.

There is also a great deal of evidence that the magnetic activity of the Sun is linked to certain alignments of the planets as seen from the Sun. We will look at this evidence, and then at my own theory which provides an explanation as to why this correlation exists.

Magnetic Tides of the Sun

In the 1940s John Nelson made the important discovery that occurrences of particularly violent events on the Sun are somehow associated with specific planetary alignments as seen from the Sun.[2] He started his investigations when he was employed by the Radio Corporation of America. Nelson was given the task of trying to find a way of forecasting the occurrence of severe increases in solar activity, since it was known that such increases were associated with the disruption of certain kinds of radio communications. Nelson found that when Venus, Earth, Mars, Jupiter, and Saturn were almost in a straight line with the Sun, or when they made angles of ninety degrees with each other as seen from the Sun, conditions were likely to be bad for radio transmission and reception. Conditions were good when the angles between these planets, as seen from the Sun, were 30, 60, 120, or 150 degrees. Nelson's work was closely scrutinized by a number of scientists who found that his claims could not be replicated.

Despite the fact that his work has been discredited, it gave rise to some more substantial work on the links between planetary configurations and solar activity.[3] Paul Jose, who worked for the

[2]J.H. Nelson, "Shortwave Radio Propagation Correlation with Planetary Position," *RCA Review*, March 1951.

[3]P.D. Jose, "Sun's Motion and Sunspots," *Astronomical Journal*, 70, 193, 1965.

U.S. Air Force, was able to find a link between the maximum of solar activity and the movement of the Sun about the common center of mass of the Solar System. The work of Nelson and Jose was carried further by J. B. Blizard and H. P. Sleeper, both of whom undertook projects on solar activity prediction on behalf of NASA. The space agency was interested in such predictions because it was known that severe activity on the Sun could damage sensitive communication satellites, so they wanted to avoid such activity when launching these devices.

Jane Blizard undertook her work in 1969.[4] She was able to show that when the planets are in conjunction or opposition, as seen from the Sun, then solar magnetic storms are very violent. However, the fact that some violent events on the Sun were associated with ninety-degree positions of the planets as seen from the Sun puzzled Blizard, and she concluded that no physical explanation was reasonable. She also concluded that two different links were involved, because all the planets seemed to play some part, not just those with the strongest gravitational or tidal tug on the Sun. Just as the Moon and Sun raise tides in the oceans, so Blizard suggested that the planets can raise tides in the gases of the Sun. Normally two objections are put forward against this idea. First, it is pointed out that tidal effects of the planets on the Sun are much weaker than the surface gravity of the Sun itself. Second, the very big gravitational tides occur when the Sun and Moon are in conjunction or in opposition, at new or full Moon, and the smallest tides occur when the Sun and Moon make ninety degrees with each other as seen from Earth. Although, some scientists argue, it might just be possible to understand how planetary conjunctions and oppositions might affect solar activity, it is completely impossible to understand these ninety-degree effects, since the gravitational tug of the planets are no longer in a straight line, but at right angles to each other.

Let us take these criticisms one at a time. First, let us consider the criticism that planetary gravitation is so weak compared with

[4] J. B. Blizard, "Long-range Solar Flare Prediction," NASA Contractor Report, CR 61316, 1969.

the innate gravitational tug of the Sun itself. Tidal activity on Earth's oceans show us that this critticism will not hold up. The tidal pull due to the gravitational attraction of the Sun and Moon on the waters of Earth is far weaker than Earth's own gravitation tug by a factor of 10 million. Yet, twice a day, all over the Earth, this relatively weak gravitational pull of the Sun and Moon is moving billions of tons of water to and fro. The tide in Canada's Bay of Fundy shifts 100 billion tons of water twice a day. The gravitational tug of the Sun and Moon can have such an effect because of a phenomenon called resonance.

As to the second criticism, that when the planets are pulling at right angles to each other, their tidal tugs cannot be simply added to produce a large tide, we have to turn to a tidal theory worked out by the astronomer royal George Biddell Airy in 1845. In fact, Airy's theory overcomes both criticisms in a very natural way, since it is what one would expect near resonance, and it allows us to understand how such resonance can exist beneath the surface of the Sun.

Airy worked out a rigorous mathematical theory which shows that it is possible to build a water canal around the Earth, parallel to the equator, in which spring tides would occur at first and last quarter, rather than at full and new Moon. This corresponds to ninety-degree positions of the Sun and Moon as seen from Earth. Such a canal would also greatly amplify the rather weak tides associated with an open ocean. The dimensions of such a canal would have to be worked out very carefully. If a rock were dropped into the canal, then the wave set up would travel along the canal at one specific speed. This is called the speed of the free wave and its value depends on the dimensions of the canal. If these dimensions were properly chosen, such that the speed of this wave was faster than the speed with which the point immediately below the Moon traveled across Earth, but slower than the speed with which the point immediately below the Sun traveled across Earth, then spring tides would occur at first and last quarters of the Moon.

The Magnetic Canals of the Sun

How are these results applicable to the Sun? It is well known from observations of sunspots that magnetic structures which resemble canals parallel to the Sun's equator exist on the Sun in the buildup to maximum sunspot activity. Such canals can greatly amplify the weak tidal forces of the planets on the Sun, because they are able to channel the very hot gases of the Sun parallel to the solar equator. The present theory of solar activity also tells us that the strength of this field increases toward solar maximum—when the number of sunspots on the Sun reaches a maximum. This strength will affect the speed with which a magnetic wave will travel along a magnetic canal. The speeds with which planets travel with respect to the material on the spinning surface of the Sun vary from one planet to the next. This means that as the speed of a free wave in the magnetic canal increases with increasing strength of the field, it will equal the speed of the tidal wave of each of the planets in turn, starting with Mercury. In other words, the magnetic free wave and the tidal wave of Mercury will, at some stage of the solar cycle, be in tune with each other. When this happens, Mercury's tidal influence on the magnetic canal will be considerably increased and it will cause disruption of the canal. The canal will then rise to the surface, causing a looped solar prominence and a sunspot pair where this loop crosses the Sun's surface.

This also means that if the tuning lies between the tidal frequencies associated with the two planets, ninety-degree configurations of these planets as seen from the Sun will mean that the tidal forces of these planets strengthen each other, giving rise to very violent activity. At other times conjunctions and oppositions will have the same effect. My theory thus proposes that we apply Airy's canal theory of the tides to the magnetic tubes of force that exist beneath the surface of the Sun in the buildup to solar maximum. These tubes of magnetic lines of force resemble canals that are parallel to the solar equator, and thus it is appropriate to use canal theory.

Just as the magnetic field of the Earth is generated by little convective eddy currents in the outer mantle, so the magnetic field of the Sun is generated by eddy currents in the convective zone of the Sun. I am further proposing that the change in direction of the eddies near the poles of the Sun, sometime before the start of the next cycle, is triggered by the movement of the Sun about the common center of mass of the Solar System. The movement is controlled by the orbiting of the outer planets: Jupiter, Saturn, Neptune, and Uranus. These planets move the Sun through a total distance of twice its own diameter (i.e., just under 2 million miles) roughly every ten and a half years.

All the planets at various stages of the solar cycle will, through their tidal tug on the magnetic canals of the Sun, contribute to the triggering of sunspot activity. At the start of the cycle, conjunction of Mercury and Venus will play the major role. Later on, as the magnetic canals drift toward the equator, ninety-degree configurations of these planets, combined with Venus-Mars conjunctions, will have the same effect. This type of sequence will progress through all the planets, until at the end of the one cycle it will be conjunctions of the outer planets that will have the dominant effect in triggering sunspot activity.[5]

Some Terrestrial Consequences of Geomagnetic Fluctuations

Some variations of the geomagnetic field can affect a few ground-based technological systems, especially in or near the auroral oval and during magnetospheric substorms. Not long after the installation of telegraph and telephone systems it became clear that serious disturbances could occur during those periods when auroras were most active. One investigator of auroral phenomena, Professor Carl Stormer, made use of currents induced in telephone wires to activate an alarm to indicate the presence of the northern lights. Telephone companies have designed and installed equipment that protects telephone networks against the possible damaging effects

---

[5]P. A. H. Seymour, "Magneto-Tidal Coupling between the Components of the Solar System" in *Proceedings of the First International Conference on Geocosmic Relations*, Pudoc (Wageningen), 1990.

of these currents. Measurable currents are also induced in power lines during severe magnetic disturbances, and there have been reports from the United States of transformer breakdowns during high solar activity periods. Currents induced in the transatlantic cable between Newfoundland and Scotland during a severe storm in 1940 led to distortion of conversation in one direction though not in the other. It has been suggested that some shipwrecks and aircraft crashes that occurred during auroral displays may have been due to the deviation of the compass needle. Auroral displays are also known to disrupt radio communications in and near the polar regions.

Magnetic fields in general are known to influence a variety of different physical and chemical systems. Even weak fields can cause some slight changes in the energy levels that exist within most atoms, and as a result, the fields will also affect the light absorbed and emitted by atoms. This is called the Zeeman effect and it has been used to detect magnetic fields of the Sun and some other types of stars. There is also evidence that certain types of chemcial reaction rates can be altered if the reactants are placed in a magnetic field. This is particularly true of reactions involving ions.

It should thus come as no surprise that the fluctuations of the geomagnetic field can have some effects on living systems; we will look at this in more detail in the rest of this chapter.

Biological Consequences of Geomagnetic Variations

Some Russian scientists have employed the technique of conditioned reflexes to investigate the effects of magnetic fields on a variety of different animals. This technique can be illustrated by the well-known example of using light or sound to condition food-seeking responses. If a light is switched on or a bell sounded whenever a group of animals is fed, then at a later stage the animals will show food-seeking behavior whenever the light is switched on or the bell is sounded, even though no food is given. The Russian biologist Y. A. Kholodov showed that magnetic fields stronger than that of the Earth could be used to condition food-seeking reflexes in fish, by exposing them to a magnetic impulse instead of light or sound, whenever food was given.

In another series of experiments Kholodov subjected rats to artificial magnetic fields similar in strength to that of Earth, but this time they were rapidly pulsating, to simulate the behavior of the Earth's field during a geomagnetic storm. The offspring of such rats were less active than normal offspring, and they committed more errors in the laboratory mazes in which they were placed. When Kholodov subjected pregnant rats to fields a hundred times stronger than that of Earth, the rats produced distinctly fewer fetuses than normal; there was an increase in the number of stillbirths; and some of the offspring were born with "ruptures of the spinal column."

Experiments on humans have shown that our reaction times, our ability to adapt to seeing in the dark, and our ability to distinguish a very rapidly fluctuating light source from a continuous one are all affected if we are shielded from the geomagnetic field. Some of this research was prompted by the start of the space age more than twenty-five years ago. Some of the first designers of spacecraft suggested that the creation of strong magnetic fields around the craft would protect the astronauts from the harmful effects of fast-moving particles in the solar wind. This initiated research into the effects such fields would have on humans. Other research was undertaken because flights to the Moon would mean that the astronauts would be separated from the Earth's field and this could affect their biological behavioral patterns.[6]

Magnetic Stimulation of the Brain

Michael A. Persinger, head of the neuroscience laboratory at Laurentian University of Sudbury in Ontario, Canada, has designed a special helmet, with the help of one of his students, that can magnetically massage the brain. He conceived of this helmet to test his theory that mystical experiences, which many people claim

[6]A. P. Dubrov, *The Geomagnetic Field and Life*, Plenum, New York, 1978.

to have had, have their origin in the temporal lobes of the brain, which are two lumps of gray matter buried under the major hemispheres of the brain. He and his colleagues suggest that these temporal lobes can be put into action in most people by subtle stimuli from the action of the magnetic field of the helmet or perhaps even vibrations of the Earth's magnetic field.

Some of Persinger's work has been done in collaboration with his wife, Gyslaine LaFreniere. He has argued, on the basis of this work, that sighting of unidentified flying objects, poltergeists, psychokinesis, and out-of-body experiences are all related to magnetic forces high in the atmosphere and deep within the Earth. Now Persinger is claiming that magnetic energy is actually responsible for inducing mystical experiences by means of the temporal lobes, which are the most electrically sensitive regions of the brain. Persinger designed the helmet to investigate these ideas. The idea came from an electromagnetic relaxing device sold openly in Canada. This device generated a wavering magnetic field that matched brain wave activity in the temporal lobes. In order to create the required magnetic fields Persinger used coils of wire, called solenoids, through which electric currents could be passed. These he made by wrapping copper wire around nails. To eliminate the possibility that the nails would injure his human subjects, he mounted the entire apparatus on a motorcycle helmet. The helmet was linked to a computer, for which one of Persinger's students had written a special program that directed the firing of the magnets in a carefully timed way. Persinger said: "This controlled pattern generated a magnetic vortex that reached the site of the temporal lobes."

One of the first experiments that Persinger carried out was to investigate claims of those people who thought they had been abducted by beings from UFOs. For a control group he used subjects who had never claimed such an encounter. When the magnetically pulsating helmet was put on their heads Persinger asked them to imagine they were emerging from a woods and could see lights in the sky. To enhance the imagery he had rigged up an overhead flashing light in the laboratory. They were then asked to a indulge in free association, giving expression to the images in their brains. These control subjects told stories that were full of the kind of detail often reported by people who had claimed close encounters with extraterrestrial aliens.

To test whether these people were just reporting what they had seen in science fiction films, Persinger used another group that had also claimed no encounters with aliens, but he did not subject them to magnetic massage, although the flashing light was still in the laboratory. The conclusions reached from these experiments was that a richer, more detailed, and more imaginative narrative came from those wearing the helmet than from those who did not. This seemed to indicate that the magnetic helmet could influence the content of perceived imagery.

The magnetic helmet was then used to study other forms of mystical experience, from déjà vu to the sense of a foreign presence. Repeatedly he found that subjects were much more likely to have a mystical experience when they donned the magnetic helmet. Persinger then observed:

The brain is like any closed system in that the area utilizing the most energy at any given time is the one that controls behavior. So it seems only reasonable that if the temporal lobes are being stimulated, then temporal lobe behavior will emerge. . . . By stimulating the temporal modes we had achieved a widening and a deepening of the emotion they associated with the experimental experience.

Many of these subjects kept coming back because they had found the experience so pleasurable. Persinger found that subjects that returned took much less stimulation on later occasions before they had some so-called mystical experience.[7]

Some of the work of Persinger has additional support from experiments carried out by Y. A. Kholodov, which showed that the brains of vertebrates that had been surgically separated from the sense organs and other parts of the nervous system responded more positively to magnetic fields. From this he concluded that the sense

[7]Michael Persinger was interviewed by *Omni* and these comments are taken from the interview (see *Omni*, "The New Transcendental Science," October, 1989.)

organs prevent the brain from fully reacting to external magnetic fields that have fluctuations imposed on them.[8]

A Theory for Links Between Biology and Geomagnetism

Dr. Robert Becker, an American medical scientist well known for his work on the use of electrical fields in bone regeneration, has suggested a mechanism for the interaction between the geomagnetic field and life. Starting with the well-known fact that electrical potential differences exist between the various parts of a living body, he goes on to suggest that this potential is the controlling influence of the activities of all living organisms. He further suggests that this direct current system of electrical potential is frequency sensitive in that it responds to some frequencies and not to others. From this he concluded that over the aeons the body of every living organism had become locked in step with specific fluctuations of the geomagnetic field, since all life had evolved in this field.[9] These fluctuation are linked, in turn, to the positions and movements of the Sun and Moon. They are also affected by the solar cycle.

According to the theory I have developed the solar cycles themselves are under the control of the positions and movements of the planets. Taken to its logical conclusions we now have a mechanism for linking solar, lunar, and planetary motions to the activities of living organisms. In other words, we have the basis for a scientific theory of cosmic effects on life.

Conclusion

In this chapter we saw that the magnetic field of Earth has a large number of fluctuations linked to the spinning of Earth on its own axis, its movement around the Sun, the sunspot cycle, and the orbiting of the Moon around Earth. I also produced evidence to

[8]Borthnothy, M. F. (editor), *The Biological Effects of Magnetic Fields*, Academic Press, New York, Vol 1 (1965), Vol 2 (1969).
[9]Becker, R. O., Seldon, G., *The Body Electric*, Morrow, NY, 1985.

show that solar activity correlated with the positions and movements of the planets, and I proposed a theory that can explain why this should be so. We also looked at the biological consequences of these variations in Earth's field. We thus have the basis for the theory that links life on Earth with the positions and movements of Earth, Sun, Moon, and the planets.

PART THREE

11

Programming by Magnetism and Light

In previous chapters we saw that several species of animal can find direction using the Sun or sky as well as the magnetic field of Earth. Thus, some animals have built-in redundancy with regard to direction finding. The question then arises how they integrate these two methods, and at what stage of their development one or the other of the methods might be dominant as a directional cue. This is the question which we will discuss in this chapter. We will address the problem with regard to bees and birds, and then we will speculate on the possible integration of the two methods by early humans. We will also look at a theory regarding the mechanism of direction finding in higher animals.

Integrated Direction Finding in Bees

We have already seen that bees can use the position of the Sun in the sky, together with their internal biological clocks, to find direction on clear days. In cloudy weather they can switch to using the changing pattern of polarization of the sky, again coupled with their internal timekeeping, to find direction. We also saw that when giving information on direction to other bees using the dance language they seem, to an external observer, to get the direction wrong by small angles that vary with the solar daily magnetic variation. The bees however seem to know what other bees are telling them with regard to direction, because they are not only being told the direction by means of the dance, but they are also picking up the associated "error" direct from the daily variations in the direction of the Earth's field that are related to the position of the Sun in the sky. If they are not actually using the magnetic field to find direction, why do they have it at all?

We saw in an earlier chapter that this is partly because they use it to orient their hives. There is, however, evidence that they use the solar daily magnetic variation for a much more important purpose: that of resetting their internal clocks. Professor James Gould of Princeton University carried out some experiments which seem to indicate that bees may well use the solar daily magnetic variation to reset their clocks. A group of bees, subject to the normal fluctuations of the geomagnetic field, were given food at a specific time of day. After a while they would show food-seeking responses even when food was not provided. Just as one can record fluctuations of sound (associated with speech and music) on a magnetic tape using a microphone and recorder, so it is possible using magnetic detectors and a special tape recorder to record the daily changes in the geomagnetic field. Professor Gould did just that, but once he had done so he used the recording to control the electric currents passing through coils of wire. Thus, he was able to artificially create, at will, the fluctuations of Earth's magnetic field. However, he "played" this artificial magnetic field to the bees at a different time of day, which was not correlated in any way with the actual position of the Sun in the sky. The bees then showed food-seeking responses at the times when the artificial field had a magnitude and direction that corresponded to those of the geomagnetic field when the food had been given. Taken in conjunction with the work on the internal clocks of bees (see page 145) and the work discussed on the previous page of this chapter, Gould's work suggests that the bees were using the artificial magnetic field to tell the time of day.

Although the evidence is as yet inconclusive, it seems that bees may, on occasion, in the absence of the Sun or the polarization of the sky, use the magnetic field to obtain some information on direction. Professor Gould had this to say:

If bees did turn out to have yet another backup, it would probably be magnetic. The system of last resort for homing pigeons under overcast skies and out of sight of familiar landmarks, for instance, is the Earth's magnetic field. And, indeed, there is plenty of evidence that bees also sense the Earth's field, though not that they use it as a compass while foraging.[1]

The question that now arises is what form the sensor might take. It could work by magnetic induction in which a current is induced in a conducting circuit within the bee when it moves or changes its orientation with respect to the field. It could work by the phenomenon of paramagnetism in which a magnetic field can temporarily induce magnetism in a substance that is neither conducting nor magnetic. The third possibility is that bees might possess some permanent magnetism. When very sensitive superconducting magnetometers, of the type normally used by geologists to search for traces of magnetism in rock, were used on bees, it turned out that they were quite magnetic. This magnetism arises from particles of lodestone, or magnetite, concentrated in front of the abdomen. Millions of these crystals are formed here during the pupal stage when the bee is no longer feeding. Thus, within the body of the bee there exist substances which can detect weak magnetic fields. How they are used to detect the field and how the field is used as an aid to navigation are questions that can only be answered by further research.

Interaction Between Magnetic and Stellar Direction Cues in Birds

A team of researchers from the University of Frankfurt—Wolfgang Wiltschko, Petra Daum-Benz, Ursula Monroe, and Roswitha Wiltschko—investigated the interaction between magnetic and stellar direction cues in some birds. They reported the findings at the Royal Institute of Navigation Conference on Orientation and

[1]J. L. Gould, C. G. Gould, *The Honey Bee*, Scientific American Library, 1988.

Navigation: Birds, Humans and Other Animals, which was held in Cardiff in April 1989.[2]

Their paper started with what we already know about each of these methods of orientation. With regard to the magnetic compass mechanism, they pointed out that work on the European robin showed that the compass of birds differed from the ordinary technological compass of navigators in two important respects. First, the range in which it functions is rather narrowly tuned to the total intensity of the ambient geomagnetic field. Second, the birds do not distinguish between magnetic north and magnetic south, but they detect the angle the field makes with the horizontal plane at a given location, and this enables them to distinguish between poleward and equatorward. It is still unclear how garden warblers master the problem they have to face when they cross the equator, where the field is parallel to the Earth's surface. With regard to stellar observational cues they mentioned the suggestion made by Emlen that birds might derive their directions from the stellar patterns in a way not dissimilar to the way in which we find north from the Big Dipper (or the Plough in Europe), regardless of its position.[3] They then reviewed some of the work we have already discussed in an earlier chapter. Their own important contribution centers on the interaction of magnetic and stellar cues during ontogeny (the development of the organism to maturity) and during the autumn and the spring migrations.

The integration of magnetic and stellar cues during ontogeny seems to vary with the species under investigation. Wiltschko and his colleagues found out that hand-raised garden warblers that had grown up under the natural sky, when tested in the geomagnetic field without visual cues, were much poorer at finding direction than those in a control group who had never seen the Sun and the stars. However, this phenomenon did not show up in pied flycatch-

[2]W. Wiltschko, P. Daum-Benz, U. Munroe, R. Wiltschko, "Interaction of Magnetic and Stellar Cries in Migratory Orientation," *Orientation and Navigation: Birds, Humans and Other Animals*, Royal Institute of Navigation, London, 1989.

[3]S. T. Emlen, "The Influence of magnetic information on the orientation of the Indigo Bunting, *Passerina Cyanea*," Animal Behavior 18, 215–224, 1970.

ers or savannah sparrows. These and other experiments seem to suggest that a view of the natural sky during early summer might affect the direction set when the birds use the magnetic compass only, although the details are still far from clear.

The Frankfurt group also investigated whether the magnetic field during ontogeny affected the later orientation by stars. They did so by raising young garden warblers under the rotating artificial sky of a planetarium. The various groups of birds were placed in the planetarium in such a way that the center of rotation lay in different directions with respect to the geomagnetic field. When later these birds were tested under a stationary sky, in the absence of magnetic information, they sought their migratory direction away from the center of rotation, regardless of what its position with respect to magnetic north had been. These experiments seem to indicate that during ontogeny the stars and celestial rotation affect the later orientation by magnetic compass, but the initial setting of the star compass seems to be independent of the direction of the magnetic field.

During the autumn migration of mature birds the relationship between the star and magnetic compass changed considerably. Wolfgang and Roswitha Wiltschko had already investigated this aspect of navigation in 1975 for the case where the magnetic field and the star compass gave conflicting information. They tested two species of the genus *Sylvia* as well as garden warblers under a clear night sky in Spain, but in the presence of an artificial magnetic field, the north of which had been turned by 120 degrees to east-southeast. Under these circumstances the birds followed the magnetic information and changed their direction of preference along with the change in magnetic north, even in the face of the natural stars. Further experiments by the Wiltschkos, with the birds in a very weak field, outside their normal range of detection, showed that the birds even reset their star compass according to the experimental magnetic field. The birds that had been tested in the altered magnetic field maintained their preferred direction now by the stars alone, without further input of magnetic directional information. Tests within a planetarium, with the situation reversed, that is altered sky but the natural geomagnetic field, yielded similar results. It thus seems as if magnetic information is dominant during migration with the magnetic field controlling the directional significance of the stars. These experiments were all carried out on wild birds caught during the migration period. In other words, the birds had grown up under natural conditions and they had already migrated some distance. When hand-raised garden warblers were used in similar experiments the results obtained were rather different. When these birds were tested under an artificial sky with an altered north but still exposed to the natural geomagnetic field, the birds followed the stars and ignored the magnetic field. Earlier experiments by Emlen on indigo buntings had yielded similar results.

The Frankfurt group explained the difference between the behavior of the wild-caught and hand-raised birds in the following words:

Celestial rotation and the stars seem to be most important during ontogeny and the start of migration when the migratory direction is first established. As the birds move south, the familiar stars of the home region descend and finally disappear below the northern horizon, while new configurations appear—the sky undergoes a slow, but continuous change. Also, the stars are frequently hidden by clouds. The wild birds had experienced all this already before they were tested, while the hand-raised birds had always been offered the same, unchanging sky that was never obscured.[4]

They further suggested that the experiences associated with migration led to a shift in the control of the star compass during ontogeny to the magnetic field during migration. The magnetic field is fairly regular at lower latitudes and it can provide a good reference for resetting new and unfamiliar star patterns which can then be used for later reference. The stars also seem to provide another function during flight. They help nocturnal migrants keep to a straight course. Some of the evidence for this has come from the use of radar, by ornithologists, to keep track of the birds during

---

[4]W. Wiltschko, P. Daum-Benz, "Interaction of Magnetic and Stellar Cries in Migratory Orientation," *Orientation and Navigation: Birds, Humans and Other Animals*, Op. cit.

flight. An analysis of these tracks has revealed that they are more scattered and less straight when the sky was overcast, or covered in patchy clouds, than they were under a clear sky. This evidence seems to show that visual cues from a clear sky are important to birds in maintaining their flight path.

There is further evidence to support this hypothesis from cage studies with captive birds. Many of the researchers in this field have found that the birds they tested showed much more scatter in the absence of visual cues, and this led them to the conclusion that the stars were essential for orientation. It now seems likely that the presence of the stars does not allow a more accurate establishment of direction of migration, but it helps to maintain the selected direction in the cage, and this is seen in a higher concentration of activity in this direction.

The general picture to emerge from these studies is that the interaction of the two systems of direction finding is extremely complex. Each mechanism on its own enables young birds to find their migratory direction. However, under normal conditions, both are integral parts of a complex system. The stars and celestial rotation seem to play a more important role during early development and in establishing the direction of migration, but the magnetic compass seems to be of increasing importance during the actual migration when the geomagnetic field is used to set the direction of the star compass as unfamiliar stars are encountered.

The Spring Migration

Although much less research has been carried out on the spring migration, and so less is known about the methods employed, it now seems as if the same navigational techniques are employed in the spring. H. Löhrl in 1959, and more recently L. V. Sokolov in 1984, carried out experiments which seem to show that birds have already selected their future breeding site in the autumn, before they set off on the migratory flight.[5] This means that in the spring the birds head for an area which is familiar to them, because they have already spent some time there. Experiments conducted

[5]Ibid.

in a laboratory with garden warblers that had been hand raised and then kept under constant conditions showed that the birds would, when exposed to the local geomagnetic field without visual cues, prefer northerly directions. This strongly indicates that the geomagnetic field can serve as a reference for direction in the spring as well as in the autumn. Other recent experiments under a planetarium sky suggests that the same might be true for the learned star compass. Wild birds also followed north in an altered magnetic field, while still having access to the real sky.

A Star Map Clock for the Birds?

I want to propose a theory that could account for the most important features of bird navigation by the stars and the magnetic field. This theory is based on a device called a planisphere, used by amateur astronomers to find their way around the sky. The most important part of this device is a circular star map able to rotate about the north celestial pole, which is very close to the Pole Star. This circular map extends across the celestial equator because some stars of the southern celestial hemisphere are visible in the Northern Hemisphere. The star map does not show all the stars visible to the naked eye, only the brighter stars in each constellation. Around the edge of the disc of this star map is marked the months of the year, further subdivided into the days of the month. Overlying this map is a slightly smaller disc, with a transparent oval-shaped window in it, and the times of the day and night marked on the edge of the smaller disc. The oval-shaped window represents the sky visible from a given latitude on the Earth's surface. Similar devices exist for Southern Hemisphere observers, but these naturally show mainly the stars of the southern celestial hemisphere and the map turns about the southern celestial pole.

To find which stars are visible at a given time of night on a particular date, the time on the overlying disc with the transparent window is lined up with the date on the circumference of the star map. The stars visible that night will be showing through the window. To find the direction and position of the stars in the real sky, the planisphere is held above the head with the star map facing downward toward the observer. The midnight mark is pointed

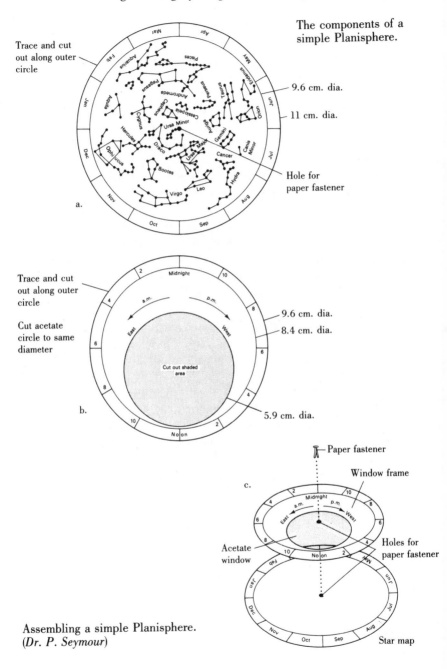

The components of a simple Planisphere.

Trace and cut out along outer circle

9.6 cm. dia.

11 cm. dia.

Hole for paper fastener

a.

Trace and cut out along outer circle

Cut acetate circle to same diameter

9.6 cm. dia.
8.4 cm. dia.

5.9 cm. dia.

b.

Paper fastener

Window frame

c.

Acetate window

Holes for paper fastener

Assembling a simple Planisphere.
(*Dr. P. Seymour*)

Star map

195

toward the north and the noon mark toward the south. The eastern and western horizons are marked at the edge of the clear window. The positions of constellations on the map that appear in the transparent window will be very similar to their position in the actual sky.

A few years ago a Japanese clock manufacturer brought out a wristwatch that incorporated a miniature version of such a planisphere, the star map being driven at the speed with which the stars move (i.e., twenty-three hours, fifty-six minutes). I am proposing that birds have genetically encoded into the brains such a star map also driven at the speed of the stars; or, to use the technical term, the star map keeps sidereal time. The young bird has initially to set the stars within its "transparent window" to correspond with the main stars in the sky that it can see, and once this is achieved the driving clock will cause it to proceed at the correct speed. This means that the bird's planispheric clock can now be used as a star compass in the same way that the Sun can be used as a compass when linked to an internal solar clock.

One needs a planisphere for each narrow range of latitudes, usually about five degrees on either side of the latitude for which it is designed. For different latitudes the position and shape of the transparent window will be different. I am proposing that the position of the "transparent window" within the bird changes with the inclination of the geomagnetic field. Each time it changes, the bird has to reset its new internal sky against the real sky. It is assisted in this by the directional information from the geomagnetic field. In flight it can use either the geomagnetic field or the star map clock-compass to find direction. As it approaches the equator the bird will begin to change over from its Northern Hemisphere planispheric clock to its Southern Hemisphere planispheric clock. At the equator the magnetic field is parallel to the surface of Earth. Since birds use the inclination of the field, the geomagnetic field is not of much use at the equator. So they can use the field sometime before reaching the equator to reset the Southern Hemisphere clock, and once this is done the compass provided by this clock can be relied upon to find direction crossing the equator.

The Use of Stellar and Solar Cues by Humans

In an earlier chapter we discussed the conscious use of the Sun, Moon, and stars for navigational purposes over the last few hundred years. Methods for using these celestial objects have been considerably refined over this period of time, and it is now possible to find direction, latitude, and longitude by making observations on the Sun, Moon, and stars. Combining measurements on the heights of these objects with information contained in the nautical almanac, and using suitable mathematical techniques, it became possible to obtain fairly accurate values for these coordinates. The nautical almanac also contains information which will allow one to obtain these parameters using the planets Venus, Mars, Jupiter, and Saturn. Mercury is not listed because this planet never gets very far from the Sun as seen from the Earth, it is not a particularly bright object even at the best of times, and so it is usually lost in the glow of sunrise and sunset. We also saw that the stars were probably used at a much earlier stage in history, by the Minoan navigators who sailed about the islands of the Aegean, to find direction, and that similar methods are still used by the islanders of the South Carolines.

We also saw that there is evidence that humans can find direction from the geomagnetic field. If bees and birds can integrate directional information from Sun, stars, and the geomagnetic field, is it not possible that early humans may have unconsciously integrated such information in the same way? With the superior brain of the human species is it also not possible that over the aeons of our evolutionary history, before our conscious interest in celestial events, we had also made use of the planets for navigational purposes? Let us now explore this possibility further.

Discovering the Rules of Astrology

The solar department at Greenwich Observatory was set up in the eighteenth century, as I have explained earlier, because solar activity caused deviations in the compass needle. I also showed that the theory of solar activity which I have developed could account for the observations that particularly violent events on the Sun were associated with planetary conjunctions, oppositions, or ninety-degree aspects of the planets as seen from the Sun. When these planets as seen from the Earth are either in opposition to the Sun or in conjunction with it, then they and the Earth will also be either in conjunction or in opposition to each other as seen from the Sun. Such a situation could give rise to violent events on the Sun. The prehistoric watchers of the sky may well have found that such events in the sky interfered with their ability to use the geomagnetic field to find direction. This I think is the most straightforward way that rules relating certain planetary alignments to disturbances of the geomagnetic field could have arisen. These rules very much later become embodied in the early development of astrology. My theory also shows that near the end of the solar cycle, ninety-degree configurations of the planets Saturn and Jupiter, as seen from the Sun, could give rise to violent events like solar flares. Because these planets are much farther from the Sun than we are, some ninety-degree configurations of these planets, as seen from the Sun, correspond to very nearly ninety-degree configurations of these planets as seen from the Earth. This could have given rise to the idea that ninety-degree configurations cause powerful influences on Earth.

I think that the awareness of changes in the magnetic field of Earth was more highly developed in prehistoric man than it is in modern human beings. This was because the finding of direction was necessary to their survival, whereas we no longer need to use this ability to the same extent. Thus, the human ability to detect magnetic fields formed a framework into which other changes, such as the meteorological effects of changes in the geomagnetic field, could be fitted. During violent sunspot activity it is not unknown for the northern lights to be seen farther south. This too would thus have been associated with those times when prehistoric man found it difficult to find direction using the geomagnetic field. I suggest it was in this way that astrology arose, a long time before it was more formally systematized by the work of the Babylonians and the Greeks.

Human Star and Planetary Compasses

During those times when prehistoric man found it difficult to find direction using the geomagnetic field he might still have to find his way home after a hunting expedition. It is possible that he could also have evolved an internal planispheric clock compass, just as birds may have done, to help him find direction on these occasions. Thus, he had some redundancy of direction-finding methods and he would switch to the star compass on those occasions when the alignments of the planets caused him to anticipate disturbances of the geomagnetic field.

Planetary configurations could only have told him that geomagnetic disturbances were more likely at such times than at other times, but when appropriate alignments existed they could still have caused him an anxiety which then became embodied in his internal cosmic almanac. This may have caused him to switch from geomagnetic to stellar direction finding, even if the alignment did not have the physical effect often associated with it.

The planets Venus and Jupiter, at their brightest as seen from Earth, are so bright that they can be seen through thin cloud, even when the stars are not visible. The same is also true of the Moon, and when Mars is nearest to our Earth it can also be seen through a veil of thin clouds. Early humans may well have used the planets as guides on those days when the cloud cover was thin enough to see bright planets. It is then quite likely that these early people evolved simple schedules that allowed them to anticipate when particular planets would have been available for use as navigational aids. Saturn is hardly ever bright enough to be seen through thin cloud, so it is unlikely to have been used in this way. However, knowledge of its movements came to the attention of early humans because of its association with those planetary configurations that were likely to lead to disturbances of the geomagnetic field. Those races who could successfully hunt far from their home base, and survive, were, I suggest, those that had evolved combined stellar, planetary, and magnetic schedules within themselves. These schedules allowed them to successfully switch between these systems at appropriate times.

It is no longer necessary for amateur sailors and professional navigators to carry a nautical almanac on board their craft. Specialized hand-held computers have programmed packages to calculate planetary and stellar positions for the appropriate date, and these can be used in conjunction with actual measurements on stars or planets, which are then manually fed into the computer, to calculate position at sea. These preprogrammed almanacs are based on a detailed and precise knowledge of the mathematics of lunar, planetary, and stellar motions that have been consciously worked out by very able astronomers over the last three hundred years.

I am not proposing that early humans had subconsciously reached this stage a long time ago. Our knowledge of biological clocks shows us that animals do not follow the complex vagaries of solar and lunar motion in those internal clocks linked to solar and lunar cycles. They follow the average periods associated with these cycles. I am suggesting natural selection favored the survival of species with inner planetary clocks which followed average periods of the planets around Earth, as seen from Earth. Such average planetary clocks would have allowed switching among stellar, planetary, and magnetic direction-finding cues, at the appropriate time. These planetary clocks would have resembled, in principle, the mechanical models of the Solar System—called orreries—which we discussed in an earlier chapter, but these internal biological orreries would have operated on the average planetary days, as seen from Earth, and would not have simulated the irregularities of planetary motion.

One question that arises about the association of visual and magnetic direction cues is whether the association between the two types of information is made before reaching the brain or after they have been independently processed in the brain. This question is closely linked with the mechanism used from detecting magnetic fields, with particular reference to human beings.

Theories on the Human Detection of the Geomagnetic Field

This subject has already been introduced in a previous chapter, but here we want to bring the various strands together and extend the ideas slightly. Since many animals that have the ability to detect magnetic fields have traces of magnetite (or lodestone) within their bodies it was thought that this might be the mechanism for magnetic field detection. Dr. Robin Baker made a search for magnetite in humans, and found that there were concentrations of the substance in our sinus bodies. However, it has since been discovered that many animals not capable of detecting magnetism also have traces of magnetite, so the correlation between magnetite and magnetic detection is no longer as convincing as it was once thought to be. Also, there are still problems about how magnetite is used to detect the field and how this information is transmitted to the brain of higher living organisms. It seems that magnetite may indeed play a part in the detection of magnetic fields in bacteria and insects, but something more complex is needed for birds and humans.

Some researchers have shown that the pineal gland is extremely sensitive to magnetic fields. This gland is an outgrowth of the forebrain. Its function in humans is obscure, but in other vertebrates it acts as an endocrine gland, secreting hormones that affect reproductive function and behavior. The ability of this organism to detect magnetic fields has been discussed by Dr. Cyril Smith and Simon Best in their book *Electromagnetic Man.*[6] Here they point out two criteria for the detection of changes in magnetic field strength by an organ the size of the human pineal gland. First, the energy in the field must be greater than the thermal (or heat) energy in the gland. The other fundamental limitation is set by the size of a discrete pack of magnetic energy—usually referred to as the quantum of magnetic flux. Some workers have already indicated that bees can respond to the very weak fluctuations of the field associated with the solar daily magnetic variation, so Smith and Best conclude on this basis, coupled with their two criteria, that pigeons with a pineal gland of 1.5 grams and humans with the pineal gland of 2 grams could do as well as the bees and may do even better in detecting weak fluctuations of the field. They also mention the work of Dr. Frank McGillion, described in more detail

[6]C. W. Smith, S. Best, *Electromagnetic Man*, St. Martin's Press, New York, 1989.

in his book *The Opening Eye*,[7] in which he proposes that the pineal gland may be involved in astrological effects because of its extreme sensitivity to weak changes in the geomagnetic field. McGillion also proposes a mechanism, involving the pineal gland, whereby visual information received via the eyes can be correlated with magnetic information coming via the pineal gland.

More recently another possibility has been explored by some biologists. This proposal does not involve a special magnetic sense organ, but proposes that the detection of the magnetic field takes place in the molecules of the retina of the human eye, as a by-product of the normal process of vision.

Conclusion

In this chapter we looked at the possibility that bees can integrate visual and magnetic cues for finding direction. We also looked at the much more extensive evidence that birds can do the same, and I proposed a theory that can explain the integrated direction finding of birds. Generalizing on the basis of this evidence I proposed that long before the conscious development of astronomy by early civilizations, people could integrate visual (including planetary) cues with geomagnetic means of finding direction. We also discussed various theories concerning the detection of the geomagnetic field by humans. In the next chapter we look at the role played by food and odor in programming our internal cosmic schedules.

[7]F. McGillion, *The Opening Eye*, Coventure, London, 1980.

12

Programming by Food and Odor

In his introduction to the book *Astronomy of the Ancients* (edited by Kenneth Brecher and Michael Feirtag)[1] Philip Morrison has this to say:

The spin and orbital motion of the Earth, whose great consequences we call day and night and the cycle of the seasons, are built biochemically deep into the function of each living thing. It goes without saying that they have meant a great deal as well within the symbol systems of our own species, we model builders, ever since we grasped the habit of thought and language. It is probably more than haphazard that the near-solstice Fourth of July is our glorious Independence Day, while in Canada they mark analogously the First of July.

One could add other significant festivals to Morrison's list, for example the association of Christmas Day with the winter solstice by the early Christian Church, and the proximity of Easter to the vernal equinox, in the Northern Hemisphere. There are a number of ways in which the movements of our Earth have been programmed into all living creatures. First, there is the variation of

[1]K. Brecher, M. Feirtag (Editors) *Astronomy of the Ancients*, MIT Press, Cambridge, Massachusetts, 1979.

light and darkness itself, and how day length is linked to the Earth's motion around the Sun. Then we have the temperatures, rainfall, barometric pressure, humidity, and other climatic factors that affect our environment, and which are linked to day and night and the seasons. There is also evidence that some creatures are tied to the cycles associated with the tides, and these are the result of the gravitational forces of Sun and Moon on the waters of Earth. We have seen the role of some geomagnetic cycles on the behavior of certain animals. However, there are other ways in which we are indirectly linked to cosmically induced cycles in our environment.

The biochemistry of the food we eat can affect our behavior to some extent, and since this food has a seasonal dependence, it is likely that this food is another way in which cosmic cycles could have been woven into the stuff of living matter. Our environment also secretes smells and pollen grains which can affect our moods, yet another way in which cycles in our environment could influence our behavior. These are the matters which we will discuss in this chapter.

The Cycles of Food

The idea that cycles in the food we eat could provide a basis for understanding some aspects of astrology came to me while I was watching a television program on which Terry Wogan was interviewing the actor Tom Conte.[2] In reply to the question about whether he believed in astrology or not, Tom Conte outlined his own theory of astrology, which he called the winter vegetable theory of astrology. He proposed that since we eat different vegetables in the summer to those we eat in the winter, and since the fetus gets its food from what the mother eats, it is not unlikely that this food could influence the personality characteristics of children born at different times of the year. My own feeling is that the influence is probably not as direct as Conte was suggesting, but the influence may well have been built into our behavior, over evolutionary time scales. Thus, if we ate a particular type of food at a certain time

[2]"The Terry Wogan Show," BBC TV, February 1985.

of year, and our bodies responded to this intake in a given way, over very long periods of time, then it is not inconceivable that the time of year could cause our bodies to react in the same way, without actually taking in the same type of food. This direct biochemical programming over aeons of time could have been reinforced by the behavioral patterns associated with the collecting of this type of food.

Hunting-Gathering Habits

In an earlier chapter we saw that long before the advent of agricultural civilizations, we had hunting-gathering cultures. These cultures depended for their food on what was available in their environment. They ate berries, nuts, and fruits that grew on trees. They also ate the eggs of wildfowl that they found in nests in trees. Perhaps they hunted birds and other small animals. With the development of simple implements for hunting they also then took to hunting larger animals. All these activities required an understanding of the life cycles and behavioral patterns of the other living creatures with which they came into contact. The cycles in these early people's living environment would thus have influenced their own cycles, not only because of the biochemistry of their food intake, but because its collection also required specific behavioral patterns. This was very graphically seen in the case of the effect that the collecting of palolo worms had on the islanders of the South Pacific. Since the palolo worm has a complex sex cycle, which depends on the time of day, the state of the tides, the time in the lunar month, and the time of year, the islanders have to adapt their eating habits to this cycle if they wish to partake of this delicacy.

Another example is provided by the people who fish for grunion.

"Grunion Run Tonight!"[3]

Grunion is a type of fish that can be found off the beaches of Southern California. The male and female fish are washed onto the

[3]Quoted by R. R. Ward, *The Living Clocks*, Collins, London, 1972.

shore in large numbers during the summer nights just fifteen minutes after high tide, in order for the female to lay her eggs and the male to fertilize them. When this happens thousands of people line the shore, from "Point Conception to Punta Abreojos—Santa Barbara to Ensenada in Baja California."According to the law the fish may only be caught with bare hands, and people use all manner of unorthodox devices to catch them. They use buckets, glass jars, and cloth sacks. The run occurs at a particular time of the lunar month, with the incoming wave rushing toward the shore when the tide is one day past its monthly high. The actual reproductive cycle is well described by Ritchie Ward in his book *The Living Clocks* in the following words:

The female grunion is the length of a man's hand. Dancing upright on her tail, she digs herself down into the sand for half the length of her body. Swaying wildly, she deposits her eggs in the cavity three inches below the surface. The male wriggles up and curves his body in a graceful arc around her as she sways. In a few seconds he has fertilized the eggs and is slithering back towards the waves. The female, now utterly exhausted, sways and wriggles to free herself. Then she flips towards the water and vanishes into the breakers; the wet sand slides into the hole and covers the eggs.

He also relates a story that shows the accuracy with which the run of grunion can be predicted:

The lady from the Middle West is still not convinced. "I think these California newspapers are pulling our leg. This afternoon they said, Grunion run expected at 10.37 tonight. I'll bet that was just a wild guess."

A balding man in damp coveralls massages white stubble on his jaw. "Well, they did come in at 10.40. That's close enough. Really, though, all you need is a tide table. The runs always come just fifteen minutes after high tide—that is, after the two highest tides of the month."

Leo the Lion in Egypt

There are other ancient stories that come from such early cultures as the Egyptian civilization that grew up along the banks of the Nile. In an earlier chapter we saw how important predicting the floods of the Nile were to the success of the crops of these people. They were not, however, the only living creatures who needed the water after the hot summer. The story goes that greats herds of deer would also trek down to the banks of the Nile to take advantage of the floodwaters. Quite naturally, lions would also be found roaming the riverbanks, to prey on the deer. As we also saw earlier, Sirius, the Dog Star, could be seen rising in the east just before sunrise at the time of year just before the annual flood. The constellation of Leo the Lion would, at that time of year, be seen setting in the west just a short while after sunset—this is how it got its name. It is thus very likely that the celestial observations were programmed into the behavior of the Egyptians, in such a way that they would have been ready to take advantage of the floods. However, the association of that time of year with lions along the banks of the Nile could well have given rise to anxieties concerning their own safety.

Leo the Lion was also very closely linked in the ancient world with another well-known constellation, Taurus the Bull. The two become part of a motif in ancient art which has since become known as the lion-bull motif, and it is often depicted as a lion devouring a bull. This particular symbol arises from the following circumstances. In the ancient world Taurus the Bull in the early morning sky marked the coming of spring. However in midwinter Leo the Lion was very close to the meridian as Taurus disappeared in the west. The lion-bull motif became a symbolic representation of the changing seasons. This particular symbol was studied in some detail by Willy Hartner, from the Johann Wolfgang Goethe University in Frankfurt, Germany. He reported his finding in the *Journal of Near Eastern Studies* in 1965. He started his article with the following words:

The symplegma of the lion and the bull [the two embracing or wrestling] as encountered in the monumental sculptures deco-

207

rating the Achaemenian palaces of Persepolis is one of the oldest motifs and undoubtedly the most tenacious traceable in the history of Near Eastern art. To witness this it will suffice to compare one of the typical Achaemenian versions with a prehistoric Elamite seal impression dating from the fourth millennium B.C., a Sumerian vase decoration, a tile from a Sumerian gaming-board, and a Persian miniature from the Mogul period. Evidently, through five thousands years, in spite of innumerable wars, the downfall of dozens of old, and the ascent of just as many new, states or kingdoms, attended by changes of the dominant races and languages, not only the symbolic combination of two combatant animals, but even some very characteristic details in the mode of representation, were carefully preserved.[4]

This is just one of many examples where the cosmic rhythms relevant to our environment became enshrined in artistic symbolism.

Internal Agricultural Calendars

With the rise of agriculture in many different parts of the world, people needed to follow a fairly rigid annual timetable of preparing the soil, sowing seeds, and reaping the harvest. This was very much associated with the constellations visible on the western horizon just after sunset, or on the eastern horizon just before sunrise. From this information the early astronomers could deduce the constellation in which the Sun would be seen, from the Earth's surface, if one could see Sun and stars at the same time. The particular constellation of the zodiac in which the Sun was at a given time of year was thus associated with the agricultural tasks that had to be carried out at that time. This link became embodied in an artistic motif which came to be called the signs of the zodiac and the labors of the month. We can find examples of this motif in many medieval churches and prayer books. One example is to be found in the Book of Hours, a prayer book which the Duc de

[4]W. Hartner, "The Earliest History of the Constellations in the Near East & the Motif of the Lion-bull Combat," *Journal of Near Eastern Studies*, 24, 1, 1965.

Berry commissioned from the Limbourg brothers. It is also to be seen in the exterior decoration of the cathedral at Amiens, in France. I found another example of the motif on the lead surrounding a baptismal font at a church in Brookland in Kent, England. The use of this particular symbolical association between zodiac signs, the labors of the month by the Christian Church, does not really imply that the Church supported astrology. It is basically a symbolic way of saying that what people do at different times of the year depends on the cycle of the seasons, and this in turn depends on the apparent position of the Sun along the zodiac.

The motif was briefly discussed by Fred Gettings in his book *Secret Symbolism in Occult Art*.[5] Here he says:

To understand something of the occult basis of astrological images, we look at them from a slightly different point of view. The Sun was visualized as passing through the equal arcs of the zodiac and marking off the passage of time. The most commonly used of all zodiacal imagery is concerned with the passage of time, which is sometimes called the "images of the seasons" or the "labors of the month." Since the Sun moves through one sign of the zodiac in approximately one month, and since a sign of the zodiac was believed to exert a particular influence on the world, it was considered reasonable to imagine that each month should have a corresponding labor or agricultural theme attached to it.

By way of illustration Gettings uses an example from another fifteenth-century French manuscript, in which the sign of Leo the Lion (through which the Sun passed in the month of August) was associated with harvesting. He then goes on to explain: "This is why a lion, standing against a backdrop of stars, is placed alongside the picture of a man reaping corn."

The Book of Hours of the Duc de Berry is discussed by Otto Neugebauer in his own book *The Exact Sciences in Antiquity*.[6] He, however, uses the illustrations for a different purpose. His interest

---

[5]F. Gettings, *Secret Symbolism in Occult Art*, Harmony Books, New York, 1987.
[6]O. Neugebauer, *The Exact Sciences in Antiquity*, Harper Torchbook, New York, 1962.

lies not in the artistic symbolism of the work, but in the light it can shed on changing practices in the exact sciences in general, and in number systems in particular. He has this to say: "A Book of Hours is a prayer book which is based on the religious calendars of saints and festivals throughout the year. Consequently we find in the book of the Duke of Berry twelve folios, representing each one of the months."

He describes the folio for the month of September:

As the work of the season the vintage is shown in the foreground. In the background we see the Chateau de Saumur, depicted with the greatest accuracy of architectural detail. For us however, it is the semicircular field on top of the picture, where we find number and astronomical symbols, which will give us some impression of the scientific background of this calendar. Already a superficial discussion of these representations will demonstrate close relations between the astronomy of the late Middle Ages and antiquity. This is indeed only one specific example of a much more general phenomenon. For the history of mathematics and astronomy the traditional division of political history into Antiquity and Middle Ages is of no significance.

Further along Neugebauer draws our attention to the fact that four different ways of writing numbers are used in this illustration:

We return once more to the diverse ways of writing numbers. Four different types of writing can be illustrated on the calendar of the Book of Hours: the place value notation still in use today; the Roman numerals operating with individual symbols for the different groups of units; complete number words; and finally alphabetic numerals.

All this indicates the great antiquity of our concern with times of the year and tasks normally associated with specific times. I would argue that it is not unreasonable to propose that these are merely conscious symbols of our internal programming that has been carried out over a much longer period of time. I would further argue that this movement from our cosmic unconscious, to the conscious development of astronomy by a few individuals within early cultures, came about as a result of the development of common needs necessitated by living in larger communities. Before this movement to larger social structures, the smaller family groups might well have been more aware of their own internal biological clocks. Such clocks could have responded to the more subtle phase-locking by the movements of the Moon, stars, and planets. It is very likely that families with certain personality traits would have followed slightly different combinations of preference for the order in which they relied on these clocks. It is not unlikely that such a system would have meant that while out hunting or foraging for food at night, different families living in the same general area would have used a shift system to avoid clashes with other families. They may thus have followed family schedules that made use of a different set of family clock compasses associated with a different combination of Moon, stars, and planets. The movement to a common system with the Sun playing a more important role would have evolved as civilization developed out of the combined needs of larger groups of people. Larger groups made it safer to hunt during the day because there could be some division of labor, with some doing the hunting and some doing sentry duty. Social concerns might well have led to a sublimation of internal biological clocks of individuals, but the aeons of time over which we may have been programmed could well have left their marks on us in the form of complex internal schedules, linked with emotional response and behavioral tendencies; that is, the cosmos programmed our internal astronomical clocks and calendars, and it is these that are responsible for our tendencies to respond in certain ways when the planets take up specific configuration. This then is how we may have become aware of the movements of the Moon, stars, and planets, and associated them with our inner emotions—our moods, hopes, and fears. Social pressures, aided by well-developed educational systems, have tended to drown out the cosmic consciousness that we acquired over the long time scales associated with the evolution of life.

Astrology, as practiced by serious astrologers, could well be one way of rediscovering our internal cosmic self—the mirror within. Evidence that we have planetary clocks within our bodies comes from Michel Gauquelin's work on planetary heredity.

Gauquelin's Work on Planetary Heredity

The idea that people tend to be born when the state of the Solar System, as seen from Earth, is the same as when their parents were born, has run through astrology for almost two thousand years, starting with Ptolemy, the great Greco-Egyptian astronomer-astrologer. Michel Gauquelin, a French statistician and psychologist with an interest in testing the validity of astrology, decided to investigate this hypothesis. He was able to show, using statistical methods, that parents and their children showed little or no tendency to be born at the same time of year. However, further investigations revealed a very significant result: If one or other parent was born with a given planet rising, or near the highest point in the sky, then there was a significant tendency for their children also to be born under these conditions of that particular planet. This tendency was increased if both parents were born with the same planet in one of these positions. The effect was most marked for the Moon, Venus, and Mars, followed by Jupiter and Saturn, but it was absent for the Sun, Mercury, and the other planets. This particular result applies to all people investigated, and, unlike some of his other work which will be discussed in a later chapter, the sample included both ordinary people, and those who had achieved eminence in a particular field. Gauquelin's conclusions, based on these results, are founded upon objectively measurable quantities, such as times of birth and planetary positions, and not on subjective criteria, such as what constitutes eminence in a profession.

In a later replication of this experiment, Gauquelin divided his sample into two categories, according to whether the births was induced or not. The results of this replication showed that the planetary heredity effect applied only to natural births. This strongly suggests that the planets are actually, in some way, influencing the natural timing of birth, making it more likely that a person of a certain type will be born at a particular time rather

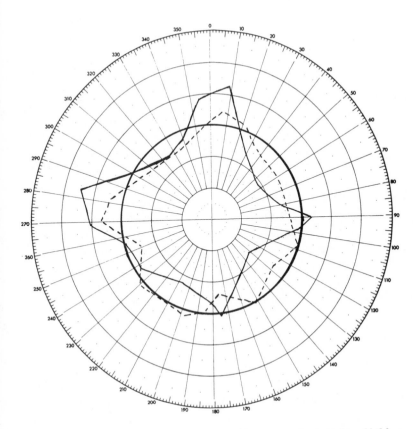

Increase in Planetary Heredity with High Geomagnetic Activity: Children born of parents who were born when a given planet had just passed the horizon (270°) or the meridian (0°) are twice as likely to be born under similar planetary configurations if they are born on a magnetically disturbed day (continuous line) than if they were born on a magnetically quiet day (broken line). The results have been combined for the Moon, Venus, Mars, Jupiter, and Saturn. (*Dr. P. Seymour*)

than another. These results, together with his earlier work, suggest that for people with different genetic constitutions, different planets will act as the signal for the moment of birth, and that these genetically inherited characteristics can also play a part in determining success in different walks of life.

In another repeat of this experiment Gauquelin divided his sample of natural births into two groups, but this time one group consisted of those born on days when storm conditions prevailed in the magnetosphere of Earth, and the other group of those born on magnetically quiet days. He was able to show that the planetary heredity effect was enhanced when the magnetic field of Earth was highly disturbed; although still present on magnetically quiet days, the effect was less evident at such times. This enhancement was apparent for Mars, Jupiter, and Saturn, it came through most strongly for Venus, but scarcely existed for the Moon. My theory for planetary heredity, which will be discussed in the next chapter, is able to explain why this should be the case.

These particular results of Gauquelin's are the most important of all his findings, as far as my theory is concerned. This is not only because they are based on objectively measurable quantities, as we have already mentioned, but because they show quite clearly that a physical agency is involved, and that this agency is the magnetic field of the Earth.

Programming by Smell

We all respond to smells, at least to some extent, in physical as well as emotional ways. The smell of a well-prepared meal can stimulate the appetite. The vapors given off by decaying leaves on a evening in autumn can induce in different people a variety of different emotions, from sadness at the end of the summer to a feeling of philosophical reverie concerning the natural cycle of decay and rebirth. Many animals have far more highly developed senses of smell than we have, and they too have have learned to respond to smell in a variety of ways. Smell is a result of the interaction between the molecules given off by certain substances in the form of vapors or gas which interact with the olfactory membrane in the noses of animals. Some smells have a seasonal dependence.

Ancient primeval memories of scents can cause certain animals to react in specific ways. Apparently when red deer smell the feces of lions, they became extremely nervous even though it has been thousands of years since the two species shared the same habitat.

A reaction like this is not really all that difficult to accept since the ability of all animals to identify their predators by smell is very much part of their survival mechanism. Less well known is that scents can also cause human beings to react in specific ways.

It has recently been discovered that women who live in hostels, prisons, and halls of residence find that their monthly periods become synchronized. Some experiments have been carried out which seem to indicate that the causal factor giving rise to this synchronization is smell. In one such experiment, the secretions from female armpits were smeared onto the upper lip of other females, who were not informed of the origin of the substances used for the smearing. The smearing was repeated each day for three months, by which time the cycles of the recipients had adjusted to the menstrual cycle of the donor. Commenting in his book *Supersense* on this and other similar experiments, John Downer has this to say:

The most interesting feature of the tests was that none of the recipients was aware of any smell coming from the smears. If these odors, operating on an unconscious level, can have such profound effects, it is likely that our lives are influenced in other ways by the human scent. [7]

Some people are affected by pollen grains given off by plants and flowers, and this too can have a seasonal dependence. Hay fever is a well-known allergy to pollen which can cause inflamed eyes, a streaming nose, and fits of sneezing. It is not unlikely that people with different personality traits would not only react to different types of pollen, but also that their mental responses to the biological condition could be different. Since in earlier times we lived in much closer proximity to our environment, and were thus more aware of the presence of pollen grains in the atmosphere, it is just possible that this could have led to some sort of evolutionary conditioning, linked to a particular time of year. We have lived in cities and inhabited insulated and air-conditioned buildings for a relatively short period of human history, and it may be that the

[7] J. Downer, *Supersense*, BBC Publications, 1988.

reference system of the seasons can invoke mental responses that were normally linked to the seasonal occurrence of certain pollens without actual physical contact with the grains.

Conclusion

In this chapter we looked at various ways in which we could have been environmentally programmed for specific seasonal responses. We considered the fact that the biochemical nature of the food we eat is to some extent linked to the seasonal availability of different types of food, and this could have been a way in which the processes of evolution gave rise to seasonal conditioning by our environment. The behavioral patterns associated with the gathering, or the hunting, of this food could have reinforced this seasonal conditioning. The seasonal odors and airborne pollen grains associated with our biological environment could have been another way in which we were conditioned by the time of year. The geometrical form and shapes of our bodies, our sense organs, and our skin coverings have evolved to help us survive in a given environment. Our movements through the three dimensions of space, and our movement through time, the internal cycles of our bodies and our behavioral patterns in space and time, give a four dimensional shape to our beings. This 4-D shape has also been molded by the processes of evolution, to ensure our survival within the four-dimensional landscape of our natural environment. The adaptation of our own 4-D shape to that of our environment has been a product of evolution, but it also offers another possiblility for understanding what may well be called astrological programming by our cosmic environment. We will discuss this further in the next chapter.

13

Maps and Shapes in Space and Time

In order to specify the position of a place on the surface of Earth we need to know its latitude and longitude. We have already seen that the circles of latitude and the meridians of longitude form a grid that envelops the Earth. Many different terrestrial quantities, for example height above sea level, average summer temperatures, annual rainfall, number of sunny days per year, and the strength of the geomagnetic field, vary with location. It is thus possible to use the grid of latitude and longitude to plot maps of all these quantities. Many terrestrial quantities are also time dependent, and some, as we have already seen, have daily and yearly cycles. These cycles can be seen to form another grid structure in time.

Using the grid structures of space and time we can plot graphs, or curves for all these quantities, and such curves will show patterns in space and time. By using each of these quantities we can then see that our environment has a complex "shape" in space and time, but within this complexity there are still discernible patterns. The shapes of our bodies and our patterns of behavior give us a complex shape in space and time, but there are also discernible patterns within this shape. The processes of evolution have, by means of known physical interactions, molded our space-time shapes to the space-time shapes of our environment. Just as the Sun, Moon, planets, and stars can be used by a navigator to find his position at sea or in the sky, so the cycles of these objects can be used to locate our own positions on the complex space-time maps of our environment.

The navigator has to combine his own direct observations on the positions of these bodies with the numerical data on these objects contained in the nautical almanac. These almanacs are now in the form of mathematical formulas stored within hand-held computers, so the necessary information on planetary positions has been programmed into the magnetic memories of this device. When the navigator fixes his position at sea he is matching the referencing system within the computer, for the appropriate date (as obtained from an external calendar) and time (obtained from the ship's chronometer), with an external referencing system as obtained from his actual observations with a sextant.

I am proposing that our astrological response to the universe is of a similar nature. We have evolved in a universe with a variety of physical rhythms, and these cycles have become part of our internal "nautical almanacs." The matching of the information within these calendars to our external cosmic environment can be done in a variety of different ways. It can be done by means of the regular pulsing of the magnetic field of Earth, which is related to the time of year, positions of the Sun and Moon, and, according to my theory of the solar cycle, the relative positions of planets as seen from the Sun. It can also be done, at least as far as the Sun and Moon are concerned, by actual observations of the light coming from these bodies. It can also be done, much less accurately, by observing meteorological conditions such as temperature, atmospheric pressure, and rainfall that prevail at a given time of year. However, for the most part our social structures and our educational system have dulled those responses to our environment which were necessary for survival in less-developed and smaller family structures of early human settlements. This means that most of us do not know how to match the internal cosmic landscape with the external one. It is quite likely that this is the role played by the serious astrologer, in that he or she can tell us where we are in the four-dimensional map of space and time, and how best to match our personal and very individual 4-D maps to that of the environment. However, just as the navigator can inform the captain of a ship of the vessel's location on a sea chart, and then it is up to the captain to decide on his or her course of action, so the "astrological navigator" can inform us of our position on the "sea chart" of space and time, but it is up to us to decide how we react to this information. Perhaps this is what H. E. Henley had in mind when he wrote:

It matters not how straight the gate,
How charged with punishments the scroll,
I am the master of my fate:
I am the captain of my soul.

In this chapter we bring the various strands of previous chapters together by further developing the analogy between the navigator and the astrologer.

Nontechnical Human Navigation

In many different parts of the world sailors and fishermen find their way around their local seas, islands, and shores using a variety of nontechnical navigational aids. Many different races and tribes find their way on land using a variety of techniques to aid navigation. In the next few sections we will look at three specific examples of navigating without tehnical aids. The first two are concerned with land navigation, and the next one is concerned with navigation at sea.

Our first example comes from the Australian aborigines. A group of these people were accompanied by David Lewis as they crossed the Central Australian Desert, because he was interested in studying their navigational skills. A number of interesting points arose from this study. He discovered that when they described direction to someone else they did not do so with reference to their own position at a given moment, but with reference to the base from which they had started, or with respect to some convenient landmark that they had encountered on the way. Most Western navigators would describe direction with respect to their own instanteous position. When the aboriginal tribesmen are out hunting or trapping it seems as if they are continually updating a mental map with reference to the changing topography of the landscape, as well as their direction with respect to base and the distance they have traveled, or the time that has elapsed, since they left base. In order to return to base they did not have to retrace their steps, but would take what was their perception of the shortest route. One aspect of their navigation that impressed Lewis was the fact that these aborigines had an almost total recollection of the geographical features of any country they had ever crossed. This was even true if several years had elapsed since they last took a particular route.

These feats of memory were aided by associating physical features in the landscape with certain mythical properties in the distant past. Some researchers in this field of investigation have reported how large tribal areas have associated stories and "spirit songs" which are totally memorized. The landscape of the desert is, for example, made up of a pattern of spiritual places linked by song lines of mythical ancestral beings. The spatial mental images built on these verbal records handed down from one generation to the next have a survival value in terms of locating water and other resources.

Lewis also found that the group that he accompanied made little or no use of celestial navigation. They did however use the temperature of the wind as an indicator of direction.

Our second example of land navigation comes from the Inuit— the Eskimos of Alaska, Canada, and Greenland. In the lowland ice-covered areas there are very few visible landmarks, so the Inuit have to rely on other navigational cues. For them the features that are the most important are ridges of snow that have been formed by prevailing winds. The direction of travel can be determined against the patterns made by the ridges, even when visibility is poor. The Inuit, like the aborigines, also use wind itself. They too have well-developed powers of observation and retention with reference to these navigational aids. There are other similarities between aboriginal and Inuit navigation. Relative positions of important geographical features are known in terms of direction and distance, which are judged in a two-dimensional mental model. They do occasionally use celestial data, but these are of secondary importance.

Our last example is provided by the native navigators of the Pacific islands. The first European explorers of these islands were very puzzled by the fact that almost every island they visited in this vast ocean was inhabited, and they suggested that one possible explanation could have been accidental colonization as a result of being driven off course by drifting and storms. Another possibility is that they were deliberately colonized.

On his visit to this area, Captain James Cook obtained a map that showed over seventy islands. The area covered almost the whole of Polynesia, except for New Zealand, Hawaii, and Easter Island. Those islands that could be identified on this map were seen to have good bearings with respect to Tahiti. The early explorers paid little attention to the navigational skills of the islanders. A great deal of modern work on this subject was carried out by David Lewis, in the 1950s and early 1960s. The work of Lewis and others was discussed by Alastair Couper at the 1989 Conference of the Royal Institute of Navigation entitled Orientation and Navigation: Birds, Humans and Other Animals. On this occasion he had this to say about the work of Lewis:

There is no need to evoke any sixth sense in the explanation of human navigation without instruments. Several of the surviving techniques used at sea have been validated and replicated, especially by David Lewis.

The most impressive intellectual aspects of way-finding in preliterate society are the remarkable feats of memory, especially of geography and astronomy; the ability to integrate this data and build mental maps, and from this to consistently orientate to a home base.[1]

W. H. Goodenough, who also did research in this field, describes the use of local star calendars by the inhabitant of the Caroline Islands, who used them to work out the best times for departures. He also describes the sidereal star compass of the Caroline navigators. This compass works in the following way. Each star will rise and set at very specific points on the horizon. For example, Mintaka, the topmost star of the belt of Orion the Hunter, will rise exactly in the east and set exactly in the west. Other stars in Orion will rise a few degrees north or south of the east, and set the same number of degrees north or south of the west. At rising and setting they can thus be used to mark specific compass directions. Stars of other constellations can be used in a similar way. From the area

[1]A. D. Couper, "Human Navigation Without Instruments" in *Orientation and Navigation—Birds, Humans and Other Animals*, Royal Institute of Navigation, London, 1989.

surrounding a given island these points of rising and setting do not change appreciably with latitude, and it is possible to give the bearings of a given island from any other island in terms of a sequence of stars that rise and set at very similar points of the horizon. Such a sequence is necessary because any star that rises in the east at a certain time on one particular night will rise four minutes earlier on the following night. Thus, a rising star will become a setting star six months later. As a star increases its altitude it become less useful for steering and another rising or setting alternative has to be used as a navigational aid. The navigators also recognized companion stars on reciprocal bearings so that in partically overcast conditions they could orient the vessel to the island by looking astern. In all there were thirty-two stars in the star compass of the Caroline navigators.

Another method used by the Polynesian navigators uses the pattern of ocean swells that exist around the islands. The waves coming from the open ocean will be reflected from the beaches of the mainland, and the incoming waves and the reflected waves will interact with each other to give rise to an "interference pattern" around the island. If there are a number of islands then there will be an even more complex interference pattern around them. The young navigators of the islands are taught how to use the bobbing up and down of their boats to detect the amplitudes and directions of the various waves, and hence to deduce from this, and a map of the interference pattern, their approximate position with respect to the islands.

A feature that the navigation of the Pacific islanders has in common with that of the aborigines is the use of mythology and song lines to aid their memories of navigational routes and methods. Once again we quote from Alastair Couper:

The aboriginal memory system appears very deeply entrenched in place mythology and complex song lines linking places. In the case of the Pacific islanders there were also factual and fabulous stories and chants known only to the navigators which helped them to learn and retain vast stores of detailed information relating to sailing directions of vital importance.[2]

[2]Ibid.

Navigating the Oceans of Space and Time

Any cyclical variations in our environment, be it temperature, availability of different types of food, rainfall, daylight, or the pulsing of the geomagnetic field, are like waves and swells in space and time. In order to have survived, prehistoric man needed to know how to use these waves and swells to successfully navigate the four-dimensional "seas" of life. It is thus very possible that we, as individuals, could read the various signs within our environment, to locate our position in space and time. The strange and mysterious properties which early man gave to the Sun, Moon, stars, and planets are no more superstition than the mythological songs and stories memorized by navigators in different parts of the world. They are also part of the memory framework that helped him to survive in the harsh conditions that reigned in times before people began to group together in larger settlements, cultures, and civilizations.

This memory framework aided survival in prehistoric times because it helped man to anticipate the possible outcome of cyclical changes in the environment. Thus, the evolution of life not only involved changes in man's anatomy and physiology, it also involved the programming of internal clocks, calendars, and cosmic almanacs, into which could be slotted personal environmental schedules. These in turn allowed man to anticipate the likelihood that certain terrestrial events would follow from particular relative positions of the Sun, Moon, and planets. This anticipatory behavior would be present even if the physical conditions that had a high probability of being associated with the particular celestial aspects and alignments did not always occur. This is rather similar to the conditioning of animals to show food-seeking responses when exposed to specifically chosen external stimuli, like light, sound, or magnetic fields. This is an example of the dictum, Once bitten, twice shy. However, this programming or conditioning has taken place over evolutionary time scales, so the relatively short periods we have spent in large civilized towns and cities have not entirely deconditioned our personal internal anticipatory schedules, which can become phase-locked to certain cosmic periods by a variety of different environmental stimuli.

As small family groups of people began to move into larger tribal groups, and then into early settlements and subsequently into large cultures which were to form the basis of the first civilizations, so they would have suppressed individual schedules, and would concentrate on those aspects of internal almanacs that were in common with other members of the society. In larger communities there would be division of labor, with people tending to do those tasks that they were good at. Parents would teach their children those tasks that they could do and also to cooperate with other people, so they could all work together for the survival of the community. Thus, the cultural framework of the community led to simple education systems that gave rise to consensus timekeeping behavior, in preference to family or individual timekeeping that had been characteristic of earlier smaller family groups. Increases in the sizes of communities led to further emphasis on collective spatial and temporal frameworks, thus leading to a further sublimation of personal internal schedules, which were partly associated with particular cosmic events.

In an earlier chapter we saw how the development of methods of travel such as the railway system, in much later periods in our technological history, led to the introduction of more uniform systems of timekeeping, which covered much larger areas of a given country. This eventually led to the introduction of Greenwich time into England and the introduction of a system of time zones into the United States. We also saw that further developments in sea travel and the introduction of the worldwide telegraph systems led to the adoption of a zone system, based on the Greenwich meridian, which envelops the whole world. The need to relate to ever larger global communities has meant that we are less and less aware of our own internal schedules, and much more aware of community, national, and global schedules, which are very necessary if we have to learn to cooperate with increasing numbers of people.

External Social Diaries

In order to keep appointments with others at certain times of particular days, we make use of diaries. The microchip revolution has recently brought about important changes in the nature of these diaries. Many wristwatches already had built-in calendars, and some also have data banks in which one can store the times and dates of various appointments. When the appropriate time is nearly due, the watch will sound a small alarm, and we can check the data bank to find brief details of a particular appointment. Some of these watches also have information on times of various large cities which are located in different time zones, so if we want to make an overseas call it is possible to check the time of the place we are calling.

Pepole who work with international organizations and businesses have to learn to live and work within an international framework of time. The jet lag suffered by people who fly across various time zones is an example of the stress that can be caused when our internal schedules are forced to cope with these international time schedules.

Prenatal Schedules

In the womb we have very little access to external social schedules. This is because the amount of information we can receive through our five senses, within the womb, is rather limited. In my book *Astrology: The Evidence of Science* I propose that the genes which we inherit contain instructions on how our nervous system should be wired, and this in turn gives us our particular collection of personality traits. I further propose that the wiring up also gives us a set of "resonant circuits" and these are tuned to certain frequencies present in the geomagnetic field: This could cause some phase-locking of our internal cosmic biological clocks. A metaphorical introduction to my theory, written by myself, is also contained in Jan Kurrels's book *Astrology for the Age of Aquarius.*[3] The following quotation is from the introduction:

There is growing evidence that the magnetic behaviour of the Sun is linked to the relative positions and motions of the planets. The magnetic field of the Earth is linked to the magnetic fluctuations of the Sun through the agency of the solar wind. The solar wind

[3]Jan Kurrels, *Astrology for the Age of Aquarius*, Anaya, 1990.

is a constant stream of sub-atomic particles flowing from the Sun's corona, 'gusting' and 'squalling' much like a real wind. It has also already been established that the magnetic field of the Earth varies in a manner linked to the motions and phases of the Moon. This means that the whole Solar System is playing a 'symphony' on the magnetic field of Earth. According to my theory, we are all genetically 'tuned' to receive a different set of 'melodies' from the symphony. While in the womb, the organs of our familiar five senses are still developing, so they are less effective in receiving information than they are once we are born. However, the womb is no hiding place from the all-pervading and constantly fluctuating magnetic field of Earth, so the symphonic tunes which we can pick up can become part of our earliest memories. It is here that some of the magnetic music of the spheres becomes etched on our brains. The first role of our particular response to this music is to provide the cue for our entry on to the stage of the world. At later stages in life, when the Solar System 'plays our tune' again on the magnetic field of Earth, it evokes these memories and our response may influence the way we react in a given situation.

Gauquelin's Evidence for Prenatal Scheduling

In an earlier chapter we looked at Michel Gauquelin's work on planetary heredity. Much of his other work has come in for a great deal of criticism, some of which will be discussed, because it involved a study of eminent individuals in particular fields of human endeavor. Some of the criticism was motivated by the fact that the critics could not conceive of a mechanism by which these results could be understood. Since I have now proposed a theory for the planetary heredity effect, and I have shown that this can be understood in causal terms by means of known physical agencies operating in a particular way, it is worthwhile to reexamine Gauquelin's work on the planetary eminence effect.

Gauquelin showed that there was no link between the position of the Moon in the sky at birth and the professions taken up by ordinary people. However, after collecting a great deal of evidence on eminent writers, he was able to show that such writers tended to be born either when the Moon was rising or when it had reached its highest point in the sky. Although these were the peak times for the birth of outstanding authors, two smaller peaks also occurred when the Moon was setting, or when it was at its highest point on the opposite side of the Earth. Later investigations showed that outstanding politicians also tended to be born with the Moon in these positions.

Most of Gauquelin's important results are discussed in full detail in his books, from which I have only extracted the salient points. Gauquelin also obtained similar results for the births of 576 members of the French Academy of Medicine. These doctors had obtained academic distinction as a result of their research work. Gauquelin selected them from medical directories, and to avoid bias he used objective criteria for the selection process. Theoretically these people could have been born at any time in the course of the day, yet these medical men tended to be born when Mars or Saturn had just risen, or had just passed the highest point in the sky. To check his results Gauquelin used another group of people chosen at random from the electoral register and covering the same period of births as the doctors. This second group did not show the same pattern as the doctors: Their birth times were evenly spread through the day. In a further experiment Gauquelin used a different set of 508 doctors, and came up with the same result as before. This showed that there was a significant correlation between particular planets and birth times for people who did outstandingly well in their professions, but no significant correlation showed up for an ordinary cross-section of the population.

Gauquelin studied many different groups of people who had obtained success in their various professions, and he came to the following conclusions. Saturn, in the positions previously mentioned, was associated with much higher than average frequencies of births of scientists and physicians; but lower-than-average frequencies of births under Saturn were obtained for actors, journalists, writers, and painters. Few scientists and physicians were born under Jupiter, but more than average numbers of actors, playwrights, politicians, military leaders, top executives, and journalists were born under this planet. For Mars the high-frequency

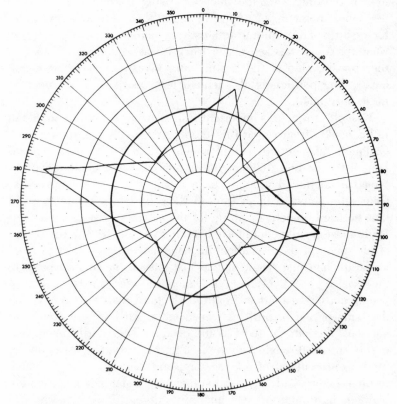

Birth Distribution of Physicians and Scientists with Saturn: The heavy black circle (third from the center) is what one would expect if there were no planetary effect. (*Dr. P. Seymour*)

groups were physicians, military leaders, sports champions, and top executives, whereas the low-frequency groups were painters, musicians, and writers.

Gauquelin found no evidence that the planets Mercury, Uranus, Neptune, and Pluto had associated with them any group of eminent individuals from a given profession. He found that there was also no evidence that the Sun played a part in determining time of birth

228

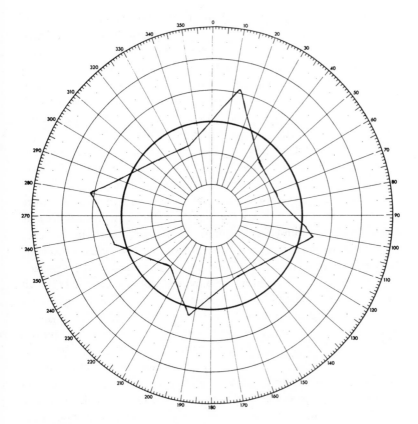

Birth Distribution of Sportsmen with Mars. (*Dr. P. Seymour*)

of any group of people, and it also did not crop up in his work on planetary heredity.

In a previous chapter I proposed that through the processes of evolution we have acquired internal biological clocks that could be phase-locked to the average solar, lunar, and stellar periods. I also proposed that human physiology had acquired more complex planetary clocks or orreries, which enabled us to use the visible planets as compass clocks when the stars or Moon were not available. I also suggested that early people became aware of planetary tides in the geomagnetic field because solar, stellar, lunar, and planetary compass clocks and the geomagnetic field were all part of an integrated navigational system. Since the planets Uranus, Neptune, and Pluto are not visible to the naked eye (they can only be seen with telescopes) they could not have been used in this way, and could not have formed part of this integrated scheme. It was also pointed out that Mercury was not a navigational planet, and was thus not listed in the nautical almanac, because it is a rather faint object, it never gets very high in the sky, and it is often lost in the glow of dawn or dusk. Mercury too would not have been very useful to navigators of prehistoric times.

I would like to propose that the Sun does not feature in the work of Gauquelin for the following reason. The basic metabolism of many species of plants and animals follow very nearly the average solar day. Many of the fundamental biochemical processes of the human body are exactly the same from one person to the next and they are largely independent of our personality traits. It is in our conscious behavioral characteristics where we differ, and where personality differences assert themselves. I have already suggested that personality traits arise from the way the nervous system is "wired up," and it is the neural network of the nervous system, which is largely independent of the basic metabolism of the body, which acts as the antenna for receiving the vibrations of the geomagnetic field associated with the Moon and the planets. Because of social convention mothers tend to follow a daily routine of working, eating, and sleeping. Thus, the overriding metabolism of the mother is constrained to follow a daily rhythm. Since the developing fetus is linked biochemically to the mother, this daily rhythm will swamp the weaker solar daily magnetic variation, but it will not swamp the resonant linking between the nervous system and certain fluctuations of the geomagnetic field, because these have slightly different frequencies. Such a proposal is thus able to explain the findings of Gauquelin.

This point has also been discussed by Professor Peter Roberts in his book *The Message of Astrology*.[4]

[4]P. Roberts, *The Message of Astrology*, The Aquarian Press, Wellingborough, 1990.

Roberts's Theory of a Preexisting Entity

In his book, Roberts gives us a thorough discussion of Michel Gauquelin's work as well as the extension of this which Roberts himself first started with John Addey, and then carried on himself after the death of Addey. He proposes a theory of his own to account for the findings of this research. This theory proposes that we can understand the available evidence in favor of astrology by postulating that there is a preexisting entity which plays a part in the birth process. He lists the properties of this preexisting entity in the following way:

1. There is a pre-existing entity which possesses qualities and these qualities will ultimately manifest in the child and the mature adult. The qualities in the entity are related to an organ which has a flower-like structure incorporating groups of petals and the prominence of each group is correlated with the strength of the associated quality.
2. The entity responds to planetary stimulation at the moment of birth when there is a joining to the physical counterpart. The stimulation enhances the prominence of specific petal groups in ways which accord with the planet involved.
3. The planetary emanations either reinforce the existing state of the entity or they may introduce a balancing effect by stimulating those groups not already prominent.

Roberts also discusses his theory in relation to my own theory:

In the later stages of the planning operating, the entity is about to enter a close (and lifelong) association with the physical body. There could be difficulties during this phase of obtaining any immediate visual clues about the position of the planets. The general rule about situations where the information flow is restricted is that the seeker turns to other methods. It seems likely that the entity in these later stages turns to a magnetic method of detection. Though there is lack of final confirming evidence, it may be that Seymour's model of geomagnetic changes generated through magnetospheric tidal effects originated by the planets explains the way in which information about planetary position can be sensed. At any rate there is the strong evidence of the Gauquelin heredity findings, in which it was observed that parent/child prominent planet correlation was twice as high on geomagnetically disturbed days as on quiet days.

Peter Roberts's approach is rather different from mine in that he proposes an entity associated with personality, but which is nonmaterial and nonphysical, that is, it is based on no known physical forces or fields. We do not have any way of knowing if he is right to invoke such an entity. What is true, as he explains in his book, is that Gauquelin's research demonstrates a clear link between sets of personality traits that promote success in given fields of human endeavor and the positions of specific planets at birth.

Conclusion

Much of what has been said in this chapter can be summed up in the words of Hüseyin Yilmaz. In the abstract to his paper "Perception and Philosophy of Science," he has this to say:

It is argued that an evolutionary theory of perception and knowledge, and a perceptual philosophy of science is, at present, a realistic and useful way of looking at the whole cognitive endeavour of living beings including man. This theory conceives perceptions, concepts and theories as ways of adapting to the useful regularities of environmental niches, and further extending these niches by exploration. This may lead, at times, to readaptation to less complex niches, etc., but in the case of man the scientific means of observation and exploration seem to lead to ever greater expansion of his environment until, at least mentally, his niche becomes the whole observable universe.[5]

[5]H. Yilmaz, *Logical and Epistemological Studies in Contemporary Physics*, edited by R. S. Cohen, M. W. Wortobsky, D. Reidel, Dordrecht, 1974.

14

Scientific Evidence and Theories

The purpose of this chapter is twofold. First we will look at available scientific evidence for and against certain aspects of astrology. Then we will see what relevance this evidence has with regard to some theories which have been proposed to account for the data, including my own theory. We will start by looking at the evidence for and against Sun-sign astrology, and then we will move on to a brief review of Michel Gauquelin's data, including the replication of these experiments by Gauquelin himself and by others. The work of Suitbert Ertel will also be discussed. John Addey used the Gauquelin data to found the subject of harmonic astrology. In this work Addey was assisted by Peter Roberts, who carried on these pioneering investigations. So we will also briefly consider the work of Addey and Roberts. Some theories have been proposed to account for the accumulated evidence collected by these various methods. Some of these theories are scientific, some of them are marginally scientific, and some of them do not pretend to be scientific at all. We will briefly review the more recent theories in the light of the evidence.

Evidence Against Sun-sign Astrology

Gauquelin's first experiments were an attempt to look for evidence in favor of Sun-sign astrology. This is the type of astrology with which most people are familiar from the horoscopes in daily news-papers, and maintains that one's personality is largely dependent on the time of year at which one is born. Since this is related to the position of the Sun along the zodiac—the apparent pathway of the Sun through the sky as seen from Earth—it became known as Sun-sign astrology. The zodiac constellation in which the Sun would have been seen at the time of year covering your birthday, in the ancient world, is called your Sun-sign. Gauquelin tested the assertion, made by astrologers, that professional soldiers are seldom born under Cancer, but often under Scorpio or Aries. He also tested many other similar assertions. Using the rigorous sta-tistical methods in which he was trained, he found that there was no evidence for any of the claims relating to Sun-sign astrology.

Sun-sign astrology was also investigated by Professor Alan Smithers of Manchester University. His work was reported over a period of four days in the *Manchester Guardian*, who, with the Koestler Foundation, provided financial support for the project.[1] Professor Smithers had started his investigation while he was still at the University of Bradford, where, with Joe Cooper, he analyzed about thirty-five thousand birth dates. This initial study seemed to provide some support for Sun-sign astrology. The *Guardian* survey used a sample that was about twice this size and this sample was taken from the United Kingdom 1971 census. This study led Smithers to some interesting results. For example, Charles Harvey, president of the Astrological Association, made two predictions:

1. Nurses would be born more frequently under alternate signs beginning with Taurus.
2. An above-average number of trade union officials would be born under Aries and alternative signs, starting with Aries.

Both these predictions turned out to be true. However, many other claims made by astrologers turned out to be contrary to the findings of Smithers. Despite the fact that this survey turned out, in many respects, to be inconclusive, it did give rise to renewed activity

[1]A. Smithers, "Articles on Astrology," *The Guardian*, March 19-22, 1984.

in the field of research. The sample used by Smithers was reanalyzed by a group of American investigators who came to the conclusion that Smithers's results could be understood in terms of statistical fluctuations and self-attribution effects. These latter effects are those that arise from the fact that many people read the daily horoscopes and sometimes act in keeping with what they know to be the personality characteristics of their Sun-sign. It thus turns out that there is still no really convincing positive evidence in favor of Sun-sign astrology. Of course newspapers carry daily horoscopes because people want to read them. But some serious astrologers feel it does a disservice to astrology to treat the subject so superficially. My own view of Sun-sign astrology is that it may still play some part in the synchronizing of the birth process, but this will be secondary to the part played by the Moon and planets.

To use a simple analogy, I would say that in the context of my theory, the Moon and the planets are actors in the cosmic drama, and the signs of the zodiac are the scenery and the sets for this drama. They could give some enhancing effect to the parts played by the Moon and the planets. The Sun, the seasons, and the planetary effects on the solar cycle provide the stage lighting for the drama. It is also likely, as I have already pointed out, that changes in the scenery, the lighting, and the drama itself could affect our moods and might influence our behavior in later life. This admittedly highly speculative possibility cannot be ruled out based on what we know at the moment, because no serious research has been carried out in this area. Neither categorical denial of this possibility by the majority of scientists, nor the counterclaims by astrologers that their work convinces them that this is definitely the case, can be treated as scientific evidence for or against this possibility.

However, according to my theory, someone born under the planet Mars would, at a given time of year, respond differently to someone born under the influence of the planet Jupiter or Saturn. But even on this basis there is no support for Sun-sign astrology. Gauquelin's work on the Moon and planets Venus, Mars, Jupiter, and Saturn remains the most important collection of data in favor of some aspects of natal astrology.

Replication of Planetary Effects by Gauquelin and Others

Gauquelin's first investigations were all restricted to data collected from France. Since it was just possible that the data reflected a peculiarity of the French, he decided to extend his studies to include Germany, Italy, Holland, and Belgium. The same pattern emerged from an analysis of these results.

In Belgium the Committee for the Scientific Investigations of Alleged Paranormal Phenomena (called the Committee Para for short) decided to see whether Gauquelin's results could be replicated in that country. They decided to test Gauquelin's work on the links between sports champions and the planet Mars. Using a new group of 535 sports champions from France and Belgium, they came up with the same result as Gauquelin. They decided not to publish the results, but issued the following statement: "The Committee Para cannot accept the conclusions of the research of M. Gauquelin based on hypotheses in which the committee has found inexactitudes."[2,3]

This is a very interesting example of how difficult people find it to get beyond their prejudices. The committee's work was presumably rigorously scientific (since they were so anxious to prove Gauquelin wrong) yet, even faced with the "scientific" fact of their own results, they were unable to bring themselves to support Gauquelin's evidence, and were even prepared to deny their own "scientific" work because of this.

A rather similar set of circumstances occurred when an American group tried to replicate these results. This group is called the U.S. Committee for the Scientific Investigation of Claims of the Paranormal. A full description of this committee's scientific ineptitude, and their prejudiced behavior in their handling of the Gauquelin affair, can be found in *The Case for Astrology* by John Antony West.[4] However, in spite of this astonishingly emotional

---

[2]H. J. Eysench, D. K. B. Nias, *Astrology: Science or Superstition?* Maurice Temple Smith, London, 1982.
[3]M. Gauquelin, *Planetary Heredity*, ACS Publications, San Diego, 1988.
[4]J. A. West, *The Case for Astrology*, Viking, New York, 1991.

and irrational activity on the part of those who wish to deny genuine questioning, some new ideas are being explained in a sincere spirit of rational enquiry.

In April 1989 I attended the First International Conference on Geo-cosmic Relations, which was held in Amsterdam. This meeting was attended by astronomers, physicians, geophysicists, physicists, meteorologists, chemists, biologists, and psychologists. At this conference I was able to hear the latest assessment of the work of Gauquelin, by Professor Suitbert Ertel of the Institute for Psychology at George-August University in Gottingen, Germany. Ertel's paper has now been published in the proceedings of the conference. In this paper he looks at a reanalysis of the replication study performed by the skeptics George Abell, P. Kurtz, and Marvin Zelen between 1979 and 1980. This is the only study so far that supposedly contradicts Gauquelin's Mars effect. He made use of his own largely objective method of grading eminence, based on a count of the citations that the various sportsmen had received in a number of publications. From this he concluded: "The sample collected by Kurtz, Zelen and Abell was indeed mediocre and did not well serve its replication purpose. The result of their study cannot throw suspicion on Gauquelin's Mars effect." Further along in the same paper he says: "The present procedure has the advantage of not presupposing any astronomical or demographic assumption, it circumvents thus all difficulties which former Gauquelin critics had regarded as severe: including astronomical (Committee Para) as well as demographic factors (Zelen)." Applying these methods to an extended sample, collected by himself, Ertel "concurs" with the findings of Gauquelin. Professor Ertel and I differ in our ideas because he concludes that there is no physical explanation for Gauquelin's observed planetary effect, while I am convinced that if there is indeed a planetary effect, then there will be (this is according to my theory) a physical explanation which can be understood in terms of the known laws of physics. However, the point which is important here is that many different people are questioning this evidence for a planetary effect and this is what we must do, and continue to do, in a rational and open-minded way, rather than trying desperately to deny the existence of this information.

Purifying Gauquelin's "Grain of Gold"

The title of this section is taken from a paper written by Professor Ertel, which appeared in *Correlation: Journal of Research into Astrology*. The subtitle of this paper was "Planetary Effects Defy Physical Interpretation." The principle conclusions of the research reported in this paper are best given in Ertel's own words, so I here quote the abstract of the paper:

The author's previous research with M. and F. Gauquelin data confirmed the existence of the planetary effects for eminent professionals. However, the present research casts doubts on Gauquelin's physical explanation. (1) For sports champions the planetary effect was unrelated to astronomical variables (distance of Mars from Earth, its angular size, apparent magnitude, declination right ascension, solar elongation and radius vector). Furthermore the effect did not diminish during Mars-Sun conjunctions. (2) For ordinary people, Gauquelin's claim that geomagnetic activity enhanced the planetary correspondence between children and parents was not supported. Nor did the planetary effect for eminent professionals covary with geomagnetic activity. It seems that Gauquelin's positive results with geomagnetism are due to random oscillations. (3) Gauquelin's claim that planetary effects decrease after 1950—a presumed side-effect of applying obstetric drugs—could not be verified with professionals' data. However, the number of post-1950 births was insufficient for a definite conclusion. (4) The accuracy of birth-times on official documents increased markedly through decades 1830–1950 but produce no corresponding increase in planetary birth frequencies. In the light of these results, Gauquelin's "midwife" hypothesis, seems to be untenable, in which case an interpretation of planetary effects in terms of physics and physiology must be replaced by something else.[5]

[5] S. Ertel, *Purifying Gauquelin's Grain of Gold*, Correlation, 9, 1, 1989.

Before discussing Ertel's conclusions in more detail, it is necessary to describe Gauquelin's "midwife" hypothesis to which Ertel refers.

Gauquelin's Planetary Midwife Hypothesis

In *Cosmic Influences on Human Behaviour* Michel Gauquelin outlines a theory to account for planetary effects on the timing of birth.[6] This theory proposes that the varying activity of the Sun is communicated to Earth by the solar wind. Together with planetary and lunar influences, this solar activity gives rise to varying intensities in the magnetic field of Earth, which is further modulated by the rotation of the Earth. These fluctuations have a selective action on the fetus, which is a function of its hereditary temperament. The magnitude of this planetary effect is controlled by the intensity of the terrestrial magnetic agitation. He further proposes that the fetal reaction is probably hormonal, and that this reaction has an influence on the mother's body during parturition, causing a contraction of the uterus hence leading to birth.

In a letter replying to Ertel's paper, also published in *Correlation*, Gauquelin further clarifies this hypothesis, calling it a "when the fetus is ready theory."

In this theory, the planets would only trigger the birth according to the genetic structure of the child. Cosmic influences at birth neither modify the heredity of the child nor add something to it; rather they would be linked to it. What about the role of geomagnetic activity or other astrophysical parameters during delivery? They would only play the role of "facilitator" or "inhibitor" of the planetary effects. For instance, sport champion Mohammed Ali was born with Mars in a "key sector." This is considered as one of the consequences of his heredity, and the strong or weak geomagnetic activity on the day of his birth would only have slightly "helped" or "impeded" Mars to appear in a key sector at his birth-time.

[6]M. Gauquelin, *Cosmic Influences on Human Behaviour*, Futura, London, 1976.

In this letter Gauquelin also comments on the indicator of geo-magnetic activity which was used by Ertel. The different indicators mentioned are different ways of averaging the complexities of the geomagnetic variations that occur during one day. Gauquelin says:

Ertel is theoretically on sounder ground when, in point (2) of his abstract, he also says, "For ordinary people, Gauquelin's claim that geomagnetic activity enhanced the planetary correspondence between children and parents was not supported." Here, working with planetary heredity, he is really testing the midwife hypoth-esis. However, one may ask why the statement of his abstract is so definite on this point. The text of his article seems to contradict that when he says: "The results taken together suggest that Gau-quelin correctly reported increased geomagnetic disturbance as the parent-child correspondences increased." At least, the ques-tion remains open to further investigation, especially since Ertel tells us he was using another indicator of geomagnetic activity than the one I used: "Mayaud's aa-indicator was chosen because it starts earlier (1868) than any others and is truly quantitative and more homogeneous than the Ci used by Gauquelin."

Gauquelin also added the following comment: "There is something ironic in the fact that it was Mayaud himself—a French scientist and priest living in Paris—who suggested in 1965 that the use of the Ci index was preferable to any other indicator of geomagnetic activity!"[7]

This is a very technical and convoluted argument, the main points of which are summarized below.

Gauquelin is saying that the genetic inheritance of the fetus will mean that it will "choose" to enter the world on a "signal" which originates in some way from a particular planet, associated with that particular set of inherited characteristics. He is also saying that geomagnetic disturbances can enhance or inhibit this "pla-netary signal."

Ertel is saying that his own work shows that geomagnetic dis-turbances have no effect on planetary heredity as reported by

[7]Letter from Michel Ganquelin, *Correlation*, 9, 1, 1989.

Gauquelin. Ertel used the aa-indicator of geomagnetic disturbances because he believed it to be truly quantitative.

Gauquelin's reply to this is that it was Mayaud himself, the originator of the aa-index, who suggested that the Ci index was preferable to any other indicator of geomagnetic activity.

My own view on the matter is, first, that Ertel's work on the effect of geomagnetism on planetary heredity can in no way be considered a replication of Gauquelin's work because they are using totally different indicators of geomagnetic activity, and second, I would agree with Mayaud, a specialist on geomagnetic disturbances, that the Ci index is indeed superior to the aa-index for this particular purpose.

Professor Ertel's paper is also criticized in the same issue of *Correlation* by Dr. Arno Muller of the Universitats of Kliniken in Germany. Muller's criticism is mainly of a technical nature concerning the statistical methods used by Ertel. However, he ends his letter with a very important general point:

Even if this result were to remain inexplicable, the possibilities for a physical explanation of the planetary effect would not be diminished by this, as Ertel states in his conclusions, at least not to a greater degree than is the case with any explanatory attempt; rather, the theory of probabilities would be in question[8]

I would agree with Muller's concluding statement. Suitbert Ertel is an extremely thorough investigator when it comes to the application of statistical methods to the human sciences. However, the very sweeping conclusions which he reaches as a result of his investigations are not in keeping with the nature and philosophy of science. It is impossible to rule out all possible physical explanations by considering a limited set of possible physical explanations. One cannot group Ertel with other scientists and science writers who are anti-astrology, because he is sympathetic enough to the work of Michel Gauquelin to give it serious scientific consideration, which is something that cannot be said of the anti-astrology scientific lobby. However, he does share with others a

[8]Letter from Arno Muller, *Correlation*, 9, 1, 1989.

too narrow view of what constitutes scientific method. This is a point I already made in my previous book on astrology, where I write: "In other words, scientists set up a very simple theory, then they shoot down their own theory, and from this they conclude that no scientific theory can be constructed to explain any part of astrology."

The point I am trying to make is that it is only possible, in any scientific investigation, either to *falsify* a theory, or to provide evidence to support a theory. Such tests can be applied to those theories that someone has already thought of, and formulated in a suitable form for scientific testing. To say that a negation of one possible theory rules out all other theories that may be thought of in the future is bad science. It also can shackle the creative imagination of scientists and impede scientific progress.

Resonance and Astrological Causation

One very obvious possibility which can explain the results of Michel Gauquelin, and which is not ruled out by any of Ertel's investigations, is that of some form of resonance effect. Ertel does not consider this possibility, although Geoffrey Dean and Arthur Mather say in their book *Recent Advances in Natal Astrology*, "Resonance is an essential consideration in any theorty of astrological causation."[9]

My own theory, as already explained, makes extensive use of resonance—resonance between the tidal tug, due to gravity, of the very hot gases trapped in the magnetic field of the Sun and Earth, and resonance between the resulting fluctuations of the Earth's magnetic field and the electrical activity of the neural network of the fetus. The fairly gross averaging of the geomagnetic aa-index used by Ertel would wash out subtle variations in the geomagnetic record due to lunar daily magnetic variation. It would also wash out any planetary variations in the solar daily magnetic variation.

[9]G. Dean, A. Mather, "Recent Advances in Natal Astrology," *The Astrological Association*, London, 1977.

Gauquelin's Recent Work on Planetary Heredity

Recently, doubt has been cast on Gauquelin's earlier work on planetary heredity by Gauquelin himself. His book *Planetary Heredity* has recently been translated into English, and the 1988 version carries information on his failure to replicate his results on planetary heredity.[10] Gauquelin carried out this experiment on three different occasions: first in 1966, then in 1976, and again in 1984. Although the first two gave positive results in favor of the planetary heredity hypothesis, the last one did not. However, although this may seem a blow to the planetary heredity hypothesis and to my theory, this turns out not to be the case. Gauquelin apparently expected the planets to have a direct influence on the time of births of babies with certain personality characteristics. In my theory there is an intermediary, the magnetic field of Earth, which can introduce a phase lag between the tidal tug due to particular planet and the actual position of the planet in the sky. What is more, the geometry of the geomagnetic field where it enters Earth is known to vary with time, on a time scale of a few years, and this variation is known to introduce a time varying phase-lag between the position of the Moon in the sky and the peaks of the lunar daily magnetic variation. It is also known that the phase-lag changes according to position on the surface of Earth, and so a further weakening of the effect will occur if parents and their children are not born in the same place. I have already discussed this possibility at the Fifth International Astrological Research Conference in London in 1986, and it is described in more detail in my monograph, *A Causal Mechanism for Gauquelin's Planetary Effect*. It is also mentioned in *Astrology: The Evidence of Science*.

The question may well be asked why planetary heredity effects are evident in some of Gauquelin's samples and not in others. This is because the secular shifts in the geomagnetic field, which result in the phase shifts, do not occur in a regular and systematic way. They can happen faster at certain times than they do at other times, and the samples used by Gauquelin do cover different periods of

[10]M. Gauquelin, *Planetary Heredity*, ACS Publications, San Diego, 1988.

time. Unfortunately we do not have sufficiently detailed data on the variations of the geomagnetic field at the places at which parents and children were born and at their respective birth times. These data are what is needed to test my theory. However, some work carried out by Gauquelin does point in this direction. Here I quote from Gauquelin's book *Cosmic Influences on Human Behaviour:*

But we were very surprised to note that the planetary effect after 1938 preceded the schedule it was following prior to 1938. The births that occurred after 1938 corresponded with planetary positions whose greatest frequencies near the horizon and the meridian no longer coincide exactly with those of their parents. Instead, they preceded their parents' planetary position by one hour. Here, for instance, is an illustration of what happened with respect to births at his hospital. If the parent was born after Mars had reached its culmination, the child would have shown a preference to be born under the same Martian schedule prior to 1938. But after 1938, we noticed that the child's birth was advanced on the hereditary calendar. The child showed the greatest tendency not to enter the outside world when Mars has just passed its culmination, but, significantly, one hour earlier. Thus the child's planetary timetable was no longer exactly the same as its parents.

Gauquelin attributes this shift to the fact that at this hospital a medicine called spasmalgin was given almost routinely during this period as soon as the woman arrived at the hospital to ease her labor pains that had already begun. This, according to Gauquelin, could have accounted for the phase-shift of one hour earlier for the children as compared to their parents. However, earlier work by Gauquelin had shown that planetary heredity did not show up in samples where the children had been born under medical intervention, so why should this substance still allow the cosmos to play its part, and only introduce a phase shift? It is just possible that the phase-shift could have been due to changes in the geometry of the geomagnetic field over the period of time between births of the parents and the births of the children. Since no controlled experiment was carried out, this possibility cannot be ruled out, although in the absence of appropriate geomagnetic records it can also not be confirmed.

I believe that this explanation is much more likely than Michel's own, because of a difficulty that Hans Eysenck and David Nias saw with Gauquelin's work, and which they mentioned in their book *Astrology: Science or Superstition?*:

> However, this solution is by no means as straightforward as it might appear. If the planet sends some kind of signal that initiates the birth process, there will obviously be a lag between the signal and the resulting birth that is equal to the duration of labour. This duration varies considerably, from a single hour to many hours, and night labours average 25 percent less than day labours. This compares with the average time between rise and culmination of about six hours. In other words, even if the births of all future sports champions began the moment that Mars was in one of certain specific positions, the resulting spread in the duration of labour should be enough to degrade the effect virtually beyond detection. This objection would be lessened if the planetary signal came after the onset of labour and closer to birth, but in that case the signal would be unnecessary!

To further clarify my own theory, I think that the birth process can be analogously compared to the launch of the *Voyager 2* space probe. This probe made a grand tour of the planets Jupiter, Saturn, Uranus, and Neptune. In order to have accomplished this the probe had to be launched within fairly narrow time limits, called a "window," which had to be carefully planned on the basis of the known schedules, or almanacs of the planets and our Earth. However, even within this window the meteorological conditions had also to be suitable for launch, so there were not only cosmic conditions that had to be satisfied, but also local conditions. Onset of labor provides the baby with the "local conditions" within which it has to plan its own entry into the world. It makes its final decision on the basis of the internal "planetary clock" that is associated with a given set of personality characteristics. This planetary clock has been programmed into the fetus over evolutionary time scales. However, it still has to be set in motion and phase-locked to the movements of a particular planet. Within the womb this phase-locking is carried out by particular variations of the geomagnetic tide to which the fetus has been genetically tuned. It is more than likely that this phase-locking has to be carried out over a few, or even several, cycles of the particular planet in question. This means that it probably takes place days or even weeks before onset of the actual birth process. This planetary birth clock then tells the baby when it should make its "launch" into the world.

Ertel's Work on Planetary Trait Analysis

Another aspect of Gauquelin's work that Professor Ertel investigated was concerned with character trait analysis. Having demonstrated that individuals who had achieved outstanding success in certain professions were born under specific planets, Michel Gauquelin decided to investigate character traits considered typical of these professions, in the hope that this would enable him to identify certain traits with the particular planets of Venus, Mars, Jupiter, and Saturn, and also with the Moon. He did this by studying biographical dictionaries and other published biographies of these eminent individuals, and then shifting out key words used to describe the characters of people following the different professions. In his book *The Truth About Astrology* he lists characteristics which he felt were associated with the Moon, and the planets Jupiter, Saturn, Mars, and Venus.[11]

Professor Ertel decided to investigate links between the planets and personality traits, using a method very similar to that of Gauquelin. He asked some of his students to pick out key words which they considered described individuals listed in biographies. He chose a subset of the data sample used by Gauquelin. These students came up with key words which described personality traits associated with the Moon and each of the four planets found to be significant by Gauquelin. However, Ertel's experiment did not confirm Gauquelin's experiment. The key words not only differed from those that Michel considered to be significant; they also difered from one student to the next. If we think about the results of this experiment it becomes quite clear that the character trait

[11]M. Gauquelin, *The Truth About Astrology*, Hutchinson, London, 1984.

JUPITER	SATURN	MARS	VENUS	MOON
ambitious	cold	active	affable	amiable
authoritarian	concentrated	ardent	agreeable	disorganized
conceited	conscientious	belligerent	ambiguous	dreamer
gay	discreet	brave	attractive	easy-going
harsh	introvert	combative	beloved	fashionable
humorous	methodical	daring	benevolent	friendly
independent	meticulous	dynamic	charming	generous
ironical	modest	energetic	considerate	good company
lively	observer	fearless	courteous	good hearted
mocking	precise	fighter	elegant	helpful
prodigal	reserved	lively	flattering	imaginative
proud	sad	offensive	gallant	impressionable
show off	simple	reckless	gracious	impulsive
social climber	somber	spontaneous	juvenile	merry
spendthrift	stiff	strong-willed	kind	nonchalant
talkative	taciturn	stormy	obliging	popular
warm	thoughtful	tireless	pleasant	socialite
well-off	timid	tough	poetic	spontaneous
witty	uncommunicative	valiant	polite	superficial
worldly	wise	vitality (full of)	seductive	tolerant

method of extracting personality characteristics is extremely suspect, but on the other hand it is not surprising that the results should have revealed this. Published biographies are very subjective, and they tell us as much about the writer as they do about the person to which the biography applies.

Also, the people that succeed in a given profession may have a set of qualities that would ensure success, but the set of qualities, even within one profession, may differ quite markedly from one individual to the next. Thus, for example, the qualities that would lead to success as an experimental biologist are not likely to be the same as those necessary to succeed as a theoretical physicist or an observational astronomer. It is quite likely, however, that there are some characteristics which all scientists share, but which will be different from those shared by artists or politicians. This leads us to some very important discoveries made by John Addey and Peter Roberts, two of the founders of harmonic astrology.

Harmonic Astrology

Working together, Addey and Roberts found that harmonics of the basic lunar and planetary periods seem to play some part in characterizing personality traits of people from the same profession, but with different sets of personality traits. Before going further, let me first explain a little about harmonics in general and how they can arise.

The first harmonic of the lunar day, say, would have a period of about 25 hours. The second harmonic would have a period of 12.5 hours, the third would have a period of 8 hours and 20 minutes, the fourth of period of 6 hours and 15 minutes, and so on. The average "planetary day" for each planet can also be divided into harmonics.

This can be clarified by looking at the tides of the ocean, and then expanding this to discuss the lunar tides in the magnetosphere. Since there are two high tides and two low tides per lunar day, we can say that the most important harmonic is the second harmonic. More detailed studies of the tides show that this is not the only harmonic present. The two high tides and the two low tides are not exactly equal. This means that there is also a first harmonic present in the tides. In other words, the tidal pull of the Moon on the waters of the oceans can be represented by two different circular waves going around the Earth: one with one maximum and minimum per lunar day and one with two maxima and two minima per lunar day.

Tides in the magnetosphere are even more complicated, and also have higher order harmonics. This is because they result from the effect of the tidal pull of the Moon on the upper atmosphere, the effect this has on barometric pressure, the movements of the atmosphere that result from these changes, and the electric current generated by these movements. This means that the effect of the Moon on the magnetic field of Earth can be described not in terms of a single note, but rather in terms of a set of notes, or "chord," with each note corresponding to a different harmonic. According to my theory, the tidal pull of the planets on the magnetosphere generates a similar set of harmonics as a result of its resonant amplification by the geometry of the geomagnetic field. Addey and Roberts, using data collected by Gauquelin, showed that certain types of personality were associated not with a particular harmonic of the Moon or one of the planets, but with a set of harmonics. To illustrate the concept, they pointed out that there are two distinct types of sportsmen: one associated largely with the third harmonic of Mars and the other more associated with the fourth harmonic of this planet. On the basis of these findings a completely different approach has been developed to the analysis of birth charts. This approach is called harmonic astrology. Although this research is still in its early days, it is quite likely that the application of harmonics to astrology will revolutionize the whole discipline.[12]

Conclusion

In this chapter we have looked at the most convincing current evidence for and against astrology. We have also looked at some of the problems presented by this evidence, and some interpretational models that have been proposed to explain this data. It is evident that traditional approaches to astrology do not have much

[12]J. Addey, *Harmonics in Astrology*, Fowler, Romford, 1976.

scientific data to support the claims made for it by its adherents. On the other hand it is also clear that there is scientific evidence that establishes links between personality and the positions of the planets at birth which cannot be ignored. Much of this evidence comes from the work of Michel Gauquelin. The foreword to Gauquelin's book *Cosmic Influences on Human Behaviour* was written by J. Allen Hynek, chairman of the Department of Astronomy, Northwestern University. In this foreword he says:

It is with considerable hesitancy nonetheless that I write this foreword, because for an astronomer to have anything whatsoever to do with anything remotely related to astrology seems enough to rule him out of the scientific fraternity. I do so, however, because as an astronomer I must discharge my duty to support any valid test of astrology, but more importantly because, quite surprisingly, the work of the Gauquelins has not thrown the baby out with the bath water, but rather has revealed an infant that may grow into a giant. This infant is "planetary heredity" and the demonstrated preferred planetary positions in the births of exceptional people.

As a professional astronomer myself I wholeheartedly support J. Allen Hynek in his statement.

15

The Astronomy–Astrology Debate

Debate and controversy is essential to scientific progress. This has always been the case. At every age in history there have been rival theories concerning a great variety of natural phenomena. Furthermore, very often the orthodox or establishment view has not been the view that remained in favor in the light of new evidence collected by later generations.

There are some scientists who believe that we have found "scientific truth," that is, that we have discovered the most important principles that govern the physical world. Such people feel that human scientific endeavor has brought us to a full understanding of the universe, and all that needs to be done now is to refine, clarify, and harmonize the various models which we already have. It does not require much reflection to see that this is a limited and dangerous point of view. It is also patently wrong, as any unbiased examination of the present state of scientific knowledge will demonstrate. But human nature craves the apparent security of certainty, and in much the same way as religious leaders can defend dogma against the opposition, so modern science has "sects" who wish to see "scientific truth" as absolute and superior to the pagan view of the "infidels" who believe that this is not the case.

Certainty in Science

Two professional astronomers, R. B. Culver and P. A. Ianna, wrote a book called *The Gemini Syndrome*, in which they roundly condemn astrology. In this book they quote Abraham Maslow's statement: "Science is the only way we have of shoving truth down the reluctant throat. Only science can overcome characterological differences in seeing and believing. Only science can progress." The authors themselves add: "The evidence—objective descriptions of nature—is the only basis of truth."[1]

The aim of these men may be a genuine wish to be objective, and to cut through muddled and half-baked thinking which can cloud judgment and deny progress. Such a laudable aim, however, is unfortunately neither simple nor easy to achieve. However much science and scientists claim to be objective, and to seek objective "truth," the task is just as difficult for them as it is for any of us.

People who are convinced that objective "truth" is available through science would do well to consider modern developments in physics and the philosophy of science, and to contemplate the history of scientific ideas. Let us look at some opinions of those who have done this.

Dr. Jacob Bronowski, in his book *The Ascent of Man*, said with reference to twentieth-century developments in physics:

There is no absolute knowledge. And those who claim it, whether they are scientists or dogmatists, open the door to tragedy. All information is imperfect. We have to treat it with humility. This is the human condition; and this is what quantum physics says. I mean that literally.

Karl Popper, the great modern philosopher of science, says in his book *The Logic of Scientific Discovery:*[2]

The game of science is, in principle, without end. He who decides one day that scientific statements do not call for any further test,

[1]R. B. Culver, P. A. Ianna, *The Gemini Syndrome*, Pachart, Tucson, 1979.
[2]K. Popper, *The Logic of Scientific Discovery*, Hutchinson, London, 1980.

and that they can be regarded as finally verified, retires from the game.

One of the most powerful and eloquent statements made in recent years on the nature of science was Richard Feynman's public address on "The Value of Science," which he delivered to the National Academy of Sciences in 1955. Here he said,

When a scientist doesn't know the answer to a problem, he is ignorant. When he has a hunch as to what the result is, he is uncertain. And when he is pretty darn sure of what the result is going to be, he is still in some doubt. Scientific knowledge is a body of statements of varying degrees of certainty—some most unsure, some nearly sure, but none absolutely certain.

He continued in the same vein:

Now, we scientists are used to this, and we take it for granted that it is perfectly consistent to be unsure, that it is possible to live and not to know. But I don't know whether everyone realizes this is true. Our freedom to doubt was born out of a struggle against authority in the early days of science. It was a very deep and strong struggle: permit us to question—to doubt—to not be sure. I think that it is important that we do not forget this struggle and thus lose what we have gained. Herein lies a responsibility to society.[3]

Speculation in Science

It is not unheard of for some scientists and science writers to dismiss as "unsupported speculation," "flimsy speculation," or "sheer speculation" new ideas with which they disagree, do not understand, or which they feel might threaten those theories that they do support. These people give the general impression that speculation has no place in science, and that those who indulge in it

[3]R. P. Feynman, *What do you care what other people think?* Hymon, London, 1989.

are being unscientific. They also quite often support the skeptical tradition as if it were the only virtue in science. Yet the history of science has provided many examples where those who dismissed new speculative ideas turned out to be wrong, although it has also happened that on many occasions they were right.

Professor Thomas Gold, from Cornell University, once said:

Whenever the established ideas are accepted uncritically, but conflicting evidence is brushed aside and not reported because it does not fit, then that particular science is in deep trouble— and it has happened quite often in the historic past. If we look over the history of science, there are very long periods when the uncritical acceptance of the established ideas was a real hindrance to the pursuit of the new. Our period is not going to be all that different in that respect, I regret to say.[4]

When Albert Einstein first proposed the general theory of relativity one British scientist called it "high finance in speculation." At first there were few observations to support the theory, but recently there have been many astronomical observations which show that Einstein's theory is the best gravitational theory we have to date. Yet, in the process of coming to accept Einstein's model, even some highly respected scientists suffered from this "hindrance to the pursuit of the new."

Enrico Fermi, the great Italian physicist, who eventually went to live and work in the United States, had a paper on a certain type of nuclear reaction turned down by the well-known scientific journal *Nature* because it involved a particle, called a neutrino, which at that stage had not yet been discovered: The journal editors thought that the ideas it contained were too speculative. The existence of this particle has been confirmed beyond reasonable doubt, and Fermi's theory is now an accepted part of nuclear physics.

On occasion the rejection of speculation can reach alarming proportions. This happened in Germany between the two world

[4]T. Gold, "The Inertia of Scientific Thought," *Speculations in Science and Technology*, 12, 4, 1989.

wars. Two German physicists, Philipp Lenard and Johannes Stark, both of whom had won Nobel Prizes for their experimental work, were supporters of Hitler and the Nazi regime. They were opposed to the quantum theory and to Einstein's theories of relativity. They tried to get theoretical physics outlawed in Germany, and branded this approach to physics as "Jewish speculation." They supported the view that all physics should be based on straightforward empirical deductions founded purely on experiment and observation.

On the whole, the great scientists and philosophers of science have appreciated the importance of speculation to the progress of science. Karl Popper said, "The essence of a good mathematical model is that it should embody the bold ideas, unjustified assumptions and speculations which are our only means of interpreting nature."

Richard Feynman said:

In our field we have the right to do anything we want. It's just a guess. If you guess that everything can be incapsulated in a very small number of laws, you have the right to try. We don't have anything to fear, because if something is wrong we check it against experiment, and experiment may tell us that it's not true. So we can try anything we want. There is no danger in making a guess. There may be a psychological danger if you bend too much work in the wrong direction, but usually it's not a matter of right or wrong.[5]

Much of the work done in theoretical physics consists of formulating models that are able to explain some of the measurements we make during experiments in physical laboratories, or some of the astronomical observations we make with telescopes or space probes. Models are a precise way of extending the data that we collect into areas that are as yet unknown. This means that models are really a way of speculating about the outcome of experiments that have not yet been made. If when these experiments and observations are carried out, we find that the predictions of the models do not

[5]R. P. Feynman, *Superstrings: Theory for Everything*, Edited by P. C. W. Davies, J. Brown, Cambridge University Press, Cambridge, 1988.

correspond to the measurements, then we have to reject the model and start again.

Different Types of Models

It may help to look at the four main types of models used by scientists: iconic, symbolic, mathematical, and analogous. Let us look at each type in turn.

(i) Iconic Models

Iconic naturally comes from the word icon, which means image or likeness. Thus an iconic model is like the real thing in every respect, although it may be a scaled-down version of the actual system being studied. Engineering prototypes are iconic models, but it is almost impossible to construct such models for natural systems. The orreries which we discussed earlier, which simulate the movements of the planets around the Sun and the Moon around the Earth, are attempts at iconic models for the Solar System. However, they can only be considered iconic to a very crude approximation. They do not simulate elliptical orbits, all the planets move in the same plane, and mechanical arms, levers, and gears keep the planets in their orbits rather than natural forces.

(ii) Symbolic Models

Symbolic models are among the most widely used class of model. Such models make no attempt at reality in a simple one-to-one way, but instead they make use of symbols to represent the actual objects of the system which it is attempting to simulate. The circuit diagrams used by electrical, electronic, and radio engineers are examples of symbolic models.

(iii) Mathematical Models

Mathematical models are really precise symbolic models. When such models are applied to physical or astronomical systems, then the symbols usually represent some measurable physical quantity. The relationships that exists between various physical quantities are represented by mathematical formulas. A mathematical model of the Solar System must be able to predict the position of the planets at any time in the future, from a knowledge of their positions in the past.

It is important to realize that mathematical models, even ones that are very sophisticated, do not represent reality. As the great mathematician John von Neumann said:

The sciences do not try to explain, they hardly even try to interpret, they mainly make models. By a model is meant a mathematical construct which, with the addition of certain verbal interpretations, describes observed phenomena. The justification of such a mathematical construct is solely and precisely that it is expected to work.

(iv) Analogous Models

Analogous models are based on the analogies that exist between many apparently different systems in the physical universe. All working scientists make extensive use of such models. The outstanding American mathematician Professor G. Polya wrote several books on mathematical thinking. In *How to Solve It* he writes:

Analogy pervades all our thinking, our everyday speech and our trivial conclusions as well as artistic ways of expression and the highest scientific achievements. Analogy is used on very different levels. People often use vague, ambiguous, incomplete, or incompletely clarified analogies, but analogy may reach the level of mathematical precision. All sorts of analogy may play a role in the discovery of the solution and we should not neglect any sort.[6]

I have made extensive use of models throughout this book and I wish to demonstrate that this approach is very much in keeping

[6] G. Polya, *How to Solve It*, Princeton University Press, Princeton, 1945

with the methodology of the sciences in general. The other very important point about all models is that they are constructs of the human mind, and thus they have their own limitations. Let me repeat the quote from Albert Einstein, given in the introduction: "The only justification of our concepts and our system of concepts is that they serve to represent the complex of our experiences; beyond this they have no legitimacy."[7]

Commenting on this statement, Professor W. H. McCrea, a well-known British astronomer and cosmologist, said:

And for Einstein it evidently meant what it means for us today: a theory is the construction of a theoretical model of the world of physics; all the mathematical discussion applies to the model; the model embodies the "system of concepts," and it serves "to represent our complex of experiences" if the experiences of the theoretical observer in the theoretical model can be put into satisfactory correspondence with the experiences of the actual observer in the actual physical world.[8]

This should be borne in mind since it demonstrates the strengths and weaknesses of all models and analogies. The arguments usually leveled against astrology are model dependent, and therefore they too have limited validity, and they do not represent a total argument against all possible models that can be thought of in the future. In particular they do not represent valid scientific arguments against the theory I am proposing.

Modern Objections to Astrology

The orthodox view of modern science is that astrology just cannot work. A variety of reasons are put forward to back this point of view. For example, it is pointed out that the gravitational pull of the Moon and planets cannot influence a fetus or baby, because the magnetic field of a doctor or midwife would completely swamp such an effect. Or it is pointed out that the lights in the delivery

[7]A. Einstein, *The Meaning of Relativity*, Science Paperbacks, London, 1967.
[8]Ibid.

room are stronger than the radiation we receive from the planets. But let us examine what is being done here in the name of scientific criticism. A scientist sets up a simple, and usually quite naive model: Then he shoots down the model, and from this he often concludes that no scientific theory can be constructed to explain any part of astrology.

Worse still, this naive and rather unscientific approach can often remain unquestioned and so it gets passed on from one generation of scientists to the next. I am here talking particularly about an attitude to astrology, although this attitude can and does occur more generally.

One of the most interesting aspects of my researches into the evidence for and against astrology has been to discover how unscientific scientists can be when addressing a problem outside their own particular field of expertise. Some scientists can also display contempt for the history, philosophy, and the methodology of science when constructing arguments about unfamiliar subjects, and this is particularly true in the case of astrology. The so-called scientific arguments with which many scholars clothe their objections to astrology are rather like the claims of those who could "see" the emperor's new clothes! And these people can resort to militancy and ridicule to hide the nakedness of their arguments.

There are normally three major flaws in arguments used to deny any validity at all to astrology. These flaws are:

(1) Denial of the existence of any scientific evidence in favor of aspects of astrology.
(2) Use of mathematical models with limited ranges of applicability to argue that astrology cannot work, but failing to point out the limitations of the models and the assumptions on which they are based.
(3) Making scientific statements which are true only under certain conditions and failing to state the conditions necessary for their validity.

Let us consider each of these flaws in turn.

The Rejection of Scientific Evidence

Denying the existence of evidence, or rejecting evidence because it conflicts with the currently accepted views in a particular area of science, is not a new phenomenon in the scientific community, nor did it stop with the debate on evolution. It is still with us today and not only with regard to astrology. In *Physics Today* (Reference Frame, September 1990) Professor Philip Anderson, a Nobel laureate in physics, was commenting on some puzzling results in solid state physics. He pointed out the difficulties encountered by experimentalists working in this field in getting their results published. He writes: "This example appears to me to reveal a major weakness in our approach as scientists: a collective unwillingness to welcome new or anomalous results." He also said: "We don't want to lose sight of the fundamental fact that the most important experimental results are precisely those that do not have a theoretical interpretation; the least important are often those that confirm theory to many significant figures."

If this is true for an established area of science, how much most so is it true for scientific enquiries into astrology, the very mention of which can cause astonishingly emotional reactions among those who would most like to consider themselves rational and objective.

I would like to return to this particular problem later in the chapter.

Calculations Based on Naive Models

Many calculations which are supposed to disprove astrology are based on simple single-link models. These normally propose a direct connection between parts of the Solar System and the fetus. The connections usually suggested are light rays, radio waves, gravitational forces, or tidal effects (which have their ultimate origin in gravitational forces). Calculations based on these models then show they cannot account for the observed effects.

It must be stressed that these results are only true for the particular models considered and within the basic assumptions that underlie these particular models. A critic using such an oversimplified model has failed to construct a model that takes account of the complex realities of science. So, conclusions based on these calculations and then used to dismiss evidence relevant to scientific enquiries on astrology demonstrate nothing more than the lack of imagination and the ineptitude of the critic.

Using Scientific Facts that Have Limited Validity

Most scientific facts have a limited range of applicability. In fact, science progresses largely by determining whether observations based on our everyday experiences are also valid under the specialized conditions available in laboratories, where situations can be set up which are different from those of common experience. For example, the statement that water boils at one hundred degrees Celsius is a common experience for many people, but it is not valid at altitudes high above sea level, or in specially constructed vessels in which pressure can be increased or decreased.

Some of the arguments against my theory make use of facts that have validity in a limited context, but these limitations are not stated. For example, reviewer Nigel Henbest has pointed out what he feels to be an insurmountable difficulty in my theory. He says, "A pregnant woman in a modern household will experience much stronger magnetic fluctuations from the washing machine and the food processor [than those coming from the lunar daily magnetic variation]. The regular rhythm of the storage heaters will swamp the weak lunar signal."[8]

As I already pointed out in *Astrology: The Evidence of Science*, the fields from most household equipment at more than two meters from the source is actually less than that associated with the lunar daily magnetic variation. However, his objection is most easily dealt with in the context of the theory of resonance, which is the physical and mathematical basis of my theory. According to the mathematical theory of resonance, if a system has a natural frequency *equal to* the frequency of an external force then the system will have a large response to that force, but its response to forces vibrating at any other frequencies will be so minute it can be ignored. This is the whole basis of radio and television systems.

[8]N. Henbest, *New Scientist*, 12 May, 1988.

Thus, a receiver will respond to the radio waves from the station to which it is tuned and ignore all others. This fact is utilized very frequently by most practicing scientists and engineers. The frequency of household equipment differs from that of the lunar daily magnetic variation by a factor of 2 million. By the same line of reasoning we do not have to switch off our radio sets every time we use household equipment because they also differ by a large factor. Since Henbest has an M.S. (Master of Science) in radio astronomy I would have expected him to realize this at once. This lapse in understanding can, I believe, be attributed to prejudice and an overeagerness to dismiss my theory of astrology.

Open-mindedness

There is a basic attitude problem which underlies these fallacious arguments. We have already seen there is a reluctance to tolerate scientific speculation which, on the face of it, appears to go beyond common sense, or beyond currently accepted scientific models. Partly this arises out of an inherent conservative tendency on the part of scientists, a tendency that is approved and fostered by training, and is, up to a point, an understandable consequence of the quest for accuracy, objectivity, and all that is generally understood by a "scientific" approach. However, as has already been stated so clearly by many great thinkers, it is essential always to remain open-minded and ready to question. It is necessary to acknowledge the *possibility* of truth in new ideas, and not to act in a way that hinders looking for evidence that could increase our knowledge and understanding.

We need to consider theories in the terms in which they are expressed. The fact that a theory, formulated in mathematical terms, may lead to conclusions that offend a prevailing view, or indeed may offend our commonsense view of how things ought to be, is not a sufficient reason for rejecting that theory. Modern physics is founded on the relativity and quantum theories, and the resistance which these theories encountered initially arose largely because their conclusions offended common sense. Yet, unless enough people have been sufficiently open-minded to dare to allow for apparently untenable hypotheses, we would not enjoy today the astonishing increase in scientific and technical knowledge which result from these new ideas.

Richard Feynman said:

We are at the very beginning of time for the human race. It is not unreasonable that we grapple with problems. But there are tens of thousands of years in the future. Our responsibility is to do what we can, improve the solutions, and pass them on. It is our responsibility to leave the people of the future a free hand. In the impetuous youth of humanity, we can make grave errors that can stunt our growth for a very long time. This we will do if we say we have the answers now, so young and ignorant as we are. If we suppress all discussion, all criticism, proclaiming "This is the answer, my friends; man is saved!" we will doom humanity for a long time to the chains of authority, confined to the limits of our present imagination.

Tuning Life to the Solar System

At this point I would like briefly to restate the general form of my theory in the light of what has been said above. It is necessary to understand which areas of the theory are based on evidence which is beyond reasonable doubt; whict parts are based on evidence that exists but is largely ignored; and lastly how the theory is speculation beyond the evidence.

It is now accepted by almost all scientists that the sunspot cycle affects the magnetic field of Earth, and the agency responsible for this effect, the solar wind, has been detected. It is also beyond doubt that the Moon causes tides in the upper atmosphere which give rise to electric currents, and these generate the lunar daily magnetic variation. There is also plenty of evidence that both the steady state as well as the fluctuating behavior of the geomagnetic field can be used by organisms, including man, for purposes of finding direction and keeping internal body time. This much is all well documented, and widely accepted.

There is evidence, largely ignored, that positions and movements of planets as seen from the Sun, play a role in the solar cycle. Furthermore, there is some evidence—highly controversial but difficult to dismiss—that some positions of the planets as seen from Earth at time of birth are linked to personality characteristics of individuals.

This evidence exists. What my theory does is to propose an interpretation, based on this evidence, which can be scientifically tested. Very briefly the steps are:

1) Planets affect the solar cycle in specific ways.
2) The solar cycle affects the geomagnetic field.
3) The geomagnetic field affects life on Earth in certain observed ways.
4) Specifically, many species, including man, can be influenced by particular states of the geomagnetic field.
5) These particular influences appear to correlate with planetary positions.
6) I propose that the behavior of the fetus at the time of birth is linked to cycles within the geomagnetic field, which in turn are influenced by the solar cycle and positions of the planets. Resonance is the phenomenon by which the fetus is phase-locked to specific cycles.

To put this in more specific terms, my theory proposes that the planets Jupiter, Saturn, Uranus, and Neptune control the direction of the convective motions within the Sun, which generate the solar magnetic field. They do so because they play the major role in moving the Sun about the common center of mass of the Solar System. As the solar cycle builds up to maximum, so certain configurations of all the planets, at different stages, play a part in disrupting the magnetic field of the sun, by means of the tidal tug (due to gravitation) of the planets on the hot gases in the Sun.

Thus, the planets play a role in the modulation of Earth's magnetic field by the solar wind. I am also proposing that the tidal tug of the planets on the hot gases trapped in our magnetosphere will, because of resonance, lock some of the vibrations of the Earth's field in step with planetary movements. The resulting fluctuations of Earth's field are picked up by the nervous system of the fetus, which acts like an antenna, and these synchronize the internal biological clocks of the fetus which control the moment of birth. The tuning of the fetal magnetic antenna is carried out by the genes which it inherits, and these to some extent will determine its basic genetically inherited personality characteristic. Thus, the positions of the planets at birth are not altering what we have inherited genetically but are labeling our basic inherited personality characteristics.

Conclusion

The purpose of this book has been to develop further the theory of astrology which I first described in lay terms in my book *Astrology: The Evidence of Science*. The main difference between this book and the earlier one is that I have placed the whole theory in an evolutionary context. Our general awareness of cosmic cycles should come as no surprise, and it follows from the evolutionary development of biological clocks, calendars, and compasses in many living forms.

This is very much in keeping with some of the views of Karl Popper. In his book *Popper*, Bryan Magee points out that Popper's theory of knowledge has close links with the theory of evolution, in that problem solving is seen as the primal activity, the primal problem being that of survival. In *Objective Knowledge*, Popper himself says, "All organisms are constantly, day and night, engaged in problem-solving; and so are all evolutionary sequences of organisms—the phyla which begin with the most primitive forms and of which living organisms are the latest members."[9]

Commenting on this point of view, Magee says:

In organisms and animals below the human level trial solutions to problems exhibit themselves in the form of new reactions, new expectations, new modes of behaviour, which, if they persistently triumph over the trials to which they are subjected, may eventually modify the creature itself in one of its organs or one of its forms and thus become (by selection) incorporated in its anatomy.[10]

[9]Karl Popper, *Objective Knowledge: An Evolutionary Approach*, Oxford University Press, Oxford, 1973.
[10]P. Magee, *Popper*, Fontana, Collins, London, 1974.

Human life has evolved from more basic forms over millions of years. It evolved in an environment in which the fundamental periodicities of the Solar System played a part, so it is likely that some of these rhythms of the Solar System have become part of our anatomy and physiology. The "music of the spheres" is, I am proposing, within each one of us.

Some of the objections of scientists to the ideas I have been promoting over the last few years, may, I think, come from a reaction to the idea that some of our basic behavioral patterns might well be similar to those of what we call lower forms of life. The Copernican revolution was fiercely resisted by the Church because it displaced the Earth from the center of the universe. The theory of evolution was also resisted by the Church because it removed man from the elevated position given to him by the Christian religion. The emotional response of the scientific community to the suggestion that we may have internal clocks linked to cosmic cycles may well come from the fact that much of science and technology has been devoted to mastery of our environment, and thus the suggestion that we may well have subtle links with cosmic rhythms in our environment will be resisted.

As I have already pointed out, many scientists see science as the pinnacle of human achievement and this places them in the role of the high priest of the scientific age of reason. Some scientists subscribe to a philosophy of science which places reason, induction, and skepticism above all else. Many of these scientists also support the common sense theory of knowledge. In the light of recent developments in the philosophy of science these attitudes are extremely suspect. Once again I quote from Popper's *Objective Knowledge:*

The essays in this book break with a tradition that can be traced back to Aristotle—the tradition of this commonsense theory of knowledge. I am a great admirer of commonsense which, I assert, is essentially self-critical. But while I am prepared to uphold to the last the essential truth of commonsense realism, I regard the common sense theory of knowledge as a subjective blunder. This blunder has dominated Western philosophy. I have made an attempt to eradicate it, and to replace it by an objective theory of conjectural knowledge. This may be a bold claim but I do not apologise for it.

Many of our prejudices stem from the common sense theory of knowledge. We do need to realize that certainty does not come from common sense, nor does it come from science, nor from astrology. Certainty cannot come from any humanly constructed system of beliefs. Recent progress in a branch of mathematics called chaos theory has shown that even systems we thought were completely deterministic can exhibit chaotic behavior at times. This has given rise to a realization that even in macroscopic systems there is a limit to how far we can predict future behavior of such systems, on the basis of past behavior and present conditions. This limit is called the predictability horizon. In quantum mechanics we have the principle of uncertainty, and in large-scale systems we have deterministic chaos which has nothing to do with quantum uncertainty. Among other things, chaos theory suggests that there is a limit to how far we can predict motions in the Solar System and how far into the future we can predict weather.

The theory developed here, by bringing aspects of astrology into the realms of scientific explanation, seems to indicate that astrology will be beset by the same uncertainties that are now seen as an integral part of the scientific enterprise. I would say that astrology can offer us little or no hope of telling us what the future will be like, because of the complexities of the forces involved, and because of deterministic chaos within the physical systems that are likely to be involved in any theory of astrology based on the known forces of physics. But if this is the case, why bother to propose such a theory? Because we have within ourselves a desire to understand ourselves, our relationships with other people, our links with our organisms that inhabit our planet, our relationship with our local environment, and our links with the cosmos. To quote from Popper's *The Logic of Scientific Discovery:*

I, however, believe that there is at least one philosophical problem in which all thinking men are interested. It is the problem of cosmology: the problem of understanding the world—including ourselves, and our knowledge, as part of the world. All science is cosmology, I believe, and for me the interest of philosophy, no less than that of science, lies solely in the contributions which it has made to it.

I leave the final word to the great American cosmologist, Edwin Hubble:

From our home on Earth we look out into the distances and strive to imagine the sort of world into which we are born. Today we have reached far out into space. Our immediate neighbourhood we know rather intimately. But with increasing distance knowledge fades, until at the last dim horizon we search among ghostly errors of observations for landmarks that are scarcely more substantial. The urge is older than history. It has not been satisfied and it will not be suppressed.

Afterword: Michel Gauquelin

Michel Gauquelin, director of the Paris Laboratoire d'Etude des Relations entre Rythmes Cosmiques et Psychophysiologiques, died in Paris on May 20, 1991, aged 62. He was born in Paris on November 13, 1928.

Michel Gauquelin was internationally renowned for his pioneering research on the relationship between planetary positions at birth and human behavior. A psychologist and statistician by training, Gauquelin worked closely together with his first wife, the psychologist and demographer Françoise Schneider. Battling with heroic courage and tenacity against the immense scientific prejudice and hostility of his colleagues in the scientific community, he was able to conclusively demonstrate, through repeated and stringently controlled experiments, that, as the ancients had believed, outstanding individuals in different professions tend to be born at times when appropriate planets were close to the horizon or the meridian. He was able to show that top military men, athletes, and entrepreneurs tend to be born "under Mars," while scientists favor Saturn, poets and politicians favor the Moon, and actors Jupiter. He was able to show that the more outstanding the individual the more likely appropriate planets would be prominent. He went on to demonstrate that, in the case of natural births, children tend to be born with the same planets prominent in the sky at birth as their parents. His later work, which has yet to be conclusively proven, focused on character traits, and suggests that strongly martial, jovial, saturnine, and lunar types in any profession will tend to be born with the appropriate planets prominent at the time of birth. Whatever the future development of his neoastrology, Michel Gauquelin's fight against scientific prejudice has been heroic in the highest traditions of scientific endeavor.

Michel Gauquelin was taught the elements of astrology by his dentist father at the tender age of ten. As he grew older his continuing studies and observations convinced him that there was an underlying truth to the traditional belief in planetary influences and he soon determined to dedicate his life to uncovering that truth. To this end in 1949 he elected to study psychology and statistics at the Sorbonne University. At the same time he started the systematic collection of the birth certificates of eminent individuals listed in various Who's Who. In 1952 he was to be joined in his work by his future wife, Françoise Schneider, whose expertise in demography was to prove invaluable.

In 1955 the newly married Gauquelin published *L'Influence des Astres* giving his first meticulously researched and documented results on over nine thousand case studies. Employing the most rigorous statistical methods it clearly demonstrated the reality of planetary effects with odds of millions to one against chance. To Gauquelin's astonishment his findings were greeted with unanimous hostility and ridicule by his colleagues, who suggested the results were an anomaly peculiar to France. Undiscouraged, Gauquelin and his wife over the next five years continued to amass fresh data from Germany, Holland, and Italy. The successful results of these fresh studies were published in *Les Hommes et les Astres* in 1960.

Repeated experiments over the next two decades, using fresh data from Belgium, France, and other countries, including the United States and Scotland, produced similar results. The only failure to replicate was that of the experiment by the Committee for the Scientific Investigation of the Paranormal in the United States in 1977. Those results it turned out had been shamelessly doctored by the CSICP investigators, as later had to be acknowledged.

From 1970 on the Gauquelins' laboratory began the publication of twenty-three meticulously documented volumes of the data involved in their experiments. In addition Michel Gauquelin wrote up the ongoing work in a series of popular accounts including *Cosmic Clocks* in 1967, *Astrology and Science*, 1965, *The Truth About Astrology*, 1985, and *Written in the Stars*, in 1988. His last book, *Neo Astrology, a Copernican Revolution*, will be published by Penguin-Arkana in August 1991. In addition to his formidable array of publications in the field of astrological research, Gauquelin was also the author and editor of some thirty books on psychology.

While not considering himself an astrologer as such, Gauquelin cooperated closely with serious astrologers both in Britain and the United States, attending their conferences and giving endlessly of his expertise for the clarification of the astrological tradition. His clarity of vision and steadfast purpose will continue to be an inspiration to his colleagues, who have already agreed to establish a Michel Gauquelin Fund under the auspices of the Urania Trust, an educational charity dedicated to the study of astrology and astronomy.

Michel Gauquelin was throughout his life a keen athlete, cyclist, and one of France's top tennis players, reaching the semifinals of the French over-fifties tennis championship.

Following his divorce from Françoise, he married Marie Catherine Cadilhac in 1986. He is survived by both, and by his son Daniel.

—Charles Harvey

Bibliography

Introduction

The Ascent of Man, J. Bronowski, Futura, London, 1987.
The Dancing Wu Li Masters, Gary Zukov, Rider-Hutchinson, London, 1979.
Speakable and Unspeakable in Quantum Mechanics, J. S. Bell, Cambridge University Press, Cambridge, 1987.
The Meaning Relativity, Albert Einstein, Science Paperbacks and Methuen, London, 1967.

Chapter 1

The Story of Greenwich Time, D. Howse, Oxford University Press, Oxford, 1980.
The Greenwich Observatory, (3 vols) E. Forbes, D. Howse & J. Meadows, Taylor & Francis, London, 1975.
The Royal Greenwich Observatory, W. H. McCrae, Her Majesty's Stationery Office, London, 1975.

Chapter 2

The History of Astronomy, A. Pannekoek, Dover, New York, 1989.
The Role of Astronomy in the Ancient World, (Ed.) F. R. Hobson, Oxford University Press, Oxford, 1974.
The Exact Sciences in Antiquity, O. Neugebauer, Dover, New York, 1969.
Science for the Citizen, L. Hogben, George Allen & Unwin, London, 1942.

Chapter 3

Adventures with Astronomy, Percy Seymour, John Murray, London, 1983.
Geared to the Stars, H. King, Adam Hilger, Bristol, 1978.
The Ascent of Man, J. Bronowski, Futura, London, 1987.

Chapter 4

The History of Nautical Astronomy, C. H. Cotter, Hollis & Carter, London, 1968.
The Greenwich Meridian, S. Malin & C. Stott, Ordnance Survey, Southampton, 1984.
Men of Mathematics, E. T. Bell, Victor Gollancz, London, 1937.
John Harrison, H. Quill, John Baker, London, 1966.
The Marine Chronometer, R. Gould, Holland Press, London, 1973.

Chapter 5

Supersense, J. Downer, BBC Publications, London, 1988.
Photoperiodism, Brian Lofts, Edward Arnold, London, 1970.

Chapter 6

Biological Clocks, Cloudesley Thompson, Weidenfeld & Nicholson, London, 1980.

Chapter 7

Cosmic Magnetism, Percy Seymour, Adam Hilger, Bristol, 1986.

Chapter 8

Living Clocks, Ritchie Ward, Collins, London, 1972.
Light and Life, L. O. Bjorn, Hodder & Stoughton, London, 1976.

Chapter 9

Science and Civilisation in China, C. Ronan & J. Needham, Cambridge University Press, Cambridge, 1978.
Cosmic Magnetism, Percy Seymour, Adam Hilger, Bristol, 1986.
Orientation and Navigation: Birds, Humans and other Animals, Royal Institute of Navigation, London, 1989.
Human Navigation & the Sixth Sense, R. Baker, Hodder & Stoughton, London, 1981.

Chapter 10

Astrology: Science or Superstition?, H. Eysenck & D. Nias, Maurice Temple Smith, London, 1982.
Recent Advances in Natal Astrology, G. Dean & A. C. Mather, Astrological Association, London, 1976.
The Geomagnetic Field and Life: Geomagnetic Biology, A. P. Dubrov, Plenum Press, New York, 1978.

Chapter 11

The Honey Bee, J. L. Gould & C. G. Gould, Scientific American Library, 1988.
Electromagnetic Man, C. W. Smith & S. Best, St. Martin's Press, New York, 1989.

Chapter 12

Astronomy of the Ancients, K. Brecker & M. Feirtag, MIT Press, Cambridge, Massachusetts, 1979.

Secret Symbolism in Occult Art, F. Gittings, Harmony Books, New York, 1987.

Written in the Stars, Michel Gauquelin, Aquarian Press, New York, 1988.

Chapter 13

Neo-astrology, A Copernican Revolution. M. Gauquelin, Penguin, London, 1991.

The Message of Astrology, Peter Roberts, Aquarian Press, Wellingborough, 1990.

Chapter 14

The Case for Astrology, John Anthony West, Viking, New York, 1991.

Cosmic Influence on Human Behaviour, M. Gauquelin, Futura, London, 1976.

Chapter 15

The Gemini Syndrome, R. B. Culver & P. A. Ianna, Pachart, Tucson, 1979.

The Logic of Scientific Discovery, K. Popper, Hutchinson, London, 1980.

What Do You Care What Other People Think?, R. Feynman, Unwin Hyman, London, 1988.

The Meaning of Relativity, Albert Einstein, Science Paperbacks & Methuen, London, 1967.

Astrology: The Evidence of Science, P. Seymour, Penguin, London, 1990.

Popper, B. McGee, Fontana-Collins, London, 1974.

Objective Knowledge, K. Popper, Oxford University Press, Oxford, 1972.

Publishers of Journals and Periodicals Quoted in the Text

Animal Navigation, Bailliere Tindall, 24–28, Oval Road, London, NW1 7DX.

Astronomical Journal, American Institute of Physics, 335 E 45th Street, New York, NY.

Astronomy and Space, David and Charles, South Deven House, Newton Abbott, Deven.

Journal of Navigation, The Royal Institute of Navigation, 1 Kensington Gove, London, SW7 2AT.

Journal of Near Eastern Studies, University of Chicago Press, Journals Division, 54205, South Woodlawn Avenue, Chicago, Illinois, 60637.

Speculation in Science and Technology. Science and Technology Letters, 12 Clarence Road, Kew, Surrey, TW9 3NL.

RCA Review, RCA Corporation, Princeton, New Jersey, 08540.

Vistas in Astronomy, Pergamon Press, Pergamon Press Place, Headington Hill Hall, Oxford, OX3 OBW, U.K.

About the Author

Dr. Percy Seymour is Principal Lecturer in Astronomy at the University of Plymouth, where he teaches astronomy and astrophysics to undergraduates and carries out research on magnetic fields in astronomy. As Director of the William Day Planetarium in Plymouth, he also regularly lectures to schools and to the general public. He is also an astronomy tutor with the Open University.

Before coming to Plymouth, Seymour was Senior Planetarium Lecturer at the Old Royal Observatory, Greenwich. There he developed an ardent interest in the history of astronomy and navigation, and introduced a series of lectures for high schools linking astronomy with other subjects in the school curriculum, such as biology and chemistry, art and literature. It was there that he first fully appreciated the interdisciplinary nature of astronomy. At Plymouth he has sought to combine his interdisciplinary approach to astronomy teaching with his research interests, by exploring the terrestrial and biological consequences of cosmic magnetic fields. This work first led him to consider the scientific links between astronomy and astrology.

Percy Seymour's other books include: *Adventures with Astronomy, Halley's Comet, Cosmic Magnetism, Astrology: The Evidence of Science*, and *The Paranormal: Beyond Sensory Science*.

He is married and has one son.